SHE WHO dreams

WANDA EASTER BURCH

SHE WHO Dreams

A JOURNEY INTO HEALING THROUGH DREAMWORK

With a Foreword by Robert Moss

NEW WORLD LIBRARY
NOVATO, CALIFORNIA

New World Library
14 Pamaron Way
Novato, California 94949

Edited by Katharine Farnam Conolly and Carol Venolia
Cover design and typography: Cathey Flickinger

The material in this book is intended for education. It is not meant to take the place of
diagnosis and treatment by a qualified medical practitioner or therapist.
No expressed or implied guarantee as to the effects of the use of the
recommendations can be given nor liability taken.

Library of Congress Cataloging-in-Publication Data
Burch, Wanda Easter
She who dreams : a journey into healing through dreamwork / Wanda Easter Burch.
p.   cm.
Includes bibliographical references and index.
ISBN 978-1-57731-426-4 (alk. paper)
1. Women's dreams—Case studies. 2. Dream interpretation—Case studies. 3.
Dreams—Therapeutic use. 4. Breast—Cancer—Psychological aspects.
5. Burch, Wanda Easter. 1947– I. Title.
BF1099.W65B87   2003
135'.3—dc21   2003011375

First printing, October 2003
ISBN 978-1-57731-426-4

10 9 8 7 6 5 4 3 2

contents

This book is for three people:
Ron, who shares my dreams;
Evan, who dreams for me; and
Robert, who partners my dreams

foreword

THROUGH DREAMING INTO HEALING

*D*reaming is healing. Our bodies speak to us in dreams, giving us early warning of symptoms we might develop, showing us what they need to stay well. Dreams give us fresh and powerful images for self-healing. Dreams are also the language of the soul; they put us in touch with wells of memory and sources of creativity and energy far beyond the clutter and confusion of the little everyday mind. Beyond this, dreams are experiences of the soul, and can take us — sleeping or hyper-awake — into realms where we can have direct access to sacred healers and teachers.

These themes and possibilities come vividly alive in Wanda Burch's brave and beautiful book *She Who Dreams*, which is both the narrative of a personal journey into healing through dreaming and an incitement to bring the gifts of active dreaming into our everyday lives.

I have been sharing dreams with Wanda since early in 1987, and I know the depth of experience and the deeps of dreaming from which this book flows. Her dreams diagnosed a life-threatening illness (breast cancer) a year before the doctors found symptoms. Her dreams guided her choice of treatment, gave her powerful imagery for self-healing and recovery, enabled her to grow a creative relationship with her physicians, and awakened her to a deeper life and a vital engagement with the world as a dreambringer — one of those who creates a safe space for others to open to the gifts of dreaming, and can bring a dream to someone in need of a dream.

Her personal story is quite fascinating. Her first dream mentor was her Irish-American grandmother, a "wise woman" of the Alabama hill country. Later she met the dreamers of the Iroquois, one of whom appeared at her back door in the form of a white wolf.

But it is the story of everyday trials, more than the extraordinary elements in this book, that will touch the hearts of many readers and bring them practical guidance that is urgently needed. Wanda shows how dreams can get us through. One of her most valuable contributions to the literature of healing and recovery is to show us how we can use the self-healing tools that flow from dreamwork to support conventional medical treatments, smoothing the process and reducing adverse side-effects. For this alone, *She Who Dreams* is an invaluable resource for healthcare professionals, therapists, healers, and caregivers.

a Dream Friendship

MY FRIENDSHIP with Wanda began with dreams, and deepened immeasurably through the sharing of dreams. Both only children, we found in each other the sister and brother that each had longed for in childhood. It is quite possible that we were dreaming of each other at that time, decades before we first met in the physical world, in March 1987.

We met in a year when (as they say in West Africa) "the ancestors move into the realm of the living" — when death is close and the veils between the worlds are thin. It was the year my father died, and the year Wanda was called to help her own father prepare for his journey beyond death. It was the year I started dreaming of people who had lived and fought and loved centuries before, on the land where I was living, and it was these ancestral dreams that led me directly to Wanda.

I had recently moved to a farm on the edge of Mohawk country, in upstate New York, to get away from the clutter of big cities. I started dreaming of people who had lived in that neighborhood in an earlier time. In some of these dreams, I met ancient healers and shamans who spoke to me in a language I did not know, which proved to be an archaic form of the Mohawk Indian language. When I had studied enough Mohawk to interpret these dreams, I learned that the Mohawk word for a healer or shaman is *atetshents*, meaning "one who dreams." I discovered that in the traditional practice of the first Peoples of the Northeast dreaming is regarded as central to healing. In Iroquois tradition, it is understood that dreams show us "the secret wishes of the soul" and it is believed that it is the duty of a caring community to gather round a dreamer, help her recognize the soul's wishes, and take action to honor them.

One of the people I met in my dreams was an imposing white man who sometimes appeared dressed like a colonial gentleman or a British general, at other times like a Mohawk Indian. Through a chance discovery in a used bookstore, I was able to identify my dream character. His name was Sir William Johnson, and he lived among the Mohawk as King's Superintendent of Indians in the time of the French and Indian Wars. I had never heard of Johnson before I started dreaming his world so vividly that I eventually wrote novels about him. My dreams spurred me to intensive research, and soon to visit Johnson Hall, Sir William's last home in the Mohawk Valley, where I first met Wanda. She was a gentle, soft-spoken Southerner who had been curator of this historic site for many years, and she knew Johnson and the Iroquois Indians very well.

We quickly discovered we had more in common than an affinity with some of the people who had lived on the Indian frontier in an earlier time.

Wanda and I had both grown up listening to our dreams. We had both known, since early childhood, that the dream world is a real world and that it is possible to travel into that world, quite consciously, in journeys beyond the body and beyond the laws of physical reality.

Soon we were sharing dreams. I told Wanda a night vision in which I flew on the wings of a red-tailed hawk to meet a healing woman who instructed me in her own language, spreading wampum belts to confirm her teachings. Wanda told me a dream in which she approached a native shaman with flowers in her hands, which turned into a baby, and then into a belt of wampum.

Within days, we were sharing as if we had known each other all our lives. We knew the colors and textures of each other's dreaming. I suspected that Wanda was the sister whose absence was so painful in childhood, yet whose presence I also sensed, behind the veil we penetrate in dreams.

I told Wanda how I survived a series of near-death experiences in childhood, and was healed through a vision of a living serpent-staff that filled the sky. We found we had both had the experience of entering other life experiences — past and future — in our dreams, and of traveling, again and again, to the same locales in the dreamspace, as if we were leading continuous lives in other realities.

Wanda told me a big dream from her childhood. Aged nine, she dreamed of a boy with brown hair who was drowning in very shallow water near a boat. In her dream, she reached in and helped pull him up. As she spoke, I was plunged back into one of the most vivid memories of my Australian boyhood. In my waking life, around that time, I fell from a gangway leading to a fishing boat into shallow water. No one above could understand that I was drowning, since the water was so shallow and I was anyway a good swimmer. But scenes of my life flashed before me and as my awareness swirled, I moved from terror into a dreamy surrender — until someone reached down and pulled me up and they pumped the water out of me. Wanda asked me several years later, "Have I been dreaming of you all my life?"

As our friendship developed, we were able to validate and confirm each other's experiences, and benefited richly from the insight and energy that flows from sharing dreams on a regular basis and helping each other to read their messages and take appropriate action to honor the dreams.

In the society in which Wanda and I had grown up, we were not often encouraged to tell our dreams, let alone honor them as gateways to soul healing, though each of us was blessed to have at least one family member who believed in dreams and intuition. So we had to improvise processes to release the gifts of our dreams. We were both avid readers and researchers, but we did not find what we needed in other people's books. We found it in our daily practice, and in our dream journals.

We noticed that both of us frequently dreamed waking events before they happened, and agreed on the importance of running a reality check on all dream material, asking "Is it possible that any of this could happen in waking life?" in order to identify messages about the future that could be life-supporting and even life-preserving.

In *She Who Dreams*, Wanda shares many instructive stories about the workings of dream precognition. She not only describes how dreams provided accurate diagnosis of a developing illness long before physical symptoms were detected; she shares many examples of dreaming incidents, large and small, before they manifested in waking life. She makes us aware that dreaming the future is entirely natural. More important, she reminds us that the future we see in dreams is actually a possible future, a future that can sometimes be reshaped for the better if we get the details clear and take appropriate action to avoid an unwanted event, or manifest a desired outcome.

As Wanda and I continued to share dreams, several times a week — in person, on the phone, and by fax or mail (in the years before we had e-mail) — I became aware that her gifts as a psychic dreamer extended beyond dreaming the future. She often had clear sightings of things happening at a distance. On many occasions, I noticed she was able to "drop in" on me and observe what I was doing, waking or sleeping. For example, after some dreams of my Scottish ancestors, I was up in the middle of the night, studying photos and descriptions of a castle in the Western Borders that had belonged to my father's clan. In the morning, I received a detailed report from Wanda of a dream in which she met me within the walls of an ancient castle; her description of the landscape closely matched the territory I had been researching.

On another night, I was caught up in a thrilling dream adventure in which I was granted a place in a circle around a purple fire in a circle of warrior-kings and given a cloak-pin that was fastened to my left shoulder. The next day — unaware of my dream, except through her own dreaming — Wanda shared a detailed account of a dream in which she saw me seated before a purple fire and watched as a cloak-pin was fastened to my left shoulder. The accuracy of her spontaneous sightings might have made me uneasy had she not become a close and trusted friend!

We began to experiment with entering each other's psychic space consciously and intentionally, and found that it is not only relatively easy to do this — with practice — but that in this way it is possible to bring through guidance, healing, and confirmation of the objective reality of experiences beyond the physical plane.

In the years after our first encounter, Wanda and I also found ourselves traveling deeper into a realm that is familiar to many dreamers, but sadly neglected by our mainstream culture: dreaming with the departed. Wanda's grandmother returned to her again and again in dreams to offer her vital guidance on modes of healing — including the use of specific herbs — and the nature of the soul, just as my father returned to me again and again (after his death in November 1987) offering help to the family.

I was privileged to share in Wanda's wonderful work with her own father as he approached death. The night before his final crisis, I dreamed that Wanda's father had become a minister of religion; Wanda called me the next morning to tell me she was flying to Memphis to be at his bedside, and that he had been praying intensely over the previous days. While Wanda played the role of guide to her father in his last months, he returned to her as a guide from the other side, giving her a clear warning about her disease, and later introducing her to other resources and allies, including an animal guardian.

We were learning and confirming so much about dreams in those early years. But neither of us had yet realized that Wanda's work with her dreams was giving her tools that would save her life.

rewriting a life contract

AFTER WANDA'S DREAMS had provided specific diagnosis of her illness — but before her doctors had confirmed that diagnosis — she followed a waking dream by flying off to West Africa as a volunteer with an archaeological team. On the eve of her plane trip, I wrote a quotation from Plotinus in my journal: "The soul has the power to conform to her character the destiny allotted to her."

This, on its deepest level, is what you will find unfolding here. Wanda tells her story with absolute candor, sometimes seasoned with sardonic humor, as she describes herself trying and rejecting fake "boobs" after her modified radical mastectomy, or hanging a wig on a stuffed bunny when her hair started falling out during the chemotherapy. She doesn't flinch from describing her moments of fear and bitter disappointment, the times when she felt her best dreams had ceased to work for her. Anyone who has undergone an illness like hers will be grateful for the honesty and practicality with which she describes the everyday ordeals and humiliations she suffered. Don't expect soap-bubble romance or easy miracles in this book. As Wanda tells it, her dreams led her down a hard road. In place of a miracle, she devised what she tellingly describes as a "healing cocktail" in which she was able to draw on her dreams and inner resources in support of the medical intervention she believed to be unavoidable. No easy road, but one that led her out of death, by giving her the courage and clarity to conform her destiny to the depth and character of soul.

Her account of the dreams in which she was reminded of the terms of her soul's contract and finally permitted (after profound ordeal and testing) to negotiate a life extension is breathtaking. She and I both believe that her terrifying dream encounter with the envoy of her personal Death literally enabled her to extend her tenure on life, and avoid the death, at age forty-three, for which her dreams had been rehearsing her for two decades.

Wanda's decision to write this book and to share her gifts as a dream helper with those around her — as she does with great generosity in many environments, with neighbors and colleagues, with cancer patients and survivors, and as a workshop leader — are part of her honoring of that tremendous dream. Her story encourages us to examine our own sacred contracts and recover the knowledge that belonged to us before we entered this life experience.

Dreaming to heal your life

WHEN YOU HAVE FINISHED reading this book, you'll have no doubt about the healing power of dreams. You'll have received powerful confirmation that in night dreams, we have access to a personal doctor who makes house calls, provides an impeccable diagnosis of our physical, emotional, and spiritual condition, and doesn't charge a cent. You'll know that dreams can provide accurate diagnosis of our ailments, often long before physical symptoms have developed. You'll have learned that dreams are a wonderful source of fresh, spontaneous imagery for healing — imagery the body believes because it comes from deep within ourselves.

You will not only be inspired by Wanda's example; you'll be able to work with effective and original meditations and exercises you can use to enter a state of wide-awake dreaming that can be profoundly relaxing and healing. My personal favorite among the guided journeys Wanda offers is "The Healing Pool," derived from her extraordinary experience of being led into an encounter with an angelic being at the pool of Bethesda. I have listened to her lead a whole group into this healing pool, and I have seen everyone present emerge refreshed and renewed.

Wanda not only offers her own example and imagery; she urges us to craft fresh visualizations for healing from our spontaneous dreams and visions, and to record our own meditations in our own voices, which may appeal to the body because they are so familiar.

Beyond all else, the message of *She Who Dreams* is that dreaming is everyday practice, a practice that can be profoundly energizing, wonderful fun, and can build deep and nurturing relationships.

— Robert Moss
author of *Conscious Dreaming*
March 2003

introduction

I have written the book I needed to read when I was diagnosed with breast cancer. It is a book based on my personal journey through dreams and experience, captured and recorded in my journal beginning with my diagnosis and continuing through surgery, chemotherapy, depression, and finally healing. It is a book for anyone who has ever remembered a dream or kept a dream journal. And yet it is not just a book about dreaming; it encompasses every common emotion shared by a person with a life-threatening illness: fear, anxiety, pain, and joy.

I am alive because I dream. Dreams come from deep within our souls, drawn from a vast repository of memory deeper than we access in our daily lives. Dreams are given to us in the context of our individual life experience; some dreams recall our simple past, and some evoke a more complex past that stirs haunting memories of places and people no longer familiar to us. Some dreams play out scenes from our busy lives, solve simple daily problems, or play back a moment of pleasure. Some dreams pull forth the secret wishes of our heart or predict events a day, a year, or a decade in the future. Other dreams, perhaps the most important ones, warn us of death and illness — and many of those dreams present paths for healing. When we discover the pattern of our dreams and how they fit into the pattern of our waking lives, we gain a deeper understanding of the complex harmony of our spirit, soul, and body. I have a story to tell of dreams, of illness, and of healing.

My dreams prepared me, twenty years in advance, for the challenge of a life-threatening illness. Dream visitors warned me of impending illness and finally pushed me to go to doctors before I developed physical symptoms. Dreams guided me in my choice of treatment, enabled me to support the medical treatments I chose, and helped me develop a creative, healing relationship with my physicians. In the aftermath of surgery, my dreams offered powerful imagery for self-healing and recovery. My adventures in dreaming took me to places of healing and transformation, and introduced me to spiritual guides and helpers who opened a path beyond fear and pain. My dreams gave me back my life. In dreaming, I found that I was able to literally renegotiate my life contract. My dreams also opened me to a deeper life and gave me gifts I could bring to others in everyday life.

As I tell the story of my dreams and their role in my healing, I must also tell the stories of my family, my grandmother, my father's death, a journey to Africa, and my dreams in the year before my diagnosis and surgery. They are all part of the history of my dreaming and my life. They form the connections to my past, and they force me to look at memories, emotions, and possibilities. I dreamed my life and my death, and I confronted both in determining which I would choose. These dreams of life and death were companions in my life, and their shared purpose allowed me to choose life and healing.

Three people, important to my waking life and to my dreaming, played pivotal roles in my recovery and healing: Ron, Evan, and Robert. I grew up with Ron, the boy who lived on the other side of the school — only slightly farther than "next door." I married him after graduate school. We had one son, Evan. Both Ron and Evan are dreamers who recall and use their dreams. They both dream with me, and I turn to them for confirmation of the life and healing in my own dreams whenever I doubt my ability to survive.

Robert Moss, the third important person in my life and in my dreaming, introduced himself in a childhood dream when I was only nine years old, but he appeared in waking reality when I was almost forty. I believe that friendships such as ours only happen to those who truly pay attention to the important "visitors" who come to us over and over in our dreams. If we do pay attention, these dream visitors are easy to recognize when they finally walk into our waking reality; they are the people with whom we feel an instant kinship. They are the ones we explain later, when asked, that "we met and felt that we had always known each other." Robert and I discovered almost immediately that we were in each other's dreams — and perhaps had been so since I dreamed as a child that I rescued a drowning boy. Robert experienced that dream in his waking life. After we met, Robert and I invested in an incomparable friendship that filled the void of having been only children, and that returned threefold dividends in dreaming dreams for one another.

These three men have formed a pyramid of healing and supportive energy for my life and my dreams. Ron built a personal haven of support within our home and community that defied statistics; an alarming percentage of spouses leave when faced with serious illness in their household. Our son Evan has taught me more about dreaming my life than I could have ever learned from my own experience, and he continues to live the life he dreams. And Robert's dreams not only matched mine in the magnitude of their healing messages — which I needed and used for my recovery — but he expanded his own journey into that of dream teacher, interpreter, and guide for me and many others.

Since our first shared dreams, Robert Moss has written three published books and numerous articles on dreaming. He also leads national and international workshops, records tapes and television shows, and works with people throughout the world to bring forward a dreaming society. I feel honored to have walked into his life in a dream when I was nine years old.

The names of these three people filled my journals; their dreams became the affirmation and confirmation of my own; their support guided me back to health.

My dreams have also provided me with guidance and support from my father and my grandmother, in ways that only those who have passed to the other side can offer. My father sometimes interfered with my journey. His fears and concern for me came through in my dreaming, and perhaps also his doubts about whether I had the strength to fight this battle. But he also performed the role of guardian and guide many times, especially when he appeared with a doctor in my first *big* warning dream, demanding that I seek help.

My grandmother played the roles of guide and teacher through my dreams. She defined spirit and soul for me. She brought me healing plants and provided memory that allowed me to reach back into my southern past and pull forward the best of my heritage. That heritage, my roots — a line of strong Irish-American women in the Alabama hills that began with my great-grandmother — encouraged me as a child to understand the importance of dreaming.

My dreams have presented me with the greatest imaginable opportunities for change and renewal. They warned me of a life-threatening illness and allowed me to view the possibility — perhaps the probability — of my death. They then helped me find the path back to life by discovering my internal resources via the inevitable review of my life. I was allowed to choose my own path to healing, using all the physical and mental resources given to me within the dreamscape and in waking reality, including the medical community.

My dreams, in fact, encouraged me to choose all the resources available to me within the medical profession. At the same time, they provided me with the dream imagery needed to guide me through aggressive chemotherapy and devastating depression. I used my dreams to devise meditations and exercises that guarded me against the more brutal side effects of chemotherapy, guiding me through the worst times of fear and anger. finally, I had a magnificent healing dream that brought a renewal of my life contract and a redirection of my life purpose.

In the aftermath of my illness, my dreams have brought change and intention to my life. Transformation is defined as "change in form, appearance, nature, or character." A second definition is "a wig or hairpiece for a woman." What a wonderful metaphor for a breast-cancer survivor who has lost her hair during chemotherapy!

I now work on a hot line for people who have been diagnosed with breast cancer. The callers always ask me three questions: how long have you survived; what did you feel when…(the blank can be filled in with endless events); and what books are available to help me feel that I'm not the only person with breast cancer? I often ask the callers about their dreams. Although some hesitate at first to share, or feel their dreams are "nonsense," they've all had at least one precognitive dream — some similar to my own — most uniquely representative of their own personal mythology. We talk about the healing opportunities presented within the dreams that have followed these precognitive dreams, and we talk about their ability to craft their own healing and transformation. They, too, can find within their dreams the ways to move from facing death to facing life, almost always with renewed purpose.

In other situations, I have met men and women who shared my experience of having specific dreams that helped them through their illnesses — but they also told me of their difficulty in finding people to talk with about healing through dreams. We all want to know that we are not alone in going through a life-threatening situation; we want to hear that someone else has shared our path to healing. A popular TV commercial for the American Cancer Society shows three frightened people who feel they are alone in their individual anguish, two with cancer, and one a spouse of someone with cancer. Although these three people have never met, they find consolation in a network link that places them in touch with one another; and the TV viewer breathes a sigh of relief as each of them finds a common bond that places them on a trail already blazed. In the same way, I knew thousands of women daily faced the same fears I faced, but I felt relief when I found just a few of them in my own journey and felt joy when I was able to share my story with others who felt that same aloneness. If there were thousands of people sharing the aloneness of cancer each day, then there must also be thousands of people dreaming important, but possibly missed, dreams of diagnosis and healing. If I could tell my story in such a way that would bring forward the importance of the healing opportunity in even just one dream for those people, then I would feel that I had helped someone find their own unique healing experience within the universal experience of dreaming.

My path to wellness has been different than your path; we are each unique individuals. As long as we look within ourselves and find our own unique abilities — the ones we call forth in any crisis, the ones that ring true in our own minds and speak to our own bodies — we will be following our individual paths to healing. Healing, like illness, takes on a different form in each person. Sometimes we must look back to our childhood, back to our roots, and rediscover our wellness — rediscover who we were when we were well — and try to recapture that state. Perhaps then, in looking back so that we may go forward, we can retrieve the best of the past and use it to transform ourselves into people who are more whole and responsible, whether we then have one more day to live or thousands.

In redefining what makes us whole or in finding our way back to who we were when we were well, we sometimes experiment with many lifestyle changes, some briefly and some more permanently. We may try out a new diet, or several diets that finally come to a moderation we can live with. We may undertake a course of medical treatment, alone or combined with alternative treatments — none of them far-fetched or hokey if they speak to us, all of them so if they do not. We may try a change of clothes, a new form of exercise, and a period of paying attention to things that do or do not make us happy. This "paying attention" period allowed me to take stock of habits that needed changing and feelings that needed restructuring. As a result of paying attention, I evaluated who I was, who I am, and who I could become.

In this book, within the context of my dreams and my life experience, I will tell you the story of who I am, where I came from, and how I chose to battle a disease that strikes one out of eight people at some point in their lifetime (150,000 a year) and kills 46,000 people each year. But more people survive than die, and they all experience their individual conflicts in the context of a common and terrifying experience. When I tell my story, I tell their story. Within each of us lies the ability to rise above the greatest challenges of our lives and choose our own way of living, our own way of healing — and possibly, for some of us, our own way of dying. All of us undertake a spiritual journey at some point in our lives; all of us recognize the common elements of our journey in those of others. I invite you to follow along my journey, to find yourself in my story and take whatever part of it makes your own journey longer or stronger, or both, and make it your own.

Part 1

Moving

through

the

Dance Hall

SOUTHERN CHILD

*D*reams have been an active part of my life for as long as I can remember. My dreaming, and my sense of the magic of dreaming, arises from my childhood in the South. For me, there has always been a magic about the South that I never found in any other part of the country — a connectedness with ancestors, with a remembered past, with traditions that go back to times before memory, and with the indomitable pull of the land itself. That magic surrounds a southern child in music, art, speech, song, and religion — in the way things are approached, in the way things are done, and even in dreaming. Being southern is more than a geographic statement; it is an inescapable state of mind, even when a person born in the South moves away. Some part of the heart or soul remains in the South and travels back to its southern past to find answers to problems, to find healing, and to find the magic that originally brought harmony to life.

My dreams were cherished and encouraged by the people I most loved. My great-grandmother, a woman I met only once, passed down to my maternal grandmother her strong belief in the reality of dreams and visions as well as her knowledge of roots, herbs, and the healing properties of woodland plants. My grandmother embraced her mother's gifts and shared them with me. In her sharing, she became a spiritual presence in my life, not only while she was alive but also after she died and appeared as a guardian and guide in my dreams.

My grandmother was a strong, proud Irish-American woman, intensely independent and resourceful. Her life combined the rigid tenets of a rural southern Protestant upbringing with Celtic and southern hill-country magic, ritual, and a gift for healing. The link between me and my grandmother seemed more genetic and intense than any of my other familial bonds. An important gift from my grandmother's past was born into me — an imprint of generations of southern women healers that seemed to skip her own children and become part of me. We were both aware of the transmission of that gift, which created an invisible, unspoken connection between us from the moment of my birth.

My grandmother was part of my birth and my growing. I was born in a small hospital in Cullman, Alabama. My mother, one of nine children, lived with my grandmother for the first year after my birth while my father looked for a job and a place for his new family to live — not an easy task in the years immediately following World War II. My parents had met in Mobile, Alabama, during wartime. My father worked as a mechanic on the *Memphis Belle,* a military aircraft, and my mother tested bomb connections in a munitions factory. They married as the war was coming to an end, at a time when housing was scarce or nonexistent and jobs were even harder to find. My mother was also ill; my birth had been difficult and not well-tended. My grandmother brought me back to her house in the Alabama mountains, bathed me and rocked me during the first year of my life, and sang lullabies to me as my mother regained her strength.

When I was one year old, my parents moved to Memphis, Tennessee. My father had found work as a mechanic in a new GE lamp plant, where Christmas-tree lights were made. Our house was in the rural outskirts of the city, a cotton-market boomtown steeped in the traditions of the Mississippi Delta: blues, Beale Street, rock 'n' roll, and the Peabody Hotel, the social embodiment of King Cotton. I grew up at a time when the city was swept away by its infatuation with one of its more famous residents, Elvis Presley — a tangible icon who signed autographs and passed out presents to throngs of children in the local five-and-dimes.

The home I grew up in was a small, government-built house that my parents purchased before the landscaping was even completed.

Engulfed by the sprawling city of Memphis, the property had originally been surrounded by dirt roads, fields, and the large old sweet-gum trees that now bordered the new driveways. One of those massive sweet-gum trees grew near the end of our driveway, where a gleaming white concrete sidewalk had just been poured. One of my earliest memories was of watching the tires of my tricycle crush the bulbous green seed bouquets of the sweet-gum tree into the white grains of the new sidewalk. The new driveways glared against the remains of the old forests that had once comprised the larger landscape of the Otsby Plantation. The plantation, already reduced to the size of a large city lot when I was a child, disappeared by the time I grew up, giving way to low-income housing, an indifferent kind of slavery perhaps just as insidious to a neighborhood as the slavery that provided the livelihood of its earlier population.

playmates in paradise

I was an only child, growing up in this close-knit suburban neighborhood of other families with solo children, all living in a maze of backyards bordering each other in a quilt-like configuration. We were a strange tribe of children, with no siblings, no stories of rivalry, no dramas of first-born, middle-born, or last-born, and no one to blame but ourselves for our joys and follies. At the time, I never considered the odds of there being so many single children in one neighborhood, all within playing range of each other. There were seven of us with interconnecting backyards — a giant jigsaw puzzle of landscape that allowed us acres of space, endless choices of climbing trees, and the push-and-shove "dare-you" joy of wriggling through the grates of the underground ditch that became our secret passageway from one yard to the next.

As a group, we were loved by our parents and abused by no one but ourselves — and then only over important things like land boundaries or the directorship of the latest play, copied from popular children's magazines (I was always the director). We constructed sets from leftover lumber scraps, set up kitchen chairs, and made costumes from scarves and old clothing, even using the huge sycamore leaves to weave headdresses or what we perceived to be native garments. I was the "middle child" of our strange community of only children, and I could outmanipulate all the others. I shouted orders, corrected lines, and even attempted to settle disputes over who was going to play what role. We put on the plays with our makeshift sets and peculiar costuming to an adoring audience of parents. We played out endless episodes of Roy Rogers and Dale Evans, gender not being an issue, and we married each other in mock ceremonies using bouquets of Queen Anne's lace.

At least three times a week, we went to the local Baptist church as a group. By the time I was twelve, I could sing every verse to every Baptist hymn. We all sang in the choir, struggled in our total-immersion baptisms, and suppressed giggles as the latest revival minister sprinted across the stage in his white-patent-leather loafers declaring his devotion to a Maker who wouldn't allow us to dance together but had the power to snatch this man or that from the bottle, or from drugs, or from wicked women, or from whatever fashionable hell was the latest style for summer saviors.

There were no air conditioners in the early fifties — certainly none that a simple working-class family could afford. Midday was too hot for hard playing, so in the heat of the day I would sit in front of the electric floor fan quietly reading the piles of books I'd checked out from the bookmobile. The droning hum of the fan blew air across my body and flipped open pages from the topmost books. Sometimes I read aloud while my mother crocheted intricate patterns of lace and flowers that became doilies and antimacassars. My father worked odd shifts at the lamp plant, and I would wait for him to come home and read to me as I curled up on the old maroon chenille sofa decorated with large white feathery plumes. As he read, I traced the plumes and grooves on the ornate wooden arms with my fingers. During the day, my friends and I read together, too, sitting in backyard swings or small sandboxes, huddled in patches of shade cast by newly planted trees. By the age of twelve, I had read every book I could borrow from the library or the bookmobile.

When the sun moved out of the midday sky I romped the neighborhood with two girlfriends who lived on either side of my house. We were more like sisters than friends. We biked and skated and played house from one porch to the next, arguing incessantly, breaking ranks only to buy ice cream from the traveling Good Humor man whose horse always stopped automatically under the large sweet-gum tree. We raced toward those wagon bells every day as though our lives depended on it. The Good Humor man waited patiently as we scrambled to mothers for dimes and nickels to buy confections on a stick that began melting before we even pulled the paper away.

There was an unspeakable sadness among us when the horse was replaced by a twirling, carnival-like ice-cream vending machine. When the horse left, the black vendors who cried their wares on the streets, with huge baskets of tomatoes and other vegetables balanced on their heads, also seemed to disappear. It was as if an era simply ended the last day the horse stopped under the sweet-gum tree. The black ladies dressed in silk and organdy, with colorful hats peppered with artificial and real flowers, also stopped singing and dancing their way to their Baptist church. The icebox disappeared and the iceman stopped delivering the huge kegs of block ice, carefully pulled out of his cart with the large black tongs. The milk bottles with paper caps and three inches of heavy cream on top disappeared from the front porch where they had always been placed in the early morning before I awoke. And an image of myself, dressed for church in white dotted swiss, sitting on the front steps bellowing with laughter at some unknown piece of joy while squeezing candy in my small hands, also disappeared. Like a special dream, I still can fill in the details missing in the photograph that captured forever the child wearing the dotted-swiss dress. I was about five years old in that photograph, the age at which I began to have dreams that I would recall in adulthood.

the ritual of dream-telling

EVERY MORNING when I was a child my mother would ask me, just as she had been asked when she was a child, "What did you dream last night?" However, the question was asked only after certain conditions were met — conditions that seemed to bear important consequences if ignored. The dream-telling could never be before breakfast; the meal had to be completed, or else some sort of bad luck would result from the improper timing. I never knew what bad thing would happen, but I never questioned the condition. And I understood that if I waited until the proper time for the dream-telling, a bad or frightening dream could not come true. On the other hand, recounting a good dream was like acting it out; the telling seemed to solidify its reality.

When I became an adult, I met people from Australia, Italy, and other cultures who recalled similar rituals of telling dreams at the breakfast table, usually after the meal. Like many such rituals, the reason for waiting until after a morning meal seems to have been lost. Even today, my own family sits down with tea, coffee, and muffins before we begin to share our dreams from the night before. Perhaps we digest dreams in telling them the way we digest the morning meal — a refreshing beginning to the day if it is a pleasant dream, an opportunity to explore and share the dream if it's disturbing. I recently became aware of the continuation of the ritual of dream-telling in my own family when my three-year-old grandson toddled in from his bedroom, sleepily stared at his morning pancake, took a bite, and then with a huge grin asked if I wanted to hear his dream. We recall dreams best in the morning when we wake up. In fact if we do not write them down, hold them in our thoughts, or share them we lose them, so we wake up, come to breakfast, a common experience for most of us, and tell the first story important to us upon waking, which is probably a dream. The habit of telling a remembered dream before it slips away then becomes a ritual.

Attaching disaster to breaking the order of a ritual — the bad thing that might happen if I told the dream before breakfast — appears over and over in the rituals of our lives. I recall, like many children, the rhyme "step on a crack/break your mother's back," chanted as we leaped over sidewalk scoring lines. At first the rhyme was silly, then it took on a realism that was threatening if I stepped on a crack while thinking of the rhyme. I would cautiously check on my mother when I came home after a harrowing two-block walk over multitudes of sidewalk lines. No wonder I still wait cautiously until I have at least taken a sip of tea before I share a dream.

My father scoffed at the daily ritual of dream-telling that my mother and I enjoyed. He never shared our enthusiasm and was reluctant to tell his own dreams. Instead, he joked about dreaming or casually quipped that he had "dreamed he was awake but woke up to find he was asleep but dreaming still" — possibly a statement that revealed more about his dreaming than he was willing to admit.

As I grew older, I became aware that my mother told her dreams because she was always expected to tell them, not because she was particularly intrigued or moved by them. Dream-telling was a tradition in her childhood home, a part of her life when she was growing up, but the individual elements of each dream held no interest for her. The importance of dreams was instilled in her by her mother, my grandmother, but she usually remembered dreams only in general terms. However, she was aware of the precognitive nature of some of her dreams, and when I was a child she shared a favorite dream of a yellow dress. When she first moved to Mobile and met the man who would become my father, she dreamed about her first date with him and the purchase of a yellow dress for the date. She left work and went to the local department store where she found the dress from the dream. She was so stunned that she traded hard-to-come-by sugar-ration and stocking stamps to buy the dress. I loved the dream of the yellow dress, not only because I was intrigued by a dream that could play itself out in such a magical fashion, but also because my mother had saved the yellow dress. In my young mind, the physical presence of the dress was the same as waking, like Sleeping Beauty, into a dream. It was a magical dress. I would play dress-up in the yellow dress and pretend that I was dancing, winning beaus on the ballroom floor or finding the man of my dreams, who was dazzled by the dress that had emerged from a dream.

Discovering meaning in Dreams

My mother believed that if she dreamed about someone, the dream indicated illness or other bad news about that person. This notion may have been translated into the southern mountains from the Celtic tradition of tragic ballads and stories. In many of these songs and stories, dreams of people spun themselves out alongside visions of owls and doves as omens of death and disaster. Lovers would see each other in dream graves or murdered in visions, then appear in the ballad or story as post-dream apparitions in bedrooms, parlors, or on gloomy hillsides on foggy nights. In my grandmother's old house, cousins often gathered at night in the warmth and light of the enormous parlor fireplace and spun tragic yarns of death and woe, reminiscent of an ancient Irish or Scots bard telling a story or singing a family ballad that inevitably ended in death and despair. After all, life was difficult on a small cotton farm in the hill country. Doctors were only available when they made their rounds; families lived miles apart; and tragedy played a major role in every family's life. I heard my mother tell stories of children who died in flu epidemics and farmers who were killed in terrible accidents with old hand-plows pulled by irascible mules, and the story of a young girl who choked to death because her brothers couldn't get her back to her family in time to save her.

If my mother's dreams were precognitive, they may have described the pain and sorrow of the families who worked difficult land in a time of economic depression and war. Pleasant dreams were incompatible with hoeing cotton in the hot, rutted fields of small, self-sufficient farms. That self-sufficiency, a seemingly sweet goal, was hard-won by the families who toiled against bad weather, insects, and the cursed invasive kudzu vine, planted across the south by order of a well-meaning president.

Little wonder my mother's dreams reflected tragedy rather than joy. Surrounded by such hard stories, I think she ceased to recognize dreams of joy and promise. We dream our lives; she was dreaming hers. She never had the luxury of recording dreams and going back to check them against the hard reality of her waking life. In fact, recording dreams would have seemed like a silly, maybe even eccentric, exercise to her. Dreams were told, not written.

My mother's dreams probably had depth beyond her tragic assumptions. That depth was never evident on the surface, nor did my mother ever talk about it with me, and it's possible that she never understood it. Yet I felt that, somewhere in the complexity of my roots, I had inherited the ability to find greater depth in my dreams. When I was a child, I began to record some of my dreams, but only those that were particularly interesting or seemed to speak to me in some special fashion. I scribbled notes about the important dreams and tucked them away in books or in the backs of drawers. Years later, I discovered and bundled together many of these dream notes.

Many of my earliest dreams reflected daily activities, much like the dreams I have as an adult. Childhood dreams were, by nature, reflective of a child's environment; I still recall dreaming about Tonto and the white horse Silver, and I remember funny dreams of TV cartoons translated from black-and-white to color in my mind.

I think we all recall a first important or unusual dream. We may not remember all the details, but there is always something special about the dream, whether delightful or frightening, that makes it stay with us into adulthood.

For example, I have a friend named Trish who grew up in a large family in the Saratoga Springs area. She had the top bunk in a room she shared with two brothers. One brother experienced what she described as a "collision" of illnesses — flu, measles, mumps, and chicken pox, all within weeks of each other. She was four years old at the time, but she still remembers how worried her family was. They were concerned that her brother might not survive. After a fretful night, she told her mother about a dream she'd had; her mother was so touched by it that Trish retained it in her own memory and shared it after the children were all grown. In this dream, Trish felt something awaken her. She looked over toward her brother and saw him surrounded by a glow that she understood to be his guardian angel. She sat up and stared at the soft green glow, and knew that her brother would recover. She told her mother the dream vision the next morning, and her mother kept the account safe for both of them so that they could share it as their private bond.

My first strongly memorable dream occurred when I was five years old. I dreamed that I was standing in my front yard playing with a doll carriage. In the dream, I looked up and saw the other children running toward me and calling to me. Several days later, I was standing beside a doll carriage in my front yard, playing with several neighborhood children. I suddenly found myself reliving the dream — hearing, seeing, and saying things that had occurred in the dream. Today I recognize this as a classic example of déjà vu, but it was profoundly disorienting to a small child who had never experienced this feeling of walking into a dream. I tried to stop the process — to change the next words — because I was both intrigued and discomforted by this feeling of losing a comfortable reality. The other children stared as I babbled nonsense to stop the flow of words I had dreamed before, and then it was over. The more comfortable, familiar reality settled in again, and I folded myself inside it.

But soon other night dreams began to foretell small events in my life. Some were extraordinary in the accuracy with which they previewed later events in waking life. In dreams, I unwrapped birthday presents before they were purchased, much less given. In a dream, I located my lost cat several blocks from my house. Some of my night dreams began to trouble me because they were "bigger" dreams; they foretold larger events and brought me to an early realization that there was a greater mystery to dreaming. When I was eleven years old, I saw a paralyzed neighbor standing before me in a dream, well and whole again, bidding me farewell. Days later my mother, stunned by my foreknowledge of our neighbor's death, listened to his grief-stricken widow tell of her husband's sudden death on the night of my dream. In another dream, which my mother and I had simultaneously, we heard my father's cries for help and awoke startled, running frightened into the hallway. At that moment the telephone rang, and the caller told us that my father had just lost a finger in an accident at work. That was when I began to understand that, even when my dreams were terrifying, they bore important messages that I needed to hear or share.

Adventures with the Drowning Boy

When I began to attend public school, my dreams and reveries helped me survive the endless days before classes were dismissed for the summer. Classrooms were too hot for concentration, and studies seemed too easy and monotonous to be worthy of attention. I was a good student, but I was bored and prone to daydreaming. When I was about nine years old, I had a night dream that I used as the nucleus of an elaborate set of daydreams. This was the night dream.

The Drowning Boy

I come to the edge of a shallow river where I find a canoe and a drowning boy. I pay no attention at first, because I think he is faking the drowning; we are not in deep water. I finally realize that he is really drowning, and I pull him to safety. He has dark hair, a pleasant face, and a sensitive disposition. I know that we will always be friends, and will always be available to help one another.

I liked the dream so much that I expanded it into a series of daydreams that helped me drift away from the boredom of the classroom into a world I created for myself and the dark-haired boy. He and I became partners — heroine and hero in a world strung between earth and sky, the two connected by magic ladders and traversed on the backs of beautiful wild horses, one white and one black, that appeared when needed and disappeared in a flash. Our friendship was real and heroic, but he had only a face, no name. In each of our adventures, we moved through requisite tests of fire, ice, wind, and water — obstacles difficult to conquer at first appearance, but easier each time thereafter. We were protected and empowered by the conquest, and we easily moved between the heavens and earth on a magic ladder through a split in the heavens. Our mission was always to save someone who had issued a call for help, sometimes rescuing each other before the adventure ended. I often asked myself, "Who is this boy?" He seemed to be an integral part of my childhood, part of my spirit, part of my waking and sleeping. It saddened me when I had to part with him and re-enter the life of the classroom. I believed that he had a waking existence somewhere and that I would grow up and find him.

As I grew older, I became embarrassed by my daydreams of the boy and our adventures. I was becoming a teenager in the 1960s — not a particularly good time in the South to learn the skills necessary for battling adversity. Before Kennedy was shot, quieting the high-school hallway chatter about what to do for the weekend; before Vietnam and world events shoved my generation into early graves, hospitals, rebellion, and the questioning of values held sacred by our parents' generation; before my generation turned back to an earlier generation — our grandmothers and grandfathers — for answers, the white female southern child was not supposed to battle the adverse conditions of her life. She bore them because they were tied unconditionally to that single-minded, sacrificial southern impression of God's will. That will rarely provided space for the strength within oneself to overcome adversity and illness.

the gifts of my grandmother

BUT IN ALL THINGS there are contradictions, and my grandmother remained that contradiction in my life. She had not only fed and nurtured me in the first year of my life, she had fed and nurtured the best part of me that was southern. She continued to be a major influence in my life even after we moved away from her house, even after I grew up and began a life independent of my birth family. We visited her in the mountains for several weeks every year of my life until she died — and even then she appeared, when needed, in my dreams. She gave me gifts of strength and generosity, as well as a stubbornness that often surfaced as defiance and obstruction. In her shadow, I breathed in and assimilated the elements of the South that both repulsed and enchanted me. The most empowering of those elements was my grandmother's strength of character, an inner strength unique to the mythology of the "southern woman."

That strength often emerged as a rejection of values held most dear to southerners. In the South, God's will could step down from the fire-and-brimstone podium and hold tenaciously to one's soul unless that soul could be shaken free and allowed space to interpret and understand the inner voice, the "big dream," the spirituality of being. Having acquired some of that inner freedom from my grandmother, there always seemed to be parts of me experimenting with different ways to look at life. I felt a need to bring all of my parts together, to interpret the diverse aspects of myself and create harmony. But it took me half a lifetime to achieve that sought-for sense of harmony and integration.

SOUTHERN ROOTS:
HEALING IN THE FOREST

*U*nderstanding and paying attention to "big dreams" was a concept my grandmother understood and imparted to me in some invisible way. When I visited my grandmother in the summers, I shared my dreams with her. I remember one particular summer when I was eight or nine years old and had been talking to my grandmother about dreams. She took my hands in hers and asked: "I know you dream, child; we all do, but tell me, what kind of dreams do you dream?" I don't recall if I answered her; I do recall, however, that I knew what she was asking. She was asking about the "big dreams," the dreams of my life that could warn, soothe, help, and heal me when I needed them.

As I mentioned earlier, my grandmother not only acknowledged the importance of my dreaming when I was a child; when I needed advice, she appeared in my dreams after she died. In these dreams, she showed me things from my southern heritage — sometimes a past more distant than my life — in new ways that allowed me to find a significance missed when I was a child.

For example, on a recent visit to the South I talked with a friend about sand yards. In rural mountain Alabama in the days before lawn mowers, homes were often surrounded by "sand yards," which were kept free of debris by sweeping. They were easier to maintain than grass yards cut with scythes, but they were more than just a convenience. The conversation with my friend triggered both a memory and a dream, in which my grandmother expanded my childhood experience of sweeping her sand yard into an understanding of possible connections with southern ritual in earlier times.

The dream recalled the magic of "yard-sweeping" — a practical mountain magic that had the power to call in the spirit. Yard-sweeping was accomplished with tough straw brooms that could make patterns and designs in the fine-grained white sand. I loved to make patterns in the soft, deep sand; they became more elaborate and evocative as I swirled and traced them. I also liked to play under the house in the sand — a place that was cool and private — with my only companion being the occasional dog or chicken curious to see who had invaded their favorite territory.

THE YARD-SWEEPER

I am back at my grandmother's old house at an earlier time. It is not my grandmother I see, but possibly my great-grandmother. The sand yard is larger than it was when I was a child, and it surrounds the house. I have been playing under the fieldstone-pillared house, and I sit watching the woman sweep the yard. She sweeps a picture border of her dream images from the night before. They mean nothing to me — just geometric shapes — but they are the expression of her dream. In the center are other symbols she has just swept; they portray stars and paths, a message from her dreams, the broom seemingly guided by the dream itself.

This dream came to me long after my grandmother died, but it illustrated the personal magic of my grandmother's influence and recalled a distant ancestral heritage. I cherished the dream because it initiated me into a better understanding of the ritual magic of sweeping yards, and because it reminded me of the first log house where my grandparents lived until I was nine years old.

the old log house

THE HOUSE was an eighteenth-century mountain house that my great-grandparents acquired when they first traveled over the Alabama mountains. They arrived with a tall-case clock, some chairs, and a wagon-load of personal possessions. They claimed the cabin and one hundred acres of land, which included a magnificent old-growth oak forest. The house had beds in the parlor and window openings without glass, which were covered by makeshift shutters attached with leather hinges. An immense stone walk-in fireplace warmed the sleeping parlor, and another held the iron crane, pots, kettles, and iron ovens for the kitchen. Nine children, seven of whom survived into adulthood, once sat at the long trestle table in the kitchen and tumbled through the parlor at night to the two large bedrooms filled with beds, pallets, and trundles. A hallway separated the bedrooms from the parlor and kitchen. This hallway, which once formed the "dog-trot" breezeway of the double-pen log cabin, a common frontier building style that looked like an H, had been enclosed and fitted with doors when the house was sided with clapboards.

My great-grandmother was still alive when I first visited the log cabin, but I only met her once; she preferred solitude. She lived alone in a one-room cabin a mile into the fields beyond my grandparents' house, where the furnishings were a bed, a rocking chair, and a few personal possessions. I walked there with my grandmother to visit her on her one-hundredth birthday. Years later, my mother told me that she visited my great-grandmother (her grandmother) almost every day when she was a child, and would follow her through the woods as she gathered special herbs and plants to make what my mother called "magic cures." In a similar fashion, I often followed my grandmother during summer visits and watched her gather special herbs and plants — a gift inherited from her mother to pass on to the next generation.

My grandfather was alive during my childhood, but he never influenced my life in the way my grandmother did. He tilled the land, tended the mules, paid the bills, and spoke little. He barely rested between chores, even on the hottest summer days, but would join us for midday "dinner," the largest meal on a southern farm. He was a large man who ate heartily and went to sleep early because a farm day began before 4:00 A.M. My favorite memories of him were visual: grandfather sitting backward astride a ladder-back chair, his arms resting on the top of the back, the chair slightly tilted; or grandfather sitting on a bench under a large oak tree, feeding the chickens. Once he reached into the sand and pulled out a black snake — the kind that liked to sun just under the surface —

and threw it far into the tall grass surrounding a field. Occasionally he would bring out an old farm sled and hitch it to the mules to give us a ride, but I didn't like the mules; they had unpleasant dispositions and would try to reach around and bite us. I liked hearing him out in the fields, though, calling "gee" and "haw" as he guided the mule-drawn plow.

My grandparents, the old double-pen log house, the forest, my southern ancestral past — all these could be found twenty miles back from the main road in rural Alabama; back into the mountains, back along dirt roads, gravel paths, and bridges that collapsed with the spring rains; back in the heart of Winston County, noted in the Civil War for its people's refusal to take sides and for its virgin oak forests, its clear springs, and the fields that once served as home for its native Indians. The Indians were now long-departed and mostly forgotten, except in the occasional genetic cheekbone or the straight lock of dark hair on a descendant of the people who once hunted in the now-plowed fields.

When I was nine, my grandmother decided it was time to have a "modern" house. Although there were still no electric lines or even the possibility of indoor plumbing, a new wood-fired cookstove and a kitchen sink with a water pump in a room no longer dominated by a walk-in fireplace and wash-tubs brought pleasure to my grandmother. At that time, my father shared one of the few dreams I ever recall him telling: a precognitive dream. He loved the old house, and he was reluctant to demolish it because he had dreamed that the beams spoke to him. In his dream, as he ripped the mortise-and-tenon joints apart he felt their strength and their pain. In waking reality, he did eventually agree to help take the house apart, but it was so strongly built that he and my uncles had to wrestle and tear at the mortise-and-tenon joints to bring the house down. I was saddened by its demolition because the house always seemed to be a physical metaphor for my grandparents' strength and endurance, and it held the memories of my great-grandparents who first moved into the Alabama mountains.

summers with my grandmother

MY GRANDMOTHER'S strength came from many generations of Irish women who had carved their lives from dense forested mountains. Like them, she carved her life from a hundred-acre cotton farm at the base of her own virgin forest. She was quiet, like me, and she had a cautious smile that seemed reserved for special moments among the dense oaks, for the smell of tall pines, for the peace of the ending of a long summer day, for the joy of new life, and for me.

I would arrive with my parents in the intense heat of July to visit my grandmother. All the local relatives would gather for our arrival, and I would approach my grandmother with the same caution and silence each year, as though it was the first time I'd ever seen her. Relatives would poke at me and tease me about my silence: "Don't you even have a kiss for your grandmother?" I did, but it was silent, and no one but my grandmother understood. She would touch my shoulders with her thin hands and look hard into my eyes. I was never really prepared for what I felt; there seemed to be a magic cord between us, drawing us inside one another.

In the hot summer evenings when I was small, I curled up in my grandmother's lap and listened as her voice rambled in a sleepy monotone reminiscent of the southern Irish hill songs. Her voice mimicked the droning rhythm of that unique beat, singing a southern child's past into the present, singing the songs that became my memory.

Field and Forest

My favorite place on the farm was a large flat field bordering an old-growth oak forest. A clear stream flowed through the forest and field and disappeared somewhere underground at the base of a rocky hillside that paralleled the forest. On top of that hill was another flat field where the house, pastures, and fields lay. Twice each day, my grandmother would take water buckets and go down the hill to the stream to get drinking water. Some of the water was poured into an iron kettle that had made the journey from her Celtic homeland and sat permanently in the field on a bed of wood coals. It was used for washing clothes and making soap, and sometimes for the healing rituals I heard about but never witnessed.

As the sultry southern summer days passed evenly one into the next, I followed my grandmother and imitated the events of her day. I picked berries with her while steam rose from the laundry in the hot wash-kettle, moving around the enormous old oaks in the forest as though I were in a fairyland. The forest arched around the cotton fields and climbed the hillside, where it became more dense and impenetrable near the freshwater spring. A special, almost sacred feeling filled my body and soul when I stood in the clearing bordering the forest, as if the trees had a life beyond their form.

There was a mythical "in the beginning" feeling around southern forests, with trees that pushed their deep roots into undisturbed fertile soil — a rich, dark soil that made them taller and stronger and able to survive more than the trees in a new forest. The trees of my grandmother's forest became a metaphor for life and healing as I returned time and again in my memory to that forest of my childhood. Clothes dried in the trees at the base of that hill, and wooden tubs sunned there in the grass. I felt complete peace and joy as I watched my grandmother climb the long, steep hill back to the house above with buckets of fresh spring water, her firm mouth set with determination. I would dance in the small clearing at the base of the hill alongside the spring, moving just to the edge of the forest , stretching my arms as wide as possible, trying to reach across the enormous breadth of the oak trunks. With each step into the shaded interior beyond the clearing, the mystery of the woods deepened. In the old-growth forest, the enormity of the oaks created such an impenetrable mass that a darkness as deep as night enveloped body and soul just steps beyond the clearing. When I looked back from behind the trees, the clearing danced with colors and the thick, humid mist of the laundry kettle's steam.

The mystery of the old forest — stories of healing, of hidden moonshine stills, and of escaped convicts and gruesome monsters too terrible to comprehend — became the stuff of tales told throughout the county. The forest both frightened and haunted me in its perceived magic. In the night as I lay half-awake, half-asleep on the lumpy old featherbed trying to be still enough to feel a cool breeze through the window, my young aunt — the last of my grandmother's nine children — would torment me with the popular stories of monsters in the woods. These monsters dug enormous pits in the deepest part of the forest, and people who happened upon them would find the bones of all their missing cattle and horses and dogs — and maybe, somewhere in one of those pits, would be the bones of missing children. Then she would tell me stories of young children who, just before nightfall, went into the forest and happened upon circles of elves dancing around the trees. The children would scramble and tumble home as fast as they could, because if they had the misfortune to be swayed by fascination and join the elves in the dance, they would never return from the forest. I would fall asleep with perspiration soaking my hair and body, dreaming of elves dancing in enchanted fairy rings in the forest. The monsters would recede, silenced by the night's humid stillness, pressed into the earth by thousands of stars in my deep dreaming sleep.

Grandmother's Magic

I KNEW THAT the forest and the clearing were magic places for me, but I did not realize at the time that the magic extended far beyond my young mind's ability to grasp. I later heard other names for my grandmother: conjure woman, healer, white witch, a woman who knew the magic from old Ireland, a woman who could cure and heal with herbs and ritual magic when doctors failed to heal. The same suspicious neighbors who called my grandmother a witch in whispers as she entered the church on Sundays would not hesitate to hand her their sick child. They would watch with complete trust as she carried the child out of sight and down the hill toward the ancient oak forest, toward the mysterious clearing where the seventeenth-century laundry kettle now served a different purpose when it accepted the special herbs, turning them into a healing brew. There my grandmother, armed with herbs, riddles, and a Bible, mixed Solomon's wisdom with ancient Celtic ritual magic and returned up the hill with the child, now well on its way to recovery. There were stories of children so ill that their parents were told they would not survive; they survived in my grandmother's hands.

Sundays provided a store of special memories. Part of the enigma of my grandmother was her silence, the wisdom in her few well-spoken words, and the sharpness of her penetrating questions. I remember the power of her silence and her words on a particular Sunday.

On Sundays just after church, all of the assorted aunts, uncles, and cousins, including me, would have an enormous dinner of fried chicken, mashed potatoes, vegetables, corn bread, biscuits, and sweet-potato pie. Each Sunday, the minister chose a different house to visit, always appearing in time for the meal. This time it was our turn to receive him.

After the meal ended, we children gathered outside and sat very still in the sand under the shelter of the old porch. The heat hung heavily and snatched breath away in short, sudden movements. We watched the Baptist preacher walk toward us to join our gathering, a gaunt young man with sunken eyes, perspiring in his worn black suit. The smells of dinner still hovered in the air as he moved stiffly toward us and sat down on the straight-backed chair. Then he looked at us as though he had just noticed we were there. We sat even more quietly in the sand, waiting to hear what he would say and fanning away insects with the long, lacy branches of a chinaberry tree. My grandmother moved slowly in the kitchen, making the minister bide his time, covering the biscuits and the pies from the completed meal with a tablecloth warmed by the kitchen sun, a country custom on Sundays in the South. Only one meal was served but enough food was prepared to last for the day. Biscuits and pies were pushed into the center of the table and covered with the ends of the tablecloth. The food would be protected from houseflies, and the family could snack at leisure or create a second meal whenever they wished. Finally, the long trestle table stood ready, with food tucked away under the gingham cover, waiting for the evening meal.

My grandmother joined us, walking barefoot on the sand and watching the young minister move uneasily in her presence. She spoke a few words, then it was his turn to speak. He spoke about things holy and made some unimportant comparisons to my grandmother's hard life. She listened. Then she began to question him — quiet, intent, hard questions. The young minister tugged uncomfortably at the old black lapels of his jacket and perspired. He finally simply rose and left — his dark suit contrasting against the white-hot day. My grandmother's strength was not matched by his words, and her questions remained unanswered. I never saw him again. We all released our breath as one, knowing we had just observed a contest of wills that, at least this time, had been won by my grandmother.

For my grandmother, man's spirit was tied to the land and the endless blue of the sky, concepts hard for a young man just out of seminary to grasp. For her, God's will was the raising of strong children who were born to carry out the kind of simple duty that God had given to the earth and the earth gave to man. At times, resentment and anger welled up inside her at what she perceived as people's inability to rise to that duty. The softness that spread across my grandmother's face when a new baby was born or healed often turned to hardness when those children grew older and seemed to respond to the world, not to God's earth. She wielded magic, the Bible, and Billy Graham together like swords of truth, reading softly, listening quietly, and then — like the ancient serpent — hissing questions at the minister or at the God of her earth, sky, and forest, knowing there were no answers to satisfy her. Nor, in those moments, were her own grown children entirely satisfying to her, so she turned back to herself, to the land, to the magic forest, to God's original commands to the earth, and finally to her grandchildren.

As she grew older, my grandmother sometimes saw her Celtic past as a poor defense against the shimmering heat of summer and the bone-chilling damp of wet, snowless winters. I cherished the stories of her past and remembered the births, deaths, and the stories of childhood, spent in my grandmother's shadow, presenting a rhythm that brought a memory to my life. In her later years, she remembered the hard living of each new day as a journey, a hard journey that required a will strong enough to survive all the joy and disappointment a day could bring. But even at the end of the hardest day, she would fold her thin hands in her lap, tell me the stories of my ancestry, and write the names of my predecessors on sheets of lined notebook paper. She looked deep into my soul, some-where behind my eyes, into the depth of my dreaming and found the child she had expected all her life among her own, but had never pro-duced. She found someone to become the bearer of the dream magic, the healer in the forest.

Dream-Telling with My Grandmother

When I followed my grandmother down to the clearing, we often talked about dreams. She talked with me about the kind of daydreams a child has: dreams of what I wanted to do when I grew up, dreams of who I wanted to marry or even whether I wanted to marry at all. We also talked about night dreams, and I remember feeling that my grand-mother never shared her dreams with anyone but me. She also helped me put my own dreams into perspective by asking me questions. Later, we would revisit our discussions after she finished her chores, sitting on the sofa in the evening and discussing the details of dreams shared in the clearing.

My grandmother often told me of her "foretelling" dreams and visions. Birds were common harbingers of death in southern mythology and in my grandmother's dreaming; dreams of owls foretold the death of both of her children who died. Because she lived on a farm, many of her dreams were of the daily farm events, but some of those fell into the category of "big" dreams: dreams of crop failure if the corn were planted at the wrong time or dreams of a fox invading the chicken house and killing all the hens. When I visited, I had similar night dreams of daily farm activity: the farm landscape, the cows in the field, watching my grandfather shoot milk from the cow's udder into the kittens' mouths, or even hearing the plaintive cry of the young calf tied to the tree by the corn crib when it was being weaned from its mother. My grandmother never used the term "big dream," but I came to recognize the difference between a dream of hauling water from the creek and a dream of a dove sitting at the head of the bed of a child who subsequently died. I began to recognize the same pattern in my own dreams, and learned to distinguish the small dreams from the larger, deeper dreams that provided a road map for my life. I began to understand that the "big" dreams were the ones that tap you on the shoulder and present a message you cannot ignore.

Dreaming of death and beyond

MY FIRST "BIG" DREAM involving my immediate family occurred in the fall when I was eleven years old. My grandfather was dying. Though he was only fifty-seven years old, his hard life and bad eating habits, combined with a history of heart problems, finally took their toll; he became the victim of an early stroke. I dreamed my grandfather's death, and found the dream more interesting than frightening.

On the day my grandfather died, I had spent several sleepless nights holding vigil with my parents in the small hospital and I finally asked if I could sleep in the car for a while. I slept fitfully in the heat, dreaming of a scene in my grandparents' house with my grandfather's body laid out in the parlor according to Irish/southern tradition. I awoke from the dream and looked out the car window, watching a small dark cloud float for a seemingly endless time across an otherwise cloudless sky. In my mind, the cloud seemed to be a waking vision having to do with my grandfather; I wondered if he could see the other side of the cloud. Just then, my parents came out to tell me that my grandfather had died.

The next few days brought all the relatives — cousins, aunts, uncles, even people I didn't know were relatives — to my grandmother's small house for the ritual of viewing the body laid out in the parlor: my dream come to reality. I sat for hours in a ladder-back chair against the parlor wall watching the people, the air thick with wood smoke and the smells of food and new clothes. The room was tense with palpable grief, the stories endless recitations of memories of my grandfather. As the children played, I moved farther back into the shadows of the room, sitting even more still. I began to visualize the forest at the base of the hill and wondered why the image had crossed my mind — perhaps an image from a forgotten dream.

When I was in my early twenties, my grandmother died. Sometimes on soft summer nights, I feel an overwhelming nostalgia for a past I only just tasted. I see my grandmother then, framed in the hallway of the old house between the clapboard wall and the doors of the enormous old pie safe, floorboards slanting, the sun casting filigreed patterns of shadows across the shelves overburdened with jars of okra, corn, tomatoes, and blackberry jam. She turns, stretching her hands toward me, speaking softly: "I know you dream, child, but tell me, what kind of dreams do you dream?"

After my grandmother died, the remains of the old log house, which had been torn down years before, were hauled away. Her grown children sold the forest to a lumber company. My heart ached for the forest, and I could never return to the place where the house and forest had stood. I could never bear to see what had happened to the place where my dreaming first had meaning. People were no longer healed there; they were no longer born in the same way, nor did they die in the same way. Owls, doves, omens, and dreams no longer foretold events there, but I still carried my grandmother's legacy in a way her children had never done. Although she was never able to teach me the riddles and mystery of her own inherited magic, her own rituals for healing, I felt that the mystery had come into me through her recognition of me as the child who would someday dream the lessons necessary to healing. I didn't need the ritual; I didn't need the riddles and herbs; I had her essence inside me, and I could call her forth in my dreams when I needed her. I could feel her magic in my life, reflected in my dreams. She had taught me how, like the trees in the oak forest, to find strength in the depth of my heart and soul, to find strength to survive in the face of daunting odds, to find healing in my dreams.

Years later, when I was diagnosed with possibly fatal breast cancer, I began to dream "big" dreams in which my grandmother helped me find my own spiritual and physical strength. The process of healing is a struggle in contradictions, in highs and lows, in defining who we are when sick and who we are when well, in finding the balance that gives life meaning. My dreams during that time investigated all the parts of my soul. They plumbed the inner regions where the darkest, most unforgiving parts of me dwelled — where passions were suppressed and depression was in control. But they also explored the high, bright parts of my soul, where joy and determination to be healed opened unusual doors and insisted that healing was at hand. In order to follow the spiritual journey to heal my body, not inseparable from my soul, I found it necessary to seek my own definition of the soul. I sought my grand-mother's help with that definition, and she came in a dream; she pre-sented me with a walnut which she peeled, layer after layer, until she held the innermost fruit in her hand. She then closed her hand over the fruit and it disintegrated into fine particles that permeated the air. I used her beautiful metaphor as a guide through my dreams to a place where I could integrate body and soul and return harmony to my life.

My grandmother taught me how to honor the dreams of my life.

Precognitive Dreaming:
The Dance Hall of the Dead

*D*reaming gifts came into my life along many paths. My grand-mother used simple questions — "what kind of dreams do you dream?" — and life stories to teach me the difference between small dreams and big dreams and to show me the importance of both in my life. My mother gave me time and space for sharing my dreams within the ritual of her own cultural tradition of dream-telling. When I began to date Ron, the neighborhood boy I eventually married, we shared stories of dreams, usually in that show-and-tell style of comparison: "Oh, yes, I had a dream like that when my mom's neighbor died..." or "Did you ever dream about something before it happened?"

While studying together for a college exam one evening, Ron fell asleep on the floor. In his sleep, he called aloud, "Whatever happened to Fairview?" When he awoke I asked him about his dream, but he recalled neither having a dream nor shouting aloud. After that evening, Fairview became a favorite joke. In later years, while driving through almost any state, a highway sign would inevitably appear with direc-tional information to that state's "Fairview," sometimes a city, sometimes a school or institution. We might never know the actual dream reference to Ron's Fairview, but every Fairview sign reminds us that even the odd little dreams can bring bits of interest to our lives. This one brought a humorous reference point to a night in our early courtship, but in the way of dreams, we might still someday find a Fairview that means something greater.

Ron was also an only child, and in the maze of education and career choices we had only one child ourselves, continuing an unplanned tradition of small families. Ron escaped the Vietnam draft by joining the ROTC program in college, entering the Air Force as an officer. We awaited our son's birth in Little Rock, Arkansas, where the Air Force planted us for four years. Two months before our son's birth, Ron and I were sitting in the large parlor of our apartment when Ron began to muse about the whereabouts of a friend who was on a month-long ice-climbing expedition in New Zealand with a popular world-class climber and instructor. I listened to Ron for a moment, then I looked up: "He died last night," I said. "I dreamed it." The next day we received the news that our friend and his instructor had plunged thousands of feet down the side of a mountain to their death. I had dreamed about the death of a neighbor when I was a child, and I had dreamed about an accident in which my father had been involved when I was a child plus I had experienced many small precognitive dreams; but I had never dreamed of someone's death who was so close to me and in such a finite manner. I was shocked, but not surprised, by a dream that declared with such certainty that our friend was dead. I don't even recall all the details of the dream now, but dreaming small precognitive dreams up to that point had prepared me for the accuracy of this larger dream.

Our son's life has been interwoven with my dreaming. I dreamed his name, Evan, dreamed his birth in 1974, and even revisited his birth after experiencing some difficulty in recovering from the delivery. I had lost consciousness in an overdose of anesthesia just before he was born and could recall nothing about his birth until I dreamed the details of the delivery weeks later. I felt I had missed something important until the dream replaced it. I also dreamed about the difficulty Evan would experience in a traditional learning environment. I recoiled from those dreams because I felt I would be unable to help a child with learning problems. I battled throughout his twelve years of education with schools and teachers and struggled against a system suited best for children who learn easily through reading and writing. I fought for my child's right to learn in a normal environment in spite of his problems with words and letters and sentences. Unlike me, Evan learned best through the spoken word; even now his letters sometimes lack punctuation and capital letters, flowing in a poetic stream of consciousness. He eventually found his own life path aided by his own dreaming.

Evan's own dreaming is phenomenal — inherited, I brag, from me. As a child, he startled me repeatedly with the intense accuracy of his dreams. Some were interesting historic dreams of life in the place where he grew up. We lived in a small nineteenth-century hamlet named Glen, nestled among rolling hills in the Mohawk Valley in upstate New York. We moved from the south to upstate New York when Evan was four. It was November 1978 and the Vietnam War had just ended and we moved into our house exactly one hundred years from the completion of its building in November of 1878. In one of Evan's more fascinating dreams he walked within the dreamscape through the hamlet as it appeared in the 1870s. He saw in the dream the location of buildings long torn down or burned down and visited inside them within the dreamscape. In dreams, he met as young children people who were now old or who had passed on. I often told people that our dreams of one another were so intensely personal that they seemed connected, as if by an umbilical cord. In my dreaming, I knew when he was suffering emotionally. In later years, I sometimes trusted his dreams of me more than my own because they had the advantage of distance from my problems. When I had a crisis, I would ask him if I was going to be okay. He usually answered via a dream the next night, and sometimes with a simple "yes" or "no." Evan would go to sleep with the intent to dream an answer to whatever question I had asked. It never failed that when given a problem, he would dream the answer or at least dream the beginning of a solution. When he simply responded "yes" or "no," he was speaking from his own intuition, which I trusted as much as I trusted his dreaming. When I became ill I often turned to Evan and asked: "Am I going to make it through this?" He always answered, "Yes."

A Wedding in Tiburon

My son and I jointly experienced a big dream that was important to his self-esteem. We dreamed the same dream, with identical details, on the same night. It was a precognitive dream of his wedding, dreamed by both of us when he was seventeen years old, years in advance of the actual event. At that time, school was not going well. He was borderline dyslexic and fighting an uphill battle with reading and writing, as well as experiencing the usual angst of being a teenager and needing confidence that seemed, in his mind, elusive for him and so easy for everyone else. I had always encouraged Evan to pay attention to his dreams, to remember them, to tell them aloud, and to find meaning for his life in them. On a bright spring morning near the end of another dreadful school year, we both ran into the hallway with a dream to share. Each of us had dreamed the same dream, with details so identical that we were excitedly completing each other's sentences:

Evan is older in the dream, perhaps in his mid-twenties. I am standing in the doorway of a beautiful chapel that sits high on a hill overlooking the ocean, apparently in California. I turn to watch Evan and his bride as they pose for the after-ceremony photographs. I know her name in the dream, but only remember when I awaken that it ends with an "ie." She is a stunning young woman, Spanish or possibly Indian; there is elegance in her features. I feel the incredible joy my son is feeling.

Evan did not recall his bride's name in his dream but also dreamed that he married a beautiful woman with long black hair who appeared to be Spanish. He saw the hill and the white church and knew that he was not in a northern landscape. He also seemed to feel that his dream took place in California. Just as he awoke my father appeared briefly in Evan's dream to offer his congratulations.

This dream gave Evan the courage he needed to look forward to a brighter future. If that had been the only gift of this dream, it would have served a useful purpose. But the complete fulfillment of this dream was not to be denied. With the help of his own dreams — several of them dramatic and precognitive — Evan forged a life and meaningful career. He had several girlfriends, one of them blond and intent on marriage. But when the relationship ended, he took it in stride. "Mom," he said, "she's not the woman in our dream." I even wondered, after a few years, if Evan was missing interesting opportunities because of his obsession with our shared dream.

Then, in 1997, Evan called to say that he was coming home for Thanksgiving and was bringing a young woman he'd met in his apartment building. Then a series of last-minute incidents prevented her from coming, but when Evan arrived he could not stop talking about another young woman he'd met in the airport. She, too, had been there without her traveling companion because of a series of incidents in her own life. Weeks later, Evan called again: "Mom!! This is her; this *is* the woman in the dream!!" Within months, she and Evan were planning their wedding. She visited her relatives in California and discovered a beautiful old chapel on one of the highest hills in Tiburon, with a view of the ocean below. In July of 1998, I stood in the doorway of that chapel, looking back at my son and his new wife as they posed for photographs. She was stunning. She was of Mexican descent and had fine, elegant features — and the nickname she used ended in an "ie." It was Ophie. I smiled when the priest said that this wedding was different — "like watching a dream or fairy tale come true." I told him he had no idea how true that was.

Evan's own career led him and Ophie to California in 2000. By that time they had two children. In 2002 when I told Evan I had sent my manuscript to a publisher in California, he told me that they were going to publish my book — months before I heard back from them. He dreamed that I had flown into the Oakland airport — not far from where he and his family now live — to see my publisher, and that he had arranged to leave work early to pick me up. He still dreams with me and for me, and I still trust his intuition.

MEETING ROBERT MOSS

IN OUR FIRST YEARS in upstate New York, Ron was in graduate school and I took a position as an historic site manager in the New York State preservation system, managing — with a small staff — an eighteenth-century house museum in the Mohawk Valley — another area rich in dreaming tradition. The house was the last home of Sir William Johnson, a colorful Anglo-Irishman who was the king's superintendent of Indian affairs. While I worked there, people of the Six Nations — particularly those from the Onondaga and Mohawk nations — became my friends and shared the importance of their strong dreaming tradition.

In addition, numerous references to dreams filled the manuscripts of Johnson's letters. He understood the importance of the dream tradition among the Iroquois, and he lived his own Celtic dreaming traditions as well. As superintendent of Indian affairs, Johnson listened to the dreams of the Iroquois representatives who came to his house. They would present a dream — "My mother is recovering from an illness, and I dreamed that you sent me back with a pot to ease her thoughts of having no pot for cooking" — and Johnson would send a new pot to ease her mind. In fact, his friendship with the Mohawk and his understanding of their dreaming was legendary. According to oral history, he once traded a bright red military coat to the Mohawk chief Hendrick in exchange for thousands of acres of land — the trade having been based on mutual dreaming. (The two then promised to curb the expression of their dreaming to avoid further uneven transactions.)

the *Drowning boy enters my waking life*

IT WAS AT Sir William Johnson's house that I met Robert Moss, who took me to the next step in understanding the nature of my dreaming. At that time, Robert was a novelist whose thrillers had topped the *New York Times* best-seller list. But synchronicity and a web of fascinating dreams changed his path, bringing him to a new home and to a dreamspace in which he visited settlers and Indians of an earlier time and moved into the voice in his historic fiction of one of the people he was dreaming, Sir William Johnson.

Robert's dreams transported both of us into deepening encounters with the ancestors of the First Peoples of the Northeast, and Robert into encounters with his own tribal ancestors — Celtic origins held in common with William Johnson. We both researched eighteenth-century documents in an effort to understand the unique relationship Johnson had with the Six Nations in the Mohawk Valley, and I role-played characters found in the Sir William Johnson documents in order for both of us to understand how diverse cultures thrived together on the New York frontier. We went to workshops on Mount Lebanon, a Sufi retreat center that was once a Shaker community, where we listened to a Mohawk speaker, Tom Porter, describe the dreaming traditions of the Mohawk people. We began sharing our own dreams as if we had known each other all our lives. Within days of meeting Robert and beginning research for his Mohawk Valley project, I called him early one morning and said, "I dreamed about someone who once worked with you; who is Sarah?" I then shared the dream with Robert: Sarah who worked with Robert; Sarah currently pregnant; and Sarah being very sad because her husband just died in a terrible ski accident. Robert confirmed that the Sarah in my dream must be the Sarah who had worked with him when he lived and worked in England years before; she was currently pregnant and her husband had indeed just died in a terrible skiing accident. That dream set in motion the most remarkable dream partnership of my life. Robert and I dreamed so accurately into each other's dreams that we checked in with each other every morning to clarify the details in each of our dreams. Checking and confirming dreams was fun and adventurous. Then we realized we were dreaming with such clarity that we could use our dreams to develop tools for helping people understand dreaming in their own lives.

We recorded all our dreams and confirmed how natural it is to move into another person's dreamspace and dream the future on an almost daily basis. In this early experience of shared dreaming, I was learning to listen to my dreams, to share them in a more meaningful fashion than simply telling a dream, to use them in discussion, and to bring dreams forward to others so that they might find common resonance between their dreams and mine or those of others. Sharing dreams with others and discussing those dreams brings clarity for both the dreamer and listener who might find elements in the dream-teller's dream useful to understanding their own dreams.

IN OUR FRIENDSHIP, Robert and I knew the color of each other's dreaming, and I felt that I had found the brother I'd longed for my entire life. In our conversations we explored the possibilities for healing that had begun to open to us in dreaming. We confirmed that we possessed the ability to enter into each other's dreams and to see the future from within the dreamspace. Robert brought me a word from the Mohawk: *atetshents*, meaning "one who dreams" or, in my case, "she who dreams." Our shared dreams became more frequent and more intense. If Robert dreamed about a castle in Scotland, I would dream about the same landscape and castle as he saw in his dreams, usually on the same night. If he dreamed about a Native American scene around a campfire, I would view the same scene in my dream with possibly different details. One of us might dream a small healing dream, but the other would supply more details within a similar dreamscape. I dreamed my foot would heal from a slight injury; Robert's dream provided the healing remedy of witch hazel. We excitedly compared notes on the telephone each morning, and we discussed our developing thoughts on the nature of dreams and their ability to present imagery that could both spontaneously heal within the dream and be brought forward to be used for active healing in waking reality.

Robert and I explored together the importance of first recording every dream, no matter how seemingly inconsequential, and then honoring the dream by sharing and exploring its possibilities with family and friends. In researching the material for his Johnson stories, Robert needed to visit the Mohawk people. I accompanied Robert and his wife, Marcia, on a visit to the Six Nations Reserve in Ontario. We spent time visiting the Mohawk people but we also spent time learning more about each other's dreams and visions. Robert revealed a series of near-death experiences in his childhood and related a vision of a living serpent-staff that filled the sky. I shared my own dreams and a poem through which we entered my grandmother's world in the southern mountains. I had written many poems from about age fifteen and into my twenties about my grandmother and brought some of the more evocative ones with me to Canada to introduce my grandmother to Robert. I was afraid I would forget how important my grandmother was to me as a child so I began writing poems when I was a teenager as a way to remember her.

Then Robert asked me to share a dream from my childhood, and I told him about the night dream of the drowning boy, which had provided the nucleus for my childhood daydreams.

Robert then told me a story from his own childhood: he had almost drowned in an accident in shallow water when he was nine years old, under circumstances that mimicked the events in my dream. I was stunned by the realization that my dream had reached across continents to touch the life of someone I would meet so many years later. I now had a name to go with the face in the dream; I had finally met the boy of my childhood earth-to-sky fantasies.

From that moment on, our dreams began to touch in the night with unswerving clarity and regularity, providing continual examples of dreaming within each other's dreams. They provided healing and assistance, sometimes offering advice before we even realized we needed it. An incomparable friendship developed between us — a friendship that continues to follow diverse paths that cross and recross along uncanny lines of dreams fulfilled and yet to be fulfilled. We go back regularly in our dream journals and find dreams dated back in the mid-eighties or early nineties that are just now coming to fruition. Each time I find a companion dream or even a single dream in my journal from five, ten, or more years ago that has just played itself out in waking reality, I understand the importance of keeping a dream journal and of questioning others who keep dated dream journals who are close friends. Inevitably I find that I am sharing dreams with those closest to me and that comparing those dreams gives each dream vivid new detail. Robert's friendship and the close relationship of our families gives us more opportunity to revisit old dreams and find their relationship to our current living. Now we use dreams, not ladders and wild horses, to bridge the gap between earth and sky.

the importance of a dream journal

ROBERT FREQUENTLY REMINDED me to record every dream until doing so became a habit. His insistence brought home to me the importance of solidifying the memory of a dream; they slip away so easily, even when we promise ourselves that we will not forget. Recording my dreams made them solid and tangible, part of the world we can touch and kick or caress. The dreams fell into patterns and became companions to my waking life. Some of my dreams were mundane, but many were "big" dreams — important dreams that predicted major events in my life. Many of those dreams would easily have disappeared from my memory; had I not recorded them, I would never have recognized their connection to events in my waking life when they were played out months or even years later. The meanings of individual dreams were often obscure; sometimes my dreams remained impenetrable until waking events caught up with them. It was always fun to dip into a dream journal and see what I found; what surfaced might be an image or a road map that could help me find my way. As I fumbled along, I found that dreams could provide instructions for living, prescriptions for healing, and choices that challenged me to move beyond habit into creative breakthroughs.

little dreams can mean a lot

IN KEEPING MY JOURNAL of dreams I discovered the majority of my dreams, big and little, were precognitive. They showed me the future, whether it be the day coming or many months or even years ahead.

Precognitive dreams can foreshadow daily events in our lives or someone else's life, or they can be complicated dreams of warning, sometimes predicting accidents, death, or illness. Precognitive dreams became important in the relationship between me and my illness so I needed to understand how important the small precognitive dreams were in making me feel secure about the bigger ones. Even the smallest dreams can give us glimpses into a possible future or serve to confirm the value of a bigger dream. For example, once I dreamed that I spilled milk on the floor; in the dream, I looked down to see the pattern of the puddle of milk on the floor. The next morning, I spilled milk on the floor and literally looked down into the manifestation of my small dream. I was fascinated by this dream not because of its value as an important dream. It wasn't. What it did was confirm in exact detail my ability to dream the future, no matter how insignificant the dream appeared to be. When I had a big dream, I could then trust that dream because I knew that the little dream of spilled milk was accurate and had happened exactly as I dreamed it. I became fascinated with the ability in sleep dreams to capture future events with such accuracy. Sometimes the dream would speak in pictures or puns, making it a bit more difficult to work with, and sometimes those pictures would not manifest themselves until the dream played out in waking reality. Those were the dreams that needed work, which could be done alone or between two people or sharing with a larger group. Even then the dreams might keep their secrets until an event unfolded, but recording the dream was still an important part of the process of understanding how a precognitive dream worked. This is another reason recording became so important — I would have never recorded a dream about spilled milk before I began to keep a daily dream journal. I would have considered it nonsense. In this search for understanding and recognizing the importance of small precognitive dreams I began asking other people about their dreams and I began to make notes about their dreams. The larger field of precognitive dreams interested me. I felt that it was important to know that we all share this gift of dreaming both little and big events in our future. I also had an important dream that I needed to understand, and I hoped that discovering how the little dreams worked in my own life and in the lives of others would bring me closer to understanding the larger precognitive dream.

Every morning when I came to work I asked those I worked with about their dreams. They began to make their own connections between their dreams and their waking reality. A colleague once told me about a dream in which she saw a man walking toward her on the road. With him was the largest German shepherd she had ever seen. Two days later, she saw a man walking toward her on the road; with him was the largest German shepherd she had ever seen. This was an example in her life of seeing the value of little precognitive dreams, which play out a simple scene that occurs in waking reality within days or weeks, which confirms in a personal way the validity of the bigger dreams. They give us familiar details that are easy to identify in waking reality: the appearance of a friend we haven't seen for a while; a dress in a department store that we are drawn to because we saw it in a dream; or the milk spilled on the floor exactly as I saw it in a dream.

Another colleague shared a dream with me that took place in her mother's house. This dream was an example of one in which the precognitive elements were disguised in her memory of the dream when she awoke. In the dream, she was standing in front of her mother's fireplace and saw what she thought was blood dripping down the bricks. She was disturbed by this brief dream until two weeks later, when she was painting her mother's mantelpiece. The excess red paint had pooled under the mantelpiece and was beginning to run down the bricks — an exact visual detail from her dream.

Dreaming large

THE IMPORTANCE of recording dreams becomes even more apparent when dreams that seem implausible eventually turn out, even though disturbing or puzzling, to become valuable predictors of health and life issues.

Our bigger dreams may be unclear to us until we are comfortable with the language of our little dreams. Sometimes a "big" dream — the one that is finally so clear that we have no question about its message — comes after many years of dreams that we have not properly worked through. For example, I recorded several precognitive dreams in the year preceding my diagnosis of breast cancer. I did not work with the dreams — I did not attempt to find out what they were trying to tell me, because I did not immediately understand them. I simply recorded the dreams. I would have never remembered the dreams had I not recorded them and could have never put together such a valuable record of my diagnosis when I began to look back through my journals. However, if I had sat down alone or with another person and gone through a process of determining what each part of the dream meant to me at the time of its dreaming, I might have discovered a diagnosis months before I dreamed the larger dreams that could not be misunderstood or ignored. This is one of many reasons why keeping a journal of dreams is so important. Many dreams spread themselves over days, months, or even years. They present ample opportunities to prepare for the big events in our lives — or time to change or even prevent the outcome of a warning dream. Some dream journeys culminate in a life-changing big dream that comes when there seems nothing left but dead-ends and uninteresting choices.

Time is sometimes difficult to determine in big dreams until we become adept at working with them. We can search for clues that might be helpful in dating the dream: a person's age in the dream, a tree that has grown, or perhaps a smaller event within the dream that might play out in a more obvious fashion in waking reality. A precognitive dream of my mother's death featured an auction that only occurs in my village every two years in the fall of the year. In waking life, the auction date had already passed and my mother was ill; I knew from that dream that she might die in two years unless something changed the outcome. My mother died within one week of the next auction.

keeping the dream journal

THE IMPORTANCE of keeping a dream journal, initially working with those dreams, and then checking and rechecking them as time distances us from them cannot be overstated. As illustrated in the spilled milk dream or the dream of the German shepherd, even the most innocuous little dream — the one most likely to be neglected because of its "oddness" or because it just doesn't seem worth the bother — often proves to be one more example of the remarkable ability of our subconscious to travel beyond the realm of our ordinary reality. If we can trust the little dreams, we can change our lives with the big dreams.

One of my favorite dreams from my own journal — one I almost didn't record — was about two dogs:

DREAM OF TWO DOGS

I am sitting at a long table in the office at work. There is a single folding chair facing me. A woman with wild red hair comes into the room, sits down in the chair, and begins to excitedly relate a story to me. I cannot hear her words, but I do see two little boxes, one on either side of her head, like dialogue boxes in a comic strip. One box has a black Lab dog in it, and the other has a yellow Lab dog. As the woman's lips move soundlessly, the box with the yellow Lab slowly fades into the background and disappears.

If I had not recorded this dream, I probably would have forgotten it. Several weeks later, a staff member at my workplace brought a visitor into the office and asked me to listen to the visitor's story. I was sitting downstairs working at a long table, and there was a folding chair near the middle of the room. The visitor came in, sat down, and began to relate an event that took place at her house in a nearby village. I was already hooked because the woman facing me had wild red hair, and I knew I was revisiting my dream in waking reality. The woman owned two dogs: a yellow Lab and a black Lab. A disgruntled neighbor hated the dogs and had threatened to call the animal control officer because they barked. The woman attempted to resolve the problem but, much to her horror, went out to the fenced backyard kennel one morning to find the yellow Lab dead; the neighbor had fed the dogs poisoned meat. The black Lab had not eaten the meat and was still alive, but the yellow Lab had eaten the meat. I was fascinated by the telling of the story, not because I knew the woman, not even because it was a distressing story, but because her story validated a dream that I would have never remembered had I not been in the habit of recording every dream. The woman's story and my dream convinced me never to neglect a dream, no matter how small or unimportant.

the red honda

ONE OF THE MOST remarkable of those "small dreams with bigger import" was a precognitive dream that I called the Red Honda dream. Robert and I had frequently discussed my style of dreaming: a gift for seeing things from a distance. We talked about the dreamer who is an observer and the dreamer who is inside the dream — those roles not being confined to one person. We all dream differently in different dreams. My particular gift of observation within a dream came alive during my illness and then kept me alive. In the context of observer and insider, Robert and I explored the gift we all have of being able to reopen a dream, walk back into it, pull together the necessary details, and then change the dream by heeding it or honoring it in waking reality.

After I awoke from the Red Honda dream, I called Robert, quite anxious, because I had dreamed that I was injured in an automobile collision but I couldn't recall any details. Robert carefully walked me back through the dream — dream reentry — and asked me questions. As he asked me questions — what was the weather in the dream, did I see anything familiar, what color was the car — my memory of the dream became clearer. By the time our conversation ended, I had all the details I needed to change the dream's ending.

THE RED HONDA

I am traveling to work in a snowstorm, and I approach a familiar bridge between two small towns. I see a red Honda coming from the opposite direction. The Honda suddenly skids into my path, slamming my car into the side of the bridge. I am injured.

I didn't know when this dream would actually play out, so I wrote it down on a piece of paper and taped it up on the dashboard of my car. Later that year, I was driving to work in a snowstorm. The road traction was good, so I wasn't concerned about my ability to arrive home safely. I was stopped at a light when I noticed a red Honda on the opposite side of the bridge. I hadn't forgotten the dream because it was in front of me every time I drove the car. I would honor my dream. I remained stopped when the light turned green, much to the annoyance of the other drivers. Then I watched as the red Honda skidded and fishtailed back and forth from one side of the bridge to the other, finally hitting the side of the bridge and coming to a stop. No one was injured. I then proceeded across the bridge, convinced that I had escaped a collision because of my remembered dream.

The Red Honda dream and the waking experience with a red Honda that followed the dream gave Robert and me a valuable lesson in our ability to change a dream. It was also a valuable lesson about the insights available from sharing a dream and asking questions that highlight and retrieve elements from that dream. I would never have recalled the color or kind of car, or even the weather conditions, had I not discussed the dream with Robert. Those important details, gleaned from reentering the dream, saved me from injury and may have saved my life.

Our dreams are real. We must look at them as another room in our life where we share and learn lessons for living, playing, communicating, healing, and even dying. We must learn from our dreams and create space for them so that they can speak to us in waking and sleeping. We not only see the future in our dreams, but dreams about the future give us the ability to make choices and shape the future for the better.

Dance hall of the dead

WORKING WITH precognitive dreams, answering Robert's questions of my dreams, and re-entering the dreamspace to investigate details in a precognitive dream were all techniques leading me back to a puzzling series of precognitive dreams that had concerned me for decades. The dream I needed to understand was actually a series of dreams that I began to call the Dance Hall dreams. I needed to understand the myriad of ways a precognitive dream played out in waking reality. Working with dreams and recording them made me well acquainted with the recurring dream that changed and grew more ominous as the years passed. Over the years, I kept notes on this dream and began to recognize its growing relevance as it shifted from a simple dream into one that predicted my death. In the 1980s, I shared this dream with Robert and told him of my firm belief that, unless I discovered the deeper meaning of the dream and how to change its outcome, it was indeed predicting my early death. Two decades passed before I unraveled the mystery of this recurring dream.

In 1972, I scribbled this short poem in the corner of a journal. It expressed my feelings about the serial dream that had haunted me for several years at that time:

What do you fear?

What do you see?

Is it a corridor that leads to a place that some men fear?

She Who *dreams*

What is there to fear?

Life is the corridor; death is only the door.

THE DREAM OCCURRED off and on throughout the 1960s and early 1970s, each recurrence presenting a slowly developing theme with increasingly troubling variations. The dream cycle of "The Dance Hall Dreams" began when I was in high school. In the earliest version, I was walking down a long hallway with rows of closed doors on either side. In later dreams, the doors along the hall swung open revealing friends, relatives, and classmates who had died since the previous occurrence of the dream. As the dream developed, I recognized the faces of boys I had known who were killed in the Vietnam War. In every version, I was moving toward a wooden door at the end of the hallway. In the dreams, I knew very clearly that if I went through the door I would exit life and pass into death. Little by little, I was moving closer to the door. I attended a large high school in suburban Memphis in the mid sixties, and I attended college in the early seventies in the same city. College classes were packed with young men trying to escape the war for a few extra years, and the ends of school terms were often sad, with many of those same young men sobbing openly when grades failed to be good enough to keep them safe for one more semester. Those years brought the shock of classmates being drafted into the unpopular Vietnam War the moment their college deferment lapsed for any reason. This was a period of draft enlistment, and the war brought death to almost every family with a son. Page after page of my high-school yearbook presented images of young men who never returned home, or who returned home with maimed bodies and minds.

Suicide took the life of one young man whose life became somehow unbearable; accidents and illness claimed other classmates. The opening pages of the yearbook were filled with memorials. A beautiful young woman was gunned down by a family member — a case of mistaken identity in a family rumored to have mob connections. The murder trial reports filled the newspaper columns for months. As soon as the furor over her death dissolved, a more evil and insidious threat gripped the entire city: a psychopathic killer, a serial murderer, was on a rampage. He preyed on women, young and old, brutally torturing and killing them. The faces of the murdered women multiplied; the murderer's rage intensified. New faces of victims appeared weekly, all women. The last victim was a high-school friend, a vibrant, talented, beautiful young woman who had been my classmate for seven years.

Each of these friends and classmates who had died appeared one at a time through the open hallway doors of my serial dream. The hallway sometimes morphed into the roadway of a parade — an avenue lined with houses on either side — and, finally, in the later dreams, into a dance hall with lines of dancers on either side of me as I waltzed alone down the center. The figures of the departed would fall back, becoming shadows, leaving me alone with a clear path to the wooden door. The image at the end of the path never changed: there was always a small wooden door. I knew that the door separated the world of the living from the world of the dead. In all of these dreams, my life was short. In one of the dreams, the hallway was littered with newspapers. I picked up a dreamscape newspaper and read the date of an obituary. It was my obituary. I was forty-three years old. The dream terrified me, but I could not understand how I was supposed to die when I was forty-three. Would I be hit by a car? Would some other terrible accident occur? Would I be ill? I told no one about these dreams because I hoped they were just anxiety dreams born out of so many friends and class-mates having died tragically. I was no longer able to say the dreams were just anxiety dreams when the date of my death was revealed. Then I seemed to simply begin to move toward that date in robotic fashion, waiting to see what the cause of my premature death might be and hoping I could find some way to prevent it. I didn't realize then that I should have been recording other dreams that might have clarified the Dance Hall dreams and given me an early warning message of prevent-ing my death or the possibility of my death. I didn't think then that a dream could be changed or looked at in any way other than how it was presented.

In 1988, just two years before my forty-third birthday, I recorded a version of the Dance Hall dream that seemed to project my death even more clearly than the previous dreams:

Bride of Death

I am walking through a forest, holding a small flower. As I walk, I begin to stroke the petals of the flower upward. As I stroke the petals the flower grows large, frilly, and more fragrant. The path becomes the familiar dance floor, and I am aware that I am dressed in a long gown, like a bride, still holding the flower. The faces of the people on either side of the hall are familiar; they are the ones who have died. I am alone, as always, dancing toward the small wooden door at the far end. The door remains far away as I dance toward it and the faces become hazy, receding into the shadows like memories. They fade into old newspaper clippings, pressed into a book in my hands. I wonder, as I often do in these dreams, what these people would have become had they lived. As I wonder about their lives, the newspaper pages become colored petals; and I drop them along the floor, still walking, still moving toward the door, wondering in the dream if I have accomplished enough in my life. I am closer to the door in this dream than I have ever been. The newspapers in this dream also announce my death. I know precisely that I am forty-three years old.

I was now dressed as a bride walking down the aisle, prepared for my death. I began to feel that I had signed a contract stating the date of my death. I found myself constantly questioning the value of my life. Had I accomplished anything worthwhile? Would I accomplish anything before I was forty-three? Did I really have to die at that age? If I did not have to die at that age, could I change the dream? If I could change the dream, how would I do so? What would precipitate my death? There seemed to be no clues in the dream about the cause of my death, but since I wasn't recording other dreams when I first began to have this dream it's hard to know if they might have offered further insight.

At the point when I had the Bride of Death dream, I was recording dreams, but I couldn't find in them answers to the further question of the cause of my death. Robert was still developing many of his own techniques for dream reentry, dream sharing, and dream-telling that would later prove invaluable in working with my dreams. However, those techniques were still in their early stages at the time, and I was fumbling with understanding this important dream. I was simply moving, seemingly inexorably, closer and closer to the wooden door.

THE YELLOW ROBE

*M*y father was dying.

The bookstores are lined with books instructing adult children on the art of dealing with less-than-perfect relationships with their parents, but no book can prepare a child for the reality of coming face-to-face with all the bumps and warts of that imperfect relationship. I had lived away from home since college — almost twenty years — and I felt that I no longer knew my father. Even growing up he was more distant than my mother. Ron, Evan, and I traveled back into the South about once every three years, or my parents visited upstate New York in between our visits south; but the visits were brief and did not seem to bring us close together any longer. It was almost as if we had forgotten how to be a family.

getting reacquainted

IN THE SUMMER of 1988, I traveled back home to the South several times for hospital visits with my father. I was trying to find a way to say good-bye before it was impossible to say it. My father was dying, but he had never found a way to say those words to me. In fact, he had not even told me he had colon cancer. The summer was painful, strained, and sad because no one would speak directly of death, yet it was constantly in our thoughts and it colored our responses to each other. Yes, I had come home to say good-bye, but before I could say good-bye I had to find a way to become reacquainted with my father. The process was slow.

My father began to talk to me about the most comfortable parts of our lives together — my childhood —then he slowly began to tell me about his own life, sharing stories from his past and revealing things about himself he had never told me. Sometimes he wanted to talk about practical matters: insurance policies, savings accounts, where he kept the checkbook. But now that he was finally talking to me, I didn't want to talk about insurance policies. I wanted to know what was in the heart of this man. I wanted to know why we had never understood each other, and I needed to know the things I could better understand about myself if I knew more about him. He seemed almost too fragile now to tell me what I wanted to know.

My father and I had always had difficulty expressing love for each other, and now time was running out. Through the years, his work schedule had made us strangers living in the same house, and I felt uncomfortable now when I was face to face with him. I did not know this man, and I needed to know him. I was furious that I was an intelligent, forty-one-year-old woman who could talk to anyone except my own father. I was angry with myself that I could feel comfortable with a stranger, but not with my own father. But finally we were talking to each other, awkwardly at first, but talking. I watched his face as he spoke and tried to recall my childhood, the time in my life when he was a special person to me. His day was never in sync with mine; his job did not follow traditional hours. He was usually awake when I was asleep, asleep when I was awake. But I had no trouble recalling vignettes of pure childhood joy: sitting in a pool of sunlight on the polished wooden floor as he repaired a toy fish that I had broken; playing with a dollhouse he had built for me; or sitting beside him as he spent endless hours assembling toys for me. A rare treat was his reading the Sunday comics to me as I cuddled in his lap between his arms, the newspaper spread open wide. I can still smell the acrid, colored inks so close to my small face.

I recalled the special love that had existed between us, but I also recalled the growing distance between us as I tiptoed through the house, whispering with friends for fear that we would wake him in the few hours he had to sleep. My friends began to play elsewhere because our house was not a place where children could play freely. I became withdrawn and even quieter than was my natural inclination, because noise was not allowed in our house during the day. I only recall a few occasions when my father lost his temper, but those times frightened me. Not only were they rare, but they seemed to come from some deep resentment and anger beyond my mother and me. They came from a childhood filled with hurt and neglect, and an adulthood in which he tried almost too hard to make up for that hurt and neglect.

Over the years, my father had become more gentle and caring, and I ached for some part of that which I would never be able to experience. Now he was telling me the stories of his childhood — stories of the strained relationship with his mother that finally resulted in his leaving home when he was still a child. He never returned, never spoke her name again to anyone. He left me one photograph, one letter, and many unanswered questions about grandparents I would never know. His father — my grandfather — had died a suspicious death on a new highway in eastern Tennessee. My grandmother had been seen in a bar convincing my grandfather to rewrite his will only moments before my grandfather wandered into the highway and was killed in a hit-and-run accident that was never investigated. The suspicions, unproven, had settled around my grandmother. As I grew up, I compared myself with her image in the photograph and realized that I had begun to look more and more like her, probably reminding my father of an unpleasant childhood.

A black family of French descent took my father into their home and raised him, but he still carried with him the southern racial prejudice inherited by my parents' generation. My father survived a brutal youth by outwitting an underworld of gamblers and thieves, gaining a reputation as a hard man to beat with a deck of cards and an even harder man to outwit across a pool table. He "rode the rails" between Chicago and the Tennessee hills, the math of the games clicking through his brain like a computer, winning and losing thousands of dollars in the crack of ball against ball, in the click of dice across a barroom floor.

My father spoke of rejection, the hard rejection he felt from a community that seemed to blame him for the disjointed lives of his family. His father had been an alcoholic; my father battled alcoholism when he was a teenager. He tried to prove to his community that he had value. Ironically, a packet of letters arrived the day he died from former classmates who had put them together during a fiftieth-year class reunion.

They all had one theme: that they actually had admired and respected my father and recognized that he had been better equipped to handle the world than they had been themselves.

I knew my father had value as a parent; he was a man with boundless pride in the child he had raised, a man who amazed me and astonished mathematicians with his ability to solve complicated math problems; the solutions seemed to flash like magic in his mind. He quoted Shakespeare and Keats to me in my crib, but he always seemed too shy and perhaps too afraid of stretching himself to succeed in business. He taught me how to find the best within myself. He believed I should do all the things that frightened him — that I should succeed in the areas where he had failed. He taught me that women should never accept artificial boundaries and should always push into fields reserved for men at that time. I succeeded in school. I did everything I felt he wanted me to do, but still the distance seemed to widen between us. In many ways — ways least beneficial to me — we were alike. My father had few close friends; friendship was difficult for me. Both of us hid our strongest feelings, wrapping our emotions tight within, reserving love and caring for only a few people. Both of us needed to break through the artificial barriers we had constructed for ourselves.

visions of change:
you can't hang a man for his past

MY FATHER WAS telling me a story that startled me out of my reverie. Several years earlier, he had been taken to the hospital — an emergency room visit in the middle of the night. While there, he'd had a classic near-death vision that changed his view of life. He told me that he had found himself near the ceiling of the room, hovering over the operating table, listening to the conversation of the physicians and watching their attempt to revive his body. Suddenly, he left the room and felt himself whirling through a tunnel that led to a beautiful meadow where he found himself face to face with a Presence that radiated light. This Presence told him that he had to return, that he had arrived too early. Then, as suddenly as he had left, he found himself back on the operating table, his body racked with pain and his mind filled with joy. He had brought back a message for living the rest of his life, and he felt that he now needed to share that message with me. He needed me to know that he had learned how to love, to really love. He didn't view people in the same way he always had. He found value in all humanity, and he desperately wanted me to know how much loving other people, no matter who they were or what they had done, had changed his life. He had feared that such a strange story would either not be believed or be too silly to tell. This was a man who had rarely shared dreams; sharing visions was almost too difficult for him. That experience had happened five years before, and he had indeed changed in that period of time.

On a hot summer evening several weeks after his return from that earlier hospital visit, my father was mugged in his driveway by two young black men. In his half-conscious state, my father heard the two young men discussing whether they should kill him. Something startled them and they snatched a few items in addition to his wallet, which was their original target, and they ran. When the police arrived to investigate the robbery and obtain a statement, my father described two young men who needed guidance, two young men who were afraid, not two young *black* men who needed prison bars. Months later, my father attracted the attention of the entire city when he became the hold-out juror in a much-publicized murder/robbery/drug case involving sons of a man noted for his mob connections. Thousands of hate-mail letters flooded his mailbox; thousands of telephone calls drove him to remove his telephone number from the book. The city wanted a conviction, but my father insisted that the evidence was not there and told the press, "You can't hang a man for his past." My father had changed more than I ever dreamed was possible. His ability to change would later give me the courage I needed to open my own life for inspection and review.

When I returned home from my first visit with my father in 1988, I hoped he would recover. I liked this man who was now willing to share his family stories, who was willing to share his heart and life with me. I dreamed about my mother when I returned home. Like many women of her generation, she was completely dependent on my father. He took care of all the daily problems of running a household: balancing the checkbook, paying the bills, calling the plumber, repairing the car, knowing when to file tax forms and pay taxes — knowing all the things considered beyond the realm of a wife and mother. I worried about my mother's ability to deal with everyday life if my father died. That worry triggered a dream:

She Who *Dreams*

I Cannot Reach My Mother

I am watching my mother. She is in a room on the upper floor of a tall building. She is opening a window and climbing out that window onto a rock-and-sand ledge. I don't understand why she is climbing out the window, and I scream for her to stop. She does not hear me. She doesn't stop, and she begins to fall, grabbing at the loose rocks and sand to stop herself. I am frightened for her, but I cannot reach her.

Several months later, my father was admitted to the hospital again, and I sought specific guidance from my dreams regarding my role in helping him and in helping my mother. I specifically went to sleep asking for dreams of assistance. The dream of my mother falling reflected her own fear and turmoil in the possibility of losing the person she had lived with her entire adult life, but the dream offered no guidance for me to offer her. I also needed dreams for my father. My small dreams began to reflect my introspection about my father's life and his illness; a large dream, a crucial dream, provided a critical emotional bond between my father and me:

The Yellow Robe

I see a large black cat. The cat gives my father two tarot cards, the first one Death, the second one The Sun. I see my father changing form slightly; he does not seem to be the same. There are no words spoken. I approach a man who is wearing a deep-blue silk jacket and deep-blue pants imprinted with symbols. He takes my hand and walks with me to a trunk and begins pulling from the trunk colored ribbons and scarves, all attached to one another like those in a magician's act. The scarves flow toward me and the man wraps them around my arms and head. Then he sits down in front of my father, continuing to wrap the ribbons and scarves, pulling a yellow one up and through my hair. He then marks a broad band of yellow across my forehead, down my nose and face to my breastbone. Then I am in my father's house, marking the band of yellow on my father's face, across his forehead and down his nose and neck. Then I see the man whirling around my father's house. As he whirls, the scarves whirl around my father and become a long yellow robe. I give my father the robe, and I leave the house.

My father called me that evening. He had grown restless and irritable in the hospital and convinced the doctors, against their better judgment, to allow him to come home. His voice was weak and far away, soft and strange. He described the physical symptoms he was experiencing from the weeks of chemotherapy and seemed particularly uncomfortable from painful mouth sores. He asked what I thought about a new mouthwash that had been advertised on television. I wasn't sure what to say. Then he laughed softly, so happy to be back in his own home. "You know, the real pain is gone," he said, "the terrible headaches, they are all gone, almost as if an invisible hand swept across my forehead." I could hardly breathe, thinking of the dream. Then he paused and said to me, almost reverently: "Thank you for the yellow robe." He laughed softly again.

I couldn't speak. The tears were flowing down my face. I couldn't find the words to express what I was feeling. I tried to open my mouth to say something, but no words emerged. My mother took the telephone away from my father, apologizing to me, explaining rapidly that she was sure the drugs were causing him to hallucinate. She told me he actually believed I sent some man into his room with a yellow robe. "He won't stop talking about the wonderful yellow robe; he tells everyone you gave him a yellow robe." I couldn't explain to my mother the incredible life-affirming connection I had made with my father; I couldn't explain to her the joy I felt at that moment. She would never have understood dreaming such as this. I didn't need to explain the joy to my father; he understood everything.

Over the next few days, my father's health declined rapidly. On a hot, humid August night I went to sleep, fitfully tossing and turning, more aware than usual of the precarious state of my father's health. I awoke off and on throughout the night, more and more exhausted by the sleepless hours but aware of snatches of dreams, the word "Gold" or "Golden" in one of them. I seemed to remember that the word was a man's name. I finally gave up on sleep and wandered around the house, trying to find something to read. At 6:30 A.M. the telephone rang; my father had been taken to the hospital in a coma several hours earlier. He was dying. A few moments later, Robert called to tell me of dreams he'd just had about a man he thought might be my father. By this time, Robert and I were routinely entering each other's psychic space. He was concerned about both me and my father; the urgent message from

Memphis was a confirmation of his dream, recorded below. I was not surprised by the level of detail in Robert's dream of my father, a man he had never met:

WANDA'S FATHER BECOMES A MINISTER

I am surprised to discover that Wanda's father is now a Protestant minister. There is a problem in one room of the house where I find him. I tell him to take his Bible and do what he can, then I will do what I have to do. He seems much more gentle and reflective than I had been led to believe. As we talk, I have trouble swallowing and talking. I remove several plates of dentures, including a plate from under my tongue. Wanda's father is leaving the house by himself. In the next scene, I am exploring the purchase of a new home that may be for him, on the outskirts of a pleasant town dominated by a huge Episcopal church where a funeral or memorial service is being conducted. A woman connected with Wanda's family resents this transaction. I walk the town, carrying an unusual cane. It is very heavy, with a weighty metal grip, as lethal as an ice-axe.

Wanda's father is now by himself. I am looking for someone to help him. My quest takes me into a diner full of rough youths, where I glean the name of someone who holds the key. He is a powerful man, something like a congressman or state senator. His name is Colson. I go looking for him at the Romeo and Juliet Hotel; he is quite a ladies' man. The porter comes up without being asked and gives me his room number, which may be 112. I meet Colson, and he delivers a helpful speech on the conduct of souls after death.

Robert recorded detailed notes from these dreams shortly after waking. Rather breathless, I told him I was rushing to catch a flight to Memphis. It seemed I had received the phone call about my father at the same time Robert was dreaming about him. I quickly explained some of the elements in Robert's dream, confirming for Robert that he had indeed been dreaming about my father. My father had been complaining of his teeth, had thrush from the chemotherapy treatments, and had been finding it difficult to swallow. These symptoms were mirrored in Robert's dream. My father had told me that he'd taken to reading the Bible and praying with my mother during the past few months. Later, I discovered that Colson was the name of a popular evangelist. Some parts of the dream mirrored my father's discussions and closeness with my mother in the last few months. Other elements might have been dream-scouting of afterlife locales, the purchase of the new "home" on the outskirts of a "pleasant town," for my father to explore.

Several hours after receiving the phone call, I stood beside my father's bed in a Memphis hospital. He had collapsed at home, drifting into a coma from which he never returned. In my opinion, he had died at home just as he had wished. When he arrived at the hospital, the attending physician had been Dr. Golden, a fact that affirmed my dream of the night before. The precognitive nature of dreams no longer startled me, but I never ceased to find the detailed accuracy amazing. That accuracy, especially in small matters such as a name, affirmed the importance of the bigger dreams whose messages were often veiled in metaphor and symbolism. At the time, I was keeping a journal of dreams and their dates, but I wasn't yet naming or recording comments on them.

My mother and I kept a vigil by my father's bedside. There was still brain activity. Monitors and life-support systems filled the room, and doctors came in and out constantly, briefly informing us of their specific activity. I closed my eyes and spoke to my father in my mind, telling him he should only come back if he wanted to or if he felt he needed to be with my mother. My mother moved close beside me and told me she'd had a wonderful last day with my father. They had sat together in a swing in the backyard, saying good-bye to each other because he knew he would leave soon. He had sung her a little love song she had never heard before; it was beautiful and she'd cried, but she could no longer remember the words. I thought that perhaps my mother's story was a message from my father that he would not be waking from the coma. We went back to my mother's house. It was late and I slept fitfully again, but on that night I remembered my dream:

MESSAGE ON THE MONITOR

I see my father, but he is not happy. I look up at the monitor on the ventilator, and the monitor lines are moving steadily in a rhythmic pattern. Then something goes wrong and the lines begin to scramble, turning into letters of the alphabet, the letters turning into words: TAKE OFF, TAKE OFF. I shout at him that there is nothing I can do.

The next day, the physician assigned to my father — Dr. Addington — walked in and out of the room with me several times and seemed to want to speak with me privately about my father's condition. Finally, at the end of the day, he asked me to wait. He was concerned that my mother might want to keep my father indefinitely on life support, and he felt that I might understand better that my father's condition was far beyond any reasonable expectation that he might return whole and well. I decided to tell him my dream, and he seemed willing to listen. He said that he felt the dream was important because he doubted that my father would want to return to his body in its current condition. He told me that if we requested that the life-support system be turned off — or at least the part of it that was providing more than was needed for comfort — he would support that decision. I talked with my mother and found her ready to listen to the prognosis. My mother and I agreed, and the order was given for no extraordinary means to be used to save my father's life. Only oxygen and necessary equipment remained.

I talked to my father, curious about his current state, asking him where he was and why he lingered, and telling him it was okay to leave. While I was talking to him, the oxygen machine began to hum louder and louder, finally blowing the tubes out of the connectors! My frightened mother called for nurses, then she laughed. "He's trying to take the last walk to Helican," she said. I didn't understand what she meant. "When we were courting," she said, "the last long, hard uphill walk on dirt roads to Helican was the last leg of the journey through the Alabama hills to reach his destination," which was then my mother's house. "This time he doesn't have to go so far," she said. "He just has to get out of this room."

That night, I dreamed that my father was holding up white cards with black figures on them, very much like the cards psychologists used for ink-blot tests. But in my dream there was a right and a wrong way to read the images. Everyone was reading them inaccurately, not comprehending my father's voiceless messages, or so he thought. He was exasperated with his inability to communicate, and he was struggling to give us messages.

In the morning, my mother talked about my father's physical symptoms and the details of his long illness, then reminisced about her mother, my grandmother. She recalled an epidemic in the Alabama hills when babies were getting terrible rashes all over their bodies that looked like thrush. The babies' mothers were unhappy with the ineffective treatment by the doctors, and they were bringing their babies to my grandmother because they'd heard that she could heal with herbs. I knew the stories about my grandmother, but my mother had not been the one who told them. This was the first time she had mentioned my grandmother's role as healer.

My mother told me that, during this epidemic, strangers were walking and riding in from hundreds of miles, sometimes days' journeys away, bringing their sick children to my grandmother. My mother was young and had charge of her brothers and sisters during this time. She watched as my grandmother took the babies in her arms, one at a time, and carried them away out of sight, down the hill where the freshwater spring flowed into the old oak forest. She would take with her a white cloth, a Bible, and some special verses that she would recite like magic formulas. She took them to the clearing where the old kettle sat on the coals near the oak forest.

My mother said she would beg to go with my grandmother, but she was never allowed because she was not the "right one." My mother then turned toward me, angrier than I had ever seen her. She shouted at me: "If my mother had given me the verses, I could have helped, maybe even cured him!!" She glared at me, livid. Apparently, she thought my grandmother had passed her over and given me her gifts. I was silent. I didn't know how such gifts were passed on, but I knew I had something from my grandmother that had eluded my mother. My mother believed that by being denied the healing information, she had been denied a secret magic that could have saved her husband.

Back at the vigils in the hospital room beside my father, I watched the monitor numbers change, the numbers on the oxygen monitor fluctuating radically. Dr. Addington, one of my father's doctors, explained that the cortex of my father's brain was severely damaged. He pressed his finger hard into the center of my father's chest. My father's hands and arms arched and moved in toward his body, an indicator of the severity of the gray matter damage. His eyes no longer moved normally or responded properly to light and movement. His kidneys still worked, and his feet still moved normally, but the heart rate, previously steady, was showing damage. The doctor explained that all unnecessary equipment had been removed, but that he could not remove the oxygen tubes until the EEG showed no brain activity. I talked to my father again. I asked if he remembered the song he sang to my mother, but I could not seem to ask him anything else. My thoughts wandered elsewhere. Numbers on the monitor changed again, and a nurse hurried in to make rapid changes on some of the equipment. She seemed concerned, and asked us to leave. She needed to isolate my father because the new bacterial readings of his blood were dangerous, indicating a highly contagious staph infection. She said that we'd have to wear suits and masks to visit inside the room in the future, then whispered to me that he wouldn't live through the night.

Back at the house, I tried to help my mother understand how to write checks and pay bills. We repeatedly became so annoyed with each other that what little progress we made seemed to come to a complete standstill. I needed to help her understand enough about the management of her expenses to stay independent, but I also tried not to push when her emotions were so raw. Even though my father responded to nothing and seemed completely unaware that we were in his room, we traveled back and forth between the hospital and the house for every set of visiting hours. We ate meals at home and I spent the little time between visits teaching her everything I could about her finances, trying not to confuse her at the same time. During the hospital visits my mother would hold my father's twisted hand and see an unrealistic glimmer of hope in some automatic body movement triggered by a fluctuating machine. During this period of seemingly endless visits to the hospital, I dreamed about a Scrabble game that was about more than Scrabble.

GAME OF LIFE

The words on the Scrabble board are ordinary at first glance, but they have double meanings. I have trouble understanding the second meaning of each word. The word "supercharge" is placed on the board. I look up the word in an enormous, larger-than-life dictionary. I have trouble reading or even seeing the meaning, so I "pick up" the word and carry it to a woman who trades it for a large tortoise-shell comb from the nineteenth century, very much like one my grandmother once gave me for my long hair. The woman then eats the word and tells me that I will understand the meaning. Then I rebuild the word on the game board and eat it.

"Supercharge" was a word that had a great deal of meaning to me at the time: the fluctuating monitors, the endless trips with no rest between visits, the raw nerves and uncertain future of my mother, nervous and afraid. Also, there were many words between my parents and me that I needed, as an adult, to "eat." Perhaps I was even running a little roughshod over my mother's emotions in my effort to help her become independent and in my effort to understand my own emotions.

The next day, my father still alive against all odds, Dr. Addington and I spoke about death. He gave me his personal definition (an interesting term to use, considering my dream of the night before); death, in his opinion, was the cessation of thought, feeling, and "mental seeing" — the loss of the quality of an individual's personal reality. The definition of "quality of life" was unique to each individual. As long as his patients were still able to make their own decisions they, of course, had the right to decide whether to prolong their own lives. If not, he felt that he had the right to sway the family to accept physical death as the least cruel decision. When families wanted to use extraordinary means to prolong a life, he accepted their decision, but reluctantly; he believed that such a decision was the most cruel restraint one could place on a spirit or a soul. He assured me once again that he was doing nothing artificial to keep my father alive. He had provided a cushion of comfort for the moment when my father would make his own decision to break the thread that held him to this world.

I stood again at my father's bedside and wondered why he stayed alive. He had always taken care of my mother and probably feared I would make changes in her life that might make her uncomfortable. She loved the South and never wanted to live in the Northeast. Perhaps he thought I might take her away from her home and her friends. Thinking, perhaps, that some part of him thought about that, I spoke aloud and promised him I would respect my mother's decision about where she wished to live and how. I told him once again that he could leave if he wished, and that I would help my mother take care of the details of life that he always took care of for her. The television turned itself on. The nurse passed by, glared at me, and turned it off. "I didn't turn it on," I said. I looked again at my father. "Did you do that somehow?" I asked. He would have found it humorous to turn mechanical things off and on to annoy the nurses; perhaps there were meanings of the word "supercharge" that I had not thought about.

I was physically and mentally exhausted. I picked up some books at a local bookstore and spent time talking on the telephone with my family and with Robert, all of whom were helping me sort out my own feelings as I went through this experience one day at a time. It had been weeks — I had lost count of how many — since my father had collapsed in his home and had been taken to the hospital. The endless trek between my childhood home and the hospital wore on my body and mind. It was now late August and I walked outside my mother's house and spent some time looking at the moon and the stars; the moon was beginning to wane. In an age before ventilators and monitors, this would be the time for death. I was too tired to return to the hospital for the evening visit. There was a knot of nerves in my body, a revulsion against the smell of the hospital, weariness for the vigil. I had never had much patience with vigils. I found myself increasingly annoyed with my father's lingering, and I wondered where such a hardened emotion came from.

The next day, while working on the checkbooks with my mother, I called the Social Security office and discovered that my mother would not have to return any portion of my father's Social Security check if he were still alive on September 3. At the foot of my father's bed hung one of those omnipresent single-day hospital calendars that the nurses changed regularly as a reference point for the patients. Was my father aware on some level of the dates on those calendar pages? He was certainly aware of the Social Security rules. Even Dr. Addington told me that there was no reason for my father to be alive and asked if I knew why he was waiting. I told him about the September 3 date, and he seemed to feel that it was as good an explanation as any other. The tubes coming from my father's body were filled with blood; the white cell count was abnormal; and the platelet count was low. His central nervous system was dead, his kidneys and brain were barely functioning, yet he was waiting for something.

Back at my mother's house, I washed the dishes and watched the water run down the drain. I recalled a small dream I'd had before I left home: In the dream, water was whirling down a sink drain and the call came from the hospital telling me that my father was dead.

That evening, still exhausted from the visits to the hospital, I dreamed about a visit to a vegetable garden where Robert and a child, possibly his daughter, were working on a "generator":

THE ENERGY PLANT

Robert has built a generator, but he does not yet have it running. A child shows me the instruction sheet used for building the machine; the sheet is old and yellow. Although the instructions are old, I seem to be able to understand how to make the machine work. I attach small wires to the machine and flat paper-like tabs to the ends of the wires. Extending from the tabs are black tine-like projections. I place them in a receptacle, and the machine works. The machine gives rise to a discussion between Robert and me about the exchange involved between energy and strength, and between energy and healing. We discuss the process of transferring energy from one person to another, and we try an experiment. We use the dream generator to transfer energy from Robert to me, at the same time using a mechanism in the generator to reserve Robert's original energy so that it is not lost in the transfer. There is an explosion, a ball of light, and an implosion of energy that shatters my body into a series of prisms, facets, and planes, almost like looking at a portrait of myself painted by Picasso. My body then seems to reassemble itself into its original form, but it retains the energy.

The dream generator, an extension of my previous dream metaphor of "supercharging," provided needed energizing of my body and mind. The dream brought me both a functional tool and a lesson in giving and receiving energy without depleting the gift or the giver. I wondered — as I did increasingly around that time — whether I had actually been with Robert in the dreamspace and whether an actual energy transference had taken place there.

I awoke feeling much less exhausted and more prepared for another visit to the hospital with my mother. My son, Evan, fourteen at the time, had arrived, and he wanted to find his own way to let his grandfather go. We looked through old photo albums, recalled special stories, and talked about plans they had made for things they would do together someday. Evan didn't want to see his grandfather in his current state — in a coma, with tubes and wires connected to his body — so he remained at my mother's house while we went to the hospital.

When we returned from our afternoon hospital visit, Evan seemed agitated. He wanted to tell me about a dream he'd had while napping. Evan had been taught to pay close attention to his dreams, and often discussed them with me. In this dream, he had found himself standing in a hospital room looking at his grandfather (in waking reality, he had not seen the isolation room where my father was, nor had I described it to him). He accurately described the room, the placement of chairs and special equipment, and the appearance of his grandfather in a level of detail that he could not have imagined. He saw me standing just outside the room, leaning over a cart and looking through the window into the room. He saw my mother putting on a mask, white gloves, and a yellow suit to go inside the room. Evan didn't know that, in reality, I hadn't gone into the room, nor had he been told that we had to wear special clothing to go in. He even repeated details of conversations I had with doctors and nurses while my mother was inside the room. I asked if, in his dream, he'd talked to anyone inside the room, but he hadn't. He had been frightened by his grandfather's appearance and by everything happening around him because he knew how real it was. He jolted himself awake and didn't want to repeat the experience of the dream. We talked about the dream until he was calm.

That evening, my mother told me that my father had visited her in a dream the night before. He was much younger, he was wearing a white shirt, and he was clean and relaxed; all the hospital apparatus was gone. He talked to my mother for a long time and comforted her. I wondered again why my father lingered. There seemed to be a reason; he had always been a practical man who carefully planned everything he did. My concern spilled over into the night and into my own dreams and translated into a disturbing dream of visiting hilly parks, cemeteries, and sleazy taverns and bars. I traveled through the dream landscape on horseback, startling some of the people in the dream when I rode the horse into the buildings they occupied. Most of the people were drinking or drunk and decided, within the dream, that they were imagining the woman on horseback.

In one particularly disturbing scene, I rode through a room and reined in the horse in front of a woman who pointed up at the ceiling, complaining to me about the tenant upstairs who was pissing through the floorboards. I awoke from the dream, disturbed by the images of honky-tonks and bars — places not so different from those my father frequented as a young man. My father had spent most of his young adulthood as a gambler in such places — honky-tonks, pool halls, and makeshift backyard shelters or outbuildings where games of dice, cards, and craps were hastily set up. He tried to protect me from that part of his life, which I regretted because when a story did slip out now and then, I was fascinated. They were stories that held just enough fascination and danger that I was intrigued and probably just a tad envious of a life so different from my own.

The next day, I stood again at the foot of my father's hospital bed and recalled a conversation we'd once had about angels. In his near-death experience, he believed he had seen angels. I was wondering when such angels appeared; were they there in the room at that moment waiting for him to make some kind of decision, perhaps helping him with that decision? My reverie was disturbed when the nurse came in to ask if my father was right- or left-handed. She was preparing to test his brain waves and that information was apparently important. My exhaustion returned, made more intense by the waiting and frustration.

Sometimes guilt took over; was I rushing my father's death in my desire to have him leave? Was I somehow more concerned with myself than with him? I didn't think so. My father had died, in my opinion, before he arrived at the hospital. Still I vacillated between feelings of peace and agitation. I read and walked and thought — perhaps too much. I was buoyed by conversations with my family, then depressed by concern about my mother and the quality of her life without my father. I had been away from Memphis so long that I didn't know if she had a network of friends who would help and support her. She needed people who would sustain her after I returned home. She would be facing a difficult period of aloneness.

These thoughts brought me back to the question of the Social Security check. It was now September 6, so September 3 had passed, but I knew my father was waiting for something. I called the Social Security office and asked again what date needed to pass for my mother to be able to keep my father's entire check. The answer changed; the date was September 6, not September 3. The first date had been inaccurate. My father would know that.

The next morning, the telephone rang at 8:00 A.M. My father's heart had ceased to beat regularly. I silently asked that he live just long enough for my mother to get to his side; it would be important to her to be there for his last heartbeat. I went into the kitchen and was startled to see the water swirling down the drain as it had been in my dream of my father's death. My mother, not me, was the one washing the dishes. I told her we needed to leave. At the hospital, the parking lot was packed and there were no parking places. I told her to get out of the car and hurry upstairs. I parked and arrived at my father's room. He had already died, but the nurse told me that his heart had continued to beat for another minute after my mother arrived. He had waited for my mother; he had waited for the Social Security date to pass. He was practical to the last moment of his life.

My mother remained in the South where she belonged. Old friends assisted her, and new friends emerged to help her with everything from writing checks to car repairs. She seemed to blossom, but she confided in me later that she had suffered through a very long year of depression. Then she began to experience memory loss and eventually drifted into some form of dementia, playing out the dream in which I could not reach her as she tumbled over the window ledge.

My dreams and my experience with my father's death not only helped me reacquaint myself with my family, but they helped me learn more about myself. My dreams gave me energy as well as imagery and vital information that opened doors to healing the flawed relationship between my father and me. They confirmed the limitless power of spirit, mind, and body working together.

Eventually, I learned that when we dream we not only encounter loved ones on the other side, but we can share with them an unending process of growth and healing. When I became ill a year later, my father returned often in my dreams to help me find the tools for my own recovery. In those dreams, he was whole and well, capable of assisting me in my difficult journey.

PACKING FOR TWIN JOURNEYS

denying the inner voice

N THE SUMMER of 1989, I began to experience physical pain. The first incident was a sharp, stabbing pain in my left breast, so severe that I could not breathe. I was frightened by the pain. I searched for a lump — anything unusual — but found nothing I could identify as "different." The pain was never constant. It was periodic, but always stabbing and intense. My inner voice began to come awake, telling me that there was a problem, that this pain was abnormal. I pushed the voice aside, ignored it, insisted that it was wrong. My father had died only half a year earlier, so my first thoughts were that I had taken on anxiety or some inner discomfort that was manifesting itself as pain. That rationalization only worked for a short time.

The pain nagged at me. I was dreaming about my illness, but my dreams had not yet shouted at me with images I recognized, so I recorded the dreams and put them away. I was an intelligent young woman who attended to my health, had regular medical exams, and read all the literature. The literature stated that pain was not associated with breast cancer. I had been diagnosed with fibrocystic breast disease — a condition that generated pain and benign lumps. There was nothing to fear from pain that was supposed to be normal, so I pushed the inner voice aside.

Throughout the summer and into the fall, the pain became more intense. There were long periods without pain, and I would lapse into feeling that I had imagined something was wrong, but intuition and barely remembered images in dreams tugged stronger. Sometimes while riding in a car or just walking or washing dishes, a sharp stab of intense pain in my left breast would cause me to bend over, gasp, and know that this was something I had never experienced before. My body was telling me something that no assurance from a physician could assuage.

Then the pain became more frequent. Murky dreams tugged at my soul but presented nothing concrete. I aggressively felt my breast for something unusual but found nothing — until I bent over and probed in a different direction, deep into an area behind the front tissue. There was a ledge with something small and hard beneath it; it was like feeling under a rock and suddenly finding something. The "something" under that ledge was a lump. Later, when two physicians described the appearance of my breast cancer, one used the image of a ledge of tissue and one described it as a globe of stars, like an old-fashioned cylindrical glass ball, only filled with dot-like stars. When I looked back through my dream journal, I found that my summer dreams had been telling me something I couldn't recognize at the time: one dream presented a ledge with debris beneath it, and another described the left side of an orb filled with stars.

Now I was more frightened than I had ever been in my life. I had followed the stabbing lines of pain to their source and found a lump. The lump moved and it was painful, both signs of a benign lump according to the literature. Then why did I not believe the literature? Why was I so terrified? My dreams, my inner voice, and my intuition were shouting "danger!" The warnings felt real, and I knew I was in trouble.

Although my dreams of ledges and globes of stars had not presented clear enough pictures for me to recognize breast cancer, they had been disturbing, gnawing away at my subconscious. They had coalesced into an intuitive feeling that something was very wrong and very dangerous. I had a sledge-hammer feeling of certainty that the lump I felt was malignant. I could no longer ignore my inner sources.

I called my gynecologist's office, but the receptionist casually informed me that there were no appointments available until 1990, almost six months away. I hung up the telephone and sat for a while, staring at the floor and thinking about nothing in particular. A stab of pain, so intense that I doubled over, frightened and angered me. I thought about the intense pain and about my dreams of the previous month; something was wrong. I called again and told the receptionist that I needed to see someone soon — that I had a lump in my breast and it might be a problem. After a few moments of juggling peoples' times and places, the receptionist managed to move my appointment into November, to a date only two weeks away.

The moment I acknowledged that I believed I had a malignancy, my murky disturbing dreams changed. The new dreams seemed more specifically about illness or an unidentified problem. In one dream my inner voice, which had tugged and shouted at me until I listened, took on two personalities. In the dream, as in waking reality, my inner voice refused to be silent but in this case split into a discussion between the two sides: one that knew there was a problem and one that denied a problem existed. In my dream journal, I referred to this denying inner voice in the dream as "her." I did not want "her" to touch me; "she" must stay away from me. I tried to run from "her." In the dream, I acknowledged that "she" did not know something about herself and that "she" would not be allowed to come near me until "she" had taken care of her medical problem. Robert appeared in the dream, walking along beside me. He assisted me in building a transparent wall that I placed between myself, the knowing dream voice, and "her," and he offered to help me find out what was wrong with "her" so that we could help "her." We walked along the top of a narrow ridge together, like children walking on a fence rail, with the invisible wall still between us and "her." We casually discussed the need for "her" to discover something important about herself, as though "she" were still not present. In the dream, neither of us named what we thought might be wrong with "her."

In waking reality I was just beginning to admit that the pain could be about something serious. I told no one else my feelings — not Ron, not Robert, and certainly not my child. Perhaps I felt that, by not talking about it, the problem would dissolve on its own. I knew that wasn't true, but sometimes we cease to think rationally when fear takes charge. If I talked about what was going on, I would definitely have to acknowledge the inner voice and my feeling of danger.

However, my intuition and my subconscious mind — the parts of the self that are most in touch with our inner body — did not stop sharing. My dreaming self was sorting out the evidence and bringing it all together. My dreaming self was no longer excluding "her"; "she" was ill, she was part of me, and she needed to be healed and brought back to wholeness. That evening I dreamed that I was traveling in an automobile — not an uncommon vehicle of exploration in my dreams, and usually a metaphor for the degree of control I had (or did not have) in a given situation. In this dream, I had no control; I was in the driver's seat, but I was not driving my vehicle:

I AM THE DREAM I CHOOSE

I am traveling in a car. Although I am in the driver's seat, I have no control. The car begins to lunge and drives itself, moving across sidewalks, streets, curbs, and lawns, moving faster and faster for several blocks. It finally stops in front of a brightly lit house, and I walk in. I pick up a small, furry kitten and I talk to a child who is sitting in a group of people. I am told to choose my favorite dream. I walk to a shelf and move my fingers over a number of jade carvings, smooth as washed stone. One fascinates me: a carving of a round-faced child standing with an abstract cat-like animal. I move my fingers over the carving, then I pick it up and hold it close. I walk halfway up a ladder-like stair and take on the characteristics of the carved child. I am an Inuit. I feel more humble, more gentle, as though I am harboring a private mystery. Everyone else is below me on the floor, seated in a circle. A leader asks each person to show his or her carving or dream. I no longer have my carving because I have become my carving. I am the dream I chose; I have become what I desired to become. As each person relates his or her dream, they become their favorite dreams, just as I have become mine. I am waiting for the complete telling of all the dreams in the room before I reveal my dream. Then I can teach the others. My dream is the full realization of myself, and that realization has brought liberty to my spirit.

The house in the dream was familiar. It looked like a house I had visited frequently as a student, a special warm place, the home of a college professor who always had people from his classes coming and going. His caring attention to each of his students had earned him the familiar nickname of "Uncle Louie." In waking reality, he had surrounded himself with objects from other cultures and with books on shelves protected by antique glass doors. He always had time to both listen to and learn from his students. His patience and kindness were legendary, and the warm gentility of his beautiful old house enhanced the experience of being in his presence. Students gathered at his house many evenings and most weekends for food and discussion. Both he and his wife nurtured and mentored those who came within their doors. They provided a spiritual and intellectual environment that fed body and soul.

The metaphor of the car driving itself mirrored my own feelings of having lost control of my health and my emotions. Control had been taken out of my hands through my own fear and anxiety. I was still in the driver's seat, but I was unable or unwilling to regain control of the vehicle, just waiting to see where the "car" would take me. When I looked more closely at this dream, I researched the general meanings of jade and Inuit carving. Inuit carvings often told stories of wisdom and healing; jade was associated with divination and healing rituals.

There was both division and unity in the dream. In order for healing to take place, the dream and the dreamer had to come together in the full realization of "self." Each image was the element of a story — a story not yet whole, and that would not be whole until all the pieces became part of the primary image. That primary image, when made whole and well, would become the teacher/healer: The Wounded Healer — the one who could lead others to a healing path because he or she had already traveled that path, suffered on it, experienced healing on it, and brought back the gift of healing. The relinquishment of the "old self" and the birth of a "new self" would soon become a familiar theme in my healing dreams — dreams of change, transformation, and the unification of dream and dreamer, all necessary in order for healing to take place.

Once the Wounded Healer became whole, she would be required to give back what she had learned. This dream became a beautiful realization of the self, of "her," who had been so separated in the earlier dream.

planning a journey to Africa

IN THE MONTHS before I had begun to experience the first shooting pains in my breast I had become intrigued by the adventures offered by a volunteer organization called Earthwatch that planned environmental, archaeological, and scientific expeditions under the tutelage of a professor or scientist. Some of the expeditions were in the United States; many of them were in foreign countries. By the time I began to grow concerned about the recurring breast pain — in the summer of 1989 — I had already applied for a trip to West Africa. My application had been accepted, and I had made all the initial preparations, including taking numerous shots needed for the journey. I had felt an unexplained pull to the West African project: a three-week archaeological study two hundred miles inland from Accra, Ghana, West Africa. The study would be directed by a University of Calgary professor whose work concentrated on the Asante culture's spiritual genesis within the forest and lands of Asantemanso, the most sacred village of the Ashanti people. The expedition was scheduled for a January 1990 departure. I felt compelled to go on this journey — almost driven, as if I would find something important in the life and culture of a people far removed from me in space and time. Usually Ron accompanied me on trips, particularly trips into another country; but he said he did not want to go on this trip with me. He was unable to explain why he did not want to go just as I was unable to explain why it was so important for me to go. Evan was still in high school and would have been unable to go.

packing for two journeys

DREAMS OF PACKING for a journey filled my nights. However, the image of "journeying" took on a deeper dream significance. Often there were images of packing for two journeys: a mental journey and a physical journey. Robert also began to appear more frequently in my dreams, often as a teacher or as a guide, instructing me in the building of things, presenting me with books to read, or guiding me through a special project.

When I made the appointment with my gynecologist for November, my plans for the winter journey to West Africa were already solidified. I had tickets, shots, and reading material, and I was already packing and repacking, just as in my dreams, attempting to organize everything I needed into a single backpack — a requirement for this journey. I was also preoccupied with thoughts about the pain and the lump in my breast.

I originally believed that my packing dreams were about the physical journey to Africa. The most evocative of the journey dreams dealt directly with images of my trip to Africa, as well as images of my healing journey:

Two Journeys

I am packing. Someone is talking to me, telling me that I am to go on two journeys, both of them important. One journey requires more preparation than the other. I find myself in the back of a large jeep, attempting to gather things together, packing and repacking. I have prepared for the trip to Africa, but I am confused. I have to repack because I have forgotten things I need: my visa, passport, and other documents. Also, much to my disappointment, someone beside me is telling me I have packed for the wrong journey. Finally, everything is together for the trip to Africa. I speak to the person who is standing beside me and tell him excitedly that I am ready to go to Ghana. The person is gentle. He tells me, softly, that of the two journeys, the second journey is more important and involves fewer things to pack. However, he says that I should go on the journey to Ghana first, because it will prepare me for the larger journey.

The dream continued into Africa:

I am in a foreign land, following steep winding roads to a market built into the side of a hill at the end of one of the roads. There are exotic foods, vegetables, and baked breads. I am choosing and placing the foods in a basket. A light-skinned woman and a man with dark features mark and wrap the purchases. To continue my journey, I need to cross a body of water. Someone appears in the dream to assist me. He or she pulls out a very long bark canoe with a seat in the middle. I hesitate because the craft appears to be ill-constructed, with gaps in the side. Unworried, the guide gives it to me, saying the water will make the boat swell back together.

I step inside the boat, and it mends itself. I have no trouble keeping the boat afloat, but some of the water leaks into the vegetables and into a parcel of clothing. There is a small makeshift line attached to poles in the center of the boat. I pin the clothing on the line to dry.

On the final mile of the journey, I leave the boat and the water and I am traveling on an old bus through a very warm country. Steep hills rise from the road and white houses nestle in the hills. Sunlight is bright — almost blinding — on the surfaces of the buildings. I am struck by the uncontrolled assemblage of structures, all sizes and shapes, the old (some with small colorful columns) with the new — and, in one case, a tent.

Many parts of this dream were identical to scenes that would become familiar to me in West Africa. On the trip between the Accra airport and Asantemanso, scenes from this dream leaped into my mind as I traveled toward Asante country. Months before my trip, the dream "saw" my surroundings in Africa; the market and village scenes were almost identical to the market and village where I would live for three weeks. The columned houses mingled with the native structures filled the brightly sunlit hillsides around Asantemanso in the same disarray as those in the dream. Crossing the body of water — a spiritual image — would repeat itself in future dreams, always in conjunction with a guide, teacher, or helper.

The dream continued, the images of illness taking priority:

I leave the village and move to the top of a hill, walking under trees, my feet crunching on something that appears to be some kind of nut, almost peanut-like in shape. I have a guide with me. He tells me to open one of the nuts. I try, but there are several layers of shell. Finally a fruit emerges, but with it a worm that is eating away at the core of the fruit. My guide tells me that there is a problem with the fruit from "my" tree, and that I must take care of the problem — that I must destroy the worm in the fruit before it destroys the tree. The guide tells me that I must look around the tree for images that I need. He says that I am on my final stop before I begin my journey, and that I must gather what I need.

In this dream, there was direct warning of illness: a worm in the fruit (my breast) that could, without intervention, destroy the tree (my life). Intuitively, I knew that I had breast cancer, but the medical community responded slowly, hesitantly, convinced that I was imagining a problem. I wanted to believe that the dreams indicated some other problem in my life. But I knew that they originated within the deepest part of my soul, some place within myself — the doctor within — that had profound knowledge of my physical and mental makeup. "Gathering what I needed" — the tools, the images to be used in my recovery —

was to become another recurring theme in my dreams. These tools would be necessary in the face of such a terrifying disease.

My Father, My Guardian

My father returned in my dream-time, now whole and cognizant of my dilemma. He still behaved like my father — a protective guardian of his daughter — in his dream attempts to change the outcome of my illness and protect me by delaying my "journey." I became annoyed with him because he was still treating me like a child and seemed to lack confidence in my ability to handle the coming crisis. His efforts to delay my journey seemed to be based on his feeling that I needed help from a parent because I would be unable to make the journey alone. He seemed frantic, perhaps not an unexpected emotion for a concerned parent to have:

My Father Meddles in My Journey

I have received an urgent telephone call from Memphis (my childhood home) to come "home." My parents arrive to take me to the airport. My father is there, checking and double-checking everything before we leave on the journey, delaying, in an annoying fashion, what I know to be an important journey. My parents are both in the airport, so I wonder what journey I am taking since everyone from my Memphis family is there with me. Finally, we arrive at the airport. We are too late for the first departure time for my journey, and there is a somewhat ominous feeling on my part because I know that delay will cause harm. We are waiting for a second opportunity for me to begin my journey.

I become increasingly annoyed with my father, who has taken shoes out of several of my suitcases and is arranging them in an orderly fashion, in pairs, in what appears to be a sample case. They are my shoes, and they are "samples" from all the years of my life, beginning with baby shoes and ranging through my teenage years and up to a current pair. I am now furious with my father because the time has arrived to get on the elevator and go up to the departure gate. My father's foolishness, his reminiscing about my life through the shoes, and even my mother's patience with his delaying my journey have left me in a rage. They have no confidence in me; they think I cannot do this without them. They are delaying, for the second time, an important journey that I must make on my own.

Delaying my healing journey became a theme of my waking life as well. Doctors called postponing appointments, moving appointments, creating delays, and wasting time — delaying the diagnosis I needed. My doctors seemed to feel that I was overreacting to what they thought was simply fibrocystic breast disease. I became increasingly concerned and increasingly frightened because I knew my life was in danger. I knew that the journey would be difficult, but that delaying the journey would be fatal. I knew that I needed to begin the journey in order to become well.

At the same time, I knew that in my dreams and in my conscious mind, I had already formed the intention of wellness; I had already begun my journey. I also knew that I could not look back; if I did, I would fall into a pattern of asking myself, "What if...," "Why didn't I...," or, even worse, "Why me?" I could not allow myself to be bogged down by what I had not done up to that point. I could not allow myself to paint a mental picture of defeat simply because I had not reacted earlier, because I had not understood the messages I was receiving.

I dreamed that I was trying to disembark from a boat and come onto an island: Easter Island. My father was already on the island and would not allow me to leave the boat or enter the island because, as he said in the dream, there was "no place for me on the island." He put me back on the boat, alone, and forced me to cross to another island far from him.

This was an important dream for me. "Easter" was my maiden name and, of course, my father's name. Easter Island was also a physical island — an ancient sacred place, a place of mystery, but now a sterile place that harbored little life. This was not like the previous dream in which my father appeared. In this dream, my father offered protection that presumed expanded knowledge of a possible future of "living" for me. I was denied admission to the island where my dead father "lived," where an ancient culture had been unable to thrive, and I was forced to go back alone to a place where there was still life. In this dream, my father had also transitioned from being a frantic parent trying to keep his child from undertaking a difficult journey into a guide and helper, willing to take protection to a more spiritual level.

la vida es sueño

WINTER APPROACHED. I tried to occupy my mind and my time with preparations for my journey to Africa. I also tried not to worry about doctor appointments. Christmas was coming, and I tried to focus on the activities of the season.

I had not yet told Ron or Robert about my medical appointments or my intuitive feelings that I had a malignancy. Deep inside, there was still some faint part of me that hoped — but did not really believe — that I would walk out of my doctor appointments with good news, and that I would never have to tell anyone about my fear, now almost terror, about my dreams. Ron knew that I had made medical appointments, but I had led him to believe that they were for ordinary annual checkups.

I experienced one of the stabbing pains in my breast on a trip with Robert to pick up one of his daughters at the airport in New York City. I had gasped from the pain, but explained it away as something I had eaten. Although my dreams were shouting "danger!" — although I had acknowledged the danger to myself — I was still keeping my information to myself, hoping in some faint, distant part of myself that I was wrong.

I made medical appointments when Ron was at work, and I kept my dream journals tucked away. I usually read my dreams to Ron and Robert, but I was reading them to no one at this time. Something private was happening that I needed to confirm before I allowed anyone else into my dilemma. Just before the holidays, I recalled an odd little dream segment from a dream several months before I began experiencing the breast pain: Robert walked into the dream and asked me to read *Life Is a Dream* (in Spanish, *La vida es sueño*), a short play by Pedro Calderón de la Barca, a seventeenth-century writer generally referred to simply as Calderón. The play had been assigned reading in my college philosophy class.

I told Robert and Ron about the dream. Both found it intriguing but not noteworthy because I had shared few, if any, of my other dreams at that time. At first I ignored the message, but then one evening I began to search for my copy of *Life Is a Dream*. Now taking my own dream literally, I looked through old boxes of books from college and finally located the play.

As directed in the dream, I read Calderón's play. The main character, Segismundo, becomes a prisoner of spiritual darkness, expressed as his captivity in a cave. His first attempt at salvation fails, but he tries again. This time he is successful — saved through faith and good works.

In the story, the conflict is between free will and predestination; the question is whether Segismundo can triumph over his predicted fate. Perhaps not coincidentally, many of Segismundo's queries and musings seemed relevant to my own questions about my dreams and about the reliability of my inner voice:

> *... because this life is short,*
> *Let's dream, my soul, let's dream again. But it*
> *Will be with prior warning that perhaps*
> *We shall awaken from this joy when least*
> *Expected, thus our disillusionment*
> *Will be less harsh, for we shall ease the pain*
> *by this anticipation. Thus forewarned*
> *That even though it seems assured, all of*
> *Our power is just lent, and must return*
> *Unto the Giver.*[1]

Segismundo admonished that even with forewarning of an event we must remember that power on earth is only lent by the Giver and must be returned. The dreamer, according to Segismundo, can do nothing about the dream until the warning has manifested into the event warned about. Then, and only then, can the dreamer begin to change the dream. I found this admonition interesting and worth some consideration but also worth some argument.

Although I had not changed my dreams up to this point, I was beginning to understand that I needed to actively work with them. I had arrived at the conclusion that Segismundo had not been able to do anything about his dream until it was fulfilled because he had not worked with his original warning dreams. Nor had I at this time; I had not understood how to work with my dreams and was still a neophyte. Reading the play was relevant to my current situation; my dreams of warning were coming to fruition because I had not understood them, but at least I was moving toward an understanding. I was fighting that understanding while moving into it. Could I now change my first

---

[1] Pedro Calderón de la Barca, *Life Is a Dream (La vida es sueño)*, trans. William E. Colford (Woodbury, N.Y.: Barron's Educational Series, Inc., 1958), Act III, page 71.

warning dreams of death into dreams of life? I must do so, or else the Dance Hall dream would come to its complete fulfillment.

Dueling with the Doctor

THE PAIN INCREASED. I was chronicling the pain in my journal, and I had begun to listen to taped meditations in the evening to lessen the pain and pinpoint its source. I kept my appointments for a gynecological exam in November and then a mammogram in December in the midst of the Christmas season. Neither exam discovered anything alarming. I was carefully assured, as though I were a troublesome child, that nothing was wrong. I insisted, in a manner uncharacteristic for me, that there was indeed something wrong. I told the gynecologist that she was wrong, that there was a problem. She was annoyed. She sighed, opened my folder, and asked, "What about the Christmas season; did you smoke, have you eaten more chocolate and perhaps more caffeine or alcohol than usual?"

"No, I don't smoke, I haven't eaten chocolate, and I don't drink coffee."

"Well, perhaps since it is the Christmas season, you have inflamed your usual cysts with too much alcohol?"

I was furious. I tried to control my emotions. "No, I have had very little alcohol during the Christmas season."

She sighed again. I stared at her for a moment and then said in the most modulated tone I could muster, "I have breast cancer and you are talking to me about chocolate, caffeine, and alcohol." I paused and spoke slowly, measuring every word: "Something is wrong with me, something very serious and very frightening, and I will find someone who will listen to me."

Now she was angry. She replied in a very controlled voice, "Would you like me to schedule an ultrasound?"

"Yes," I said, finally satisfied that an ultrasound might confirm what I already knew. The ultrasound was ordered, but problems arose with scheduling; available dates conflicted with my trip to Africa. I remembered my dreams of two journeys, which indicated that I was to go to Africa first and then attend to the more difficult journey. Besides, I was determined to make the trip to Africa. The ultrasound was scheduled for the day after my return home.

shadowed by wings

AT ABOUT THE SAME TIME, Robert appeared in a small dream and handed me a Bible turned to a specific chapter in Isaiah. In this dream, Robert played the role of a teacher or guide, somewhat older than he was in waking reality. Robert assumed this role in many of my dreams before and during my illness. I woke up quoting the chapter number aloud, immediately found a Bible, and looked up the words. They meant nothing to me:

Woe to the land shadowing with wings; which is beyond the rivers of Ethiopia; That sendeth ambassadors by the sea, even in vessels of bulrushes upon the waters, saying, Go, ye swift messengers, to a nation scattered and peeled, to a people terrible from their beginning hitherto; a nation meted out and trodden down, whose land the rivers have spoiled.[2]

I went to the library after work and found a Bible history. "The land shadowing with wings" referred to the ancient lands of the Ashanti people. The dream was yet another confirmation of my decision to go to Africa before I embarked on my spiritual journey, which would begin while I was in Africa.

Scheduling the trip and then rescheduling the ultrasound left me even more frightened and uncomfortable. I told no one about the extent of my fear. Perhaps I had made a mistake. Perhaps I should not go to Africa. I was so convinced of my illness that I was afraid to delay any medical appointments. But I also wanted the doctors to be right; I wanted them to prove me wrong and tell me that I was not ill. In the next instant, I wondered how many women had died because they never insisted on having their inner voice heard, never listened to their dreams. How many women had been intimidated into believing that they had no inner source of knowledge?

At the end of December the pain became more constant. I dreamed of an orb-like ball filled with stars. I later found in my dream journal that I had dreamed during the summer about an orb filled with stars. But in this new dream a child explained the stars as a concept of space. The child drew the stars on a blackboard and circled nebulae on a large chart, showing me with a pointer a confined mass with one large bright

---

[2] Isaiah 18:1–2, King James Version.

star and smaller stars radiating from it. It was on the left side of the blackboard. The child explained that it was on the left and that it was a set of stars that belonged to me. There was no mistaking the message in this dream: This dream, like the earlier "orb" dream I would later rediscover, pinpointed the location of the malignancy but described the radiating cancer cells in the language of a biopsy.

The new year began — 1990 — and my departure date for Africa approached. I finally told friends and family about my dreams, about the Dance Hall dream, and about my fears. I could no longer make the second journey — the more important spiritual journey — alone, and I now knew strongly that, no matter how much I hoped there would be no malignancy, my dreams and intuition were correct.

Ron had always gone on vacations and physical journeys with me. But for some reason, he had not wanted to travel with me to Africa. He later told me, after reading all my summer and fall dreams, that he finally understood why he could not go with me to Africa; I needed time and space in the country of my dreams to discover something deep within myself that would help me through my spiritual journey to wellness. If he had gone with me, he would have interfered with my discovery of what I needed. This was a physical journey that I needed to make alone.

Robert was intrigued with my trip to Africa because he had studied West African culture, written about it, and always felt spiritual connections to Africa, but he had never taken his own physical journey to the sacred places of the Asante and Yoruba.

My son Evan told me, as he continued to tell me throughout my illness, that I would come back and do whatever I needed to do to become well and whole again.

The three most special people in my life — my husband, my son, and my friend — sent me off, probably with concern, but certainly with their love and support. They encouraged me to follow my dreams of taking both journeys: the journey to Africa, and then the journey of spirit and soul.

Besides, I was not ready to die. There was too much I wanted to do, and there were too many places I hadn't seen. My son needed my help in growing up, and I needed to know that he would get beyond the teenage years and find a responsible path for himself. I needed to be there to help him, and I needed to know what he would do with his life. I also needed time for myself, time to not think about my illness. And that was the kind of time that Africa would give me.

More important than needing to live for the other people in my life, I needed to remember who I was in a place far removed from where I lived and far away from the people who knew me best. I needed to remember in a different way — a way that could bring me strength and stability — and I needed to find these things in a new environment. Some of the tools I needed would be found in the unfamiliar culture of Africa just as they had been in my dreams. I was also convinced that I was already beginning to change the outcome of my illness. I had made my intention known to the universe of my dreaming. I had identified a problem, and my mind and body were already beginning to deal with it. I was ready for my journey. I was ready for both of my journeys.

A Journey into the Sacred Forest

*"Woe to the land shadowing with wings
which is beyond the rivers of Ethiopia..."*

(Isaiah 18:1)

I was about to leave for the land of my first journey, where I would meet people who not only lived their dreams but could look into someone else's heart and *know* what kind of dreams they dreamed. Perhaps the lesson of this journey would be the reality of the dream world.

On January 25, 1990, I determined that I would erase from my mind all thoughts of cancer, mammograms, doctors, illness, fear, and all the anxiety associated with those thoughts. I was leaving for Africa — an adventure unlike any I had ever attempted, an escape from any routine that I had established in my life. My dreaming came with me, often in unexpected ways. I was embarking on the first journey I'd encountered in my dreams of two journeys — and, for some reason, I was expected to take this first journey before I kept my next medical appointment. The second journey would begin when I returned home in three weeks.

SHE WHO *Dreams*

<u>*"no condition is permanent"*</u>

THE JOURNEY WAS LONG: thirty-five hours on airplanes including a layover in Switzerland. Most of us who were coming as volunteers met in New York City, but a few arrived from other destinations and met us at the airport in Switzerland. I had never slept well on airplanes, so the trip seemed even longer than thirty-five hours.

We arrived in West Africa in the capital city of Accra, Ghana, late at night after the grueling, seemingly endless trip. The Earthwatch volunteers, seven of us, stepped from the airplane into a burst of hot, humid air, walking single-file across the tarmac like refugees. Our guide was a young man who led us toward a black hole in a square, lime-green building lit by a glaring blue floodlight. Immigration proceedings seemed interminable. We were herded, still in single file, from booth to booth through the oppressive heat. The only light came from unshielded fluorescent tubes attached precariously to makeshift fixtures. Cultures seemed to blend in odd mixtures of clothing. Multitudes of deep black faces demanded papers, their bureaucratic shouting occasionally interrupted by crying blond Swiss babies being handed over the gates to await their parents' clearance. Other children, whose adoption papers had been cleared, were in the process of being introduced to their new European parents, who would have an hour of acquaintance before leaving with them on outgoing flights.

At any other time in my life I would have been annoyed by the endless procedures, but not this time. In a place so far away from familiar surroundings, the process took my mind farther and farther away from the reality of my illness. I basked in the unfamiliarity of this foreign place and imprinted every word, every scene, as though the newness itself could wash me clean. Small, poorly lit offices lined the long hall; their curtains were dirty strips of calico suspended from sagging strings. Men — too many men for the tasks at hand — rushed about waving papers at each other or at passengers, shouting in their own language, in unintelligible English, or in German. I smiled. Sleepiness began to overcome me; the trip, including the interval in Switzerland, had been thirty-five hours long. The heat and humidity were suddenly unbearable. There was an acrid smell in the air that I eventually associated with the African body — not unpleasant a few days later, but difficult to assimilate in the heat and confusion.

A Journey into the Sacred Forest

At last the final stamp in my currency book released me into a large lobby. There we were greeted by Dr. Peter Shinnie, chief archaeologist, and his Asante wife Ama. Ama was diminutive and soft-spoken, quiet but regal in bearing. She wore glasses much too large for her beautiful face. Her skirt of traditional Kente cloth was topped with a University of Calgary T-shirt, the outfit completed with fluorescent-blue sneakers. Dr. Shinnie was considerably older than Ama. He was comfortable in his position of authority among the professionals in his field, but he easily deferred to Ama's matrilineal position among her own people and her royal natal position in the Queen's family. The Queen Mother of Asantemanso, the sacred village of the Asante, was also Ama's mother and Peter Shinnie's mother-in-law. Since the first people of West Africa, the Asante families held the royal descent. Like the Iroquois in the Mohawk Valley, the authority was matrilineal; and the royal line came down from the first people to Ama. Ama rapidly moved us past the customs officials with few words and a defiant look to the officials.

After introductions, we piled into University of Calgary pickup trucks. It was much too late to begin a journey to Asantemanso, so the first evening was spent at the Star Hotel. The ride to the hotel was brief but refreshing after so many hours in an airplane. Stars seemed close to the earth, and gray branches of enormous trees stretched into the sky and outward for what appeared to be thirty or forty feet in all directions from their trunks. People were everywhere, waving to us from sidewalks and bare city lots.

The Star Hotel was better than I anticipated and worse than many of the older volunteers expected. Ama had described the hotel as "scruffy," but I found it a welcome accommodation; the bed was clean and comfortable, the water worked in a more or less consistent fashion in one faucet (plus it was potable), the air conditioner was noisy but functional, and the one bare light bulb remained lit when needed. There was no handle on the toilet, but a bucket of water took care of that problem. I slept soundly, exhausted after so many waking hours, and woke early enough for a brief walk.

Across the street from the Star Hotel was a small booth, probably set up to attract business from hotel visitors. There were displays of carved masks and beads, and nearby was a prayer rug where the owner of the booth, a Muslim, could retire several times each day to pray. Near the prayer rug was a garishly painted blue "disco" van, spray-painted with gyrating bodies and musical instruments, the band sleeping on the ground nearby. I ate, then found a place to exchange money — dollars for *cedes* — picked up my backpack from the hotel, tossed it on my back, and strolled down the road to the National Museum of Ghana, where we were to meet Peter and Ama to depart for the village. From there, we would travel via Kumasi to Esumeja, where we were to live for three weeks — a long ride on over 150 miles of badly rutted African highway.

The vans were in place, but Ama was not, so we had to wait. In West Africa, the Ashanti royal family's spiritual and hereditary control was all-encompassing, even in the smallest details. Power was also matrilineal, so although Peter was married to Ama, he did not have the power to even move vans because the drivers had not been told by Ama that they should obey his instructions. During this delay, we explored the museum, which housed a diverse collection of Asante weavings, gold work, swords, stools, staffs, gold weights, and religious artifacts. The staffs were captivating, with decorative birds and lions that combined Christian symbolism and tribal motifs to illustrate proverbs and adages.

A bird known as the Sankofa appeared as a motif on many objects. It was derived from motifs of King Adinkera of the Akan people of West Africa, and it served as a reminder that "it is not shameful or taboo to look back to recollect or to remember one's past" *(se wo were fi na wosan kofa a yenki)* — an admonition to recall one's past or what one has forgotten and use it to face the future armed and ready. This proved to be the first healing tool given to me in this journey in a foreign land.

The lion, another symbol evident on many items, appeared on the royal stools and carved on staffs, a symbol of authority among the Asante people. It was often accompanied by a man whose hand rested lightly above the animal's head, signifying innocence, virtue, and respect as true companions to authority.

At last Ama returned and the vans were ready. We squeezed ourselves into the vans and began the 150-mile trip to Asantemanso. The weather was hot and the driving was very slow as our driver dodged potholes, stalled trucks, and throngs of people carrying baskets on their heads moving in single file down the roads. A fine red sand sifted over people, vehicles, houses, the landscape — everything. On either side of the highway were miles of low tropical brush, interrupted in places by stands of banana trees and coconut palms.

A Journey into the Sacred Forest

The people who lined the roads between villages carried firewood, food, market items, water, and even animals on their heads. Roadside villages were compact and crowded. Village huts and small houses constructed of sun-baked clay bricks were grouped in compounds, some painted white, some decorated with Mediterranean blue borders and glowing pink trim. Most had sheet-metal roofs, and some had thatched roofs of palm grass. I later learned that in earlier times all the huts had been thatched, but the metal roofs reduced insect infestation and prevented showers of bugs and spiders from descending on the inhabitants when the roof was disturbed. The thatch, however provided a cooler interior environment than the metal.

About halfway to Kumasi, I noticed an entire village of joined buildings made in the earlier style, still bearing thatched roofs. Personal possessions were few. There was an occasional palace for the governing family, and a few other elegant houses appeared to be left from the English colonial period. These houses usually had pink or blue columns and were painted white with a pink border and pink or blue shutters. The window openings had no glass, and they were usually shuttered against the bright, hot sun. Doors were sometimes carved with elaborate reliefs illustrating hunting, religious, or biblical scenes. For me, the domestic dwellings, the shrine houses — small, conical-shaped buildings reserved for spiritual ceremonies — and the landscape were familiar; they were almost identical to the scenes in my dream of a "foreign country."

We stopped at a "chop bar" for lunch, where we ate fried yams with hot sauce and drank orange soda. The chop bars, shops, vans, and buses all bore hand-lettered names and shorthand proverbs: "IS UNKNOWN," "NO PROBLEM," "WHO IS," "EXODUS." Some declared African unity, many in English and some in *Twi*, the Asante language. Our van announced "GOD PROVIDES ALL NEEDS" on the front and "NO CONDITION IS PERMANENT" on the rear, apparently covering all bases.

Kwasi, our driver, was also a member of the Asante royal family and a resident of the village of Esumeja, where we would be housed. There was always quiet deference to those who were of the royal family, but they dressed and presented themselves as part of the village culture. Only in the larger ceremonies would the special dress, canes, fans, and scepters give them away. Kwasi had remained quiet throughout the drive, concentrating on the treacherous roads that had enormous ruts and were busy with people walking between villages. Occasionally the vans were stopped at impromptu checkpoints where Kwasi explained our presence in West Africa. At any other time, these stops would have made me nervous. But this was a journey I was supposed to take, so I just watched the proceedings from my seat, completely trusting Kwasi to answer the questions to their satisfaction.

Kwasi himself relaxed a bit as we approached his home, Esumeja, and his spiritual birthplace, Asantemanso, both important villages of the Asante and just a mile apart. As we neared the sacred forest at Asantemanso, Kwasi turned toward us, nodded, and began to speak of the history of his people and their association with the sacred forest and the sacred village of Asantemanso, where we would be working for three weeks. Any anxiety I felt about being so far from home, any fear I felt about breast cancer dissolved in the melodious depth of his voice. He told his story in the recitative style of the Asante. His voice was fluid and evocative, filling my head with images as one would a vessel. Words flowed like poetry through the hot air, enveloping everyone with the mood of the tale. His voice changed and took on a rhythm, like the beat of a drum, beating the rhythm of the story, making the air vibrate with the tones of its telling. As we drove, taller trees began to appear, many accompanied by nearby termite hills. Small animals darted about — egrets, lizards, black-and-white crows, and weaverbirds. Magnificent sunbirds darted back and forth in front of the van. Kwasi's voice droned on and on, pulling me into the trees, which were now thicker and taller. Suddenly the sacred forest appeared beside our bus, thick with brush. Enormous trees and palms towered against the sky, sculpting it with their magnificent, ancient branches.

I had my own spiritual ties to the old-growth forest on my grandmother's land, and my deep feelings of reverence for her healing gifts were intertwined with the nearness of her forest. However, Kwasi's stories were of creation — of the very beginning of a people in the depths of this even more ancient forest. This was my first experience with such a powerful symbol of the source of what a people believed to be the beginning of humanity. There was palpable magic in this forest — one mile of sacred land, the forest where the Asante believed time began, the place where the first two of seven clans emerged, one from a hole in the earth, one from the sky on a golden chain. Kwasi's voice drifted away as we passed the forest.

to home

Only one mile from the sacred forest was the village of Esumeja. We were to be housed at the "motel" in Esumeja, where we found our rooms by kerosene light the first evening. Throngs of children and members of the archaeology crew greeted us, asking our names and jockeying to carry our bags. Dinner was waiting for us at the communal table — pasta with a spicy pepper-and-tomato sauce — and the children hovered around us, telling us their names again and asking ours. They liked to say "Wan-da."

Sleep was difficult the first night in Esumeja. I was unaccustomed to the unrelenting heat without relief from fans or breeze. Sounds were also different: sheep sometimes wandered, bleating, into the communal "motel"; frogs, thousands of them it seemed, croaked through the night; and an unfamiliar animal produced a loud, harsh, crackling sound. Just before finally drifting off to sleep, I heard an angry woman shouting and banging on a nearby door.

The next morning — Sunday — was not a work day, so I was able to explore my surroundings. I felt comfortable. I walked around the village, curious about what brought me to this country so far from my own. I had been drawn to this place in an inexplicable way that I still did not understand. Perhaps I would never fully understand, but I knew that I needed a place so foreign from my own environment that I could be myself, begin to understand myself, without the encumbrance of a familiar setting. The decision to take this trip had been impulsive, but it had been the right decision — and perhaps not as impulsive as I thought.

On my walk, I met people who were on their way to church. They were friendly and stopped to ask me questions. They already knew why I was there, but they wanted to know who I was, whether I had a family, where I lived, and what I thought of their village. Several people asked if I were Asian. The fourth person who asked me that question — an old man — seemed willing to walk with me for a moment. I asked him, "Why did you think I might be Asian?" He grinned a large toothless grin. "You have funny eyes, like Asian eyes; you are different behind your eyes. You hear what people really say. You answer them, but you are in two places. Part of you goes far away when you talk, perhaps to home." "To home?" I asked, "To my home?" He grinned again. "No, you know by 'home.'" Deep inside I felt that, indeed, I knew "by home"

— a spiritual place where we go when we need to find healing, when we need to find solace and refuge, when we need to remember, like the Sankofa, how to find our way back.

I left the man near the church and walked on to the sacred forest. The two villages sat on different points of a gradually rising hill that became even more steep as it continued into the countryside and another mile toward a small settlement of cloth weavers. Asantemanso was near the base of the hill and across from the sacred forest. When I got there, I stood and stared at the enormous, smooth gray trunks of the magical trees. The upper branches, which were more bare, were hung with hundreds of weaverbirds' nests. I closed my eyes and listened carefully to their haunting tones, the harmonies drifting down the side of the hill and filling the branches of the trees. Two vultures sat in one of the trees near the nests, lulled into a peaceful coexistence with the weaverbirds.

Kwasi had told us that people believe Eden and the beginning of time are somewhere lost in that forest — the origin of all humanity, the mythology of all humanity lying somewhere in there. "Home" for every person who had ever been born, who would ever be born, was somewhere deep in that forest. Perhaps all of us needed to go "to home" when we became lost or just sidetracked by illness or change. A small boy interrupted my reverie and asked if I would walk with him to the village market for *pano*, a sweet tea bread that was a favorite for morning toast or for jams and peanut butter. He seemed to enjoy holding my hand and introducing me to his family and friends.

A Terrible Wednesday had just passed. Terrible Wednesdays occurred every forty days and commemorated something "too terrible" that had happened sometime in the peoples' unrecorded past. No one recalled any longer exactly what that terrible event was; it could have been a disaster that wiped out village crops, an illness, or some such thing. No one was allowed to work on a Terrible Wednesday, and the Queen Mother would ask people to stop whatever they were doing if they were unaware of the day. "Too terrible" also became a joking response if someone wished not to do something, like work, for some trivial reason. It would then be "too terrible" or "too too terrible" to work. When the Terrible Wednesday came, it would be announced by the beating of drums, and libations would be poured to prevent disasters from coming again to crops, to families, and to the village.

the village of life

OUR ARCHAEOLOGY SITE was located in the ancient sacred Asante village of Asantemanso, home to the Queen Mother (called Nana), her immediate family, and Crazy John, the seer, who lived in a small hut alone where he practiced practical magic with plants and amulets. Crazy John could "see" into the spirit world and was sought by those who wished to receive messages. Hanging from his hut were gourds, plants, and old tools; and the village children always approached him with respect and awe. The sacred forest stood on the edge of and across the road from Asantemanso, and one entered the forest only when invited and only in the company of the Queen Mother. All of Asantemanso and its surroundings were sacred — the village, the forest — and all was tied to the concept of beginnings. Asantemanso was a village of life, not of death. No one was allowed to die within its boundaries. In fact, if someone were near death, that person was taken away from Asantemanso to Esumeja or another village to die.

The archaeology crew gathered each morning to receive a blessing from the Queen Mother and to learn a new phrase from her. One person at a time, she would hold our hands together in hers and keep them there until we had pronounced the syllables of the new phrase correctly. We learned proper greetings for the morning and evening (*N-kyea* for both, with slight variations) and a special blessing for the night: *sum-day-a papa* (have beautiful dreams).

The sharp stabbing pain in my breast came and went, but I pushed it aside. I would breathe deeply in and out, working mentally to expel the pain and bring in healing. At night, I would raise my arms above my head, breathing in and out deeply, asking that the need for a second journey be dissolved somewhere in this country so far away from my home. I tried not to feel the pain in this place where I needed to make my first journey. I would attend to the pain when I returned to the place where I would begin my second journey, back in my own home.

Each morning we gathered to receive our instructions for the day. The archaeologists had been looking for an *ansanse*, a place for mourning pots. They were searching just beyond the boundaries of Asantemanso because death and mourning were not permitted in the village. They had not found the ansanse they'd originally sought, but they did find an even more important site near the village compound, which we called "the place of pots." This site contained an enormous cache of sacred pots, which had been "killed" with holes pierced through their bases, remnants of thousands of years of ceremonies. The site had never before been explored by archaeologists, and the stories surrounding its use were numerous.

Most of the stories indicated that medicine men used this location for destroying disease and evil intentions. The disease (or evil) was ritually placed in the pot by spiritual practitioners. Libations were poured and potions were boiled in larger pots, which were blessed and presented to the person who was ill. The nature of the person's illness would determine how the potion was used: ingested, inhaled, or poured over the body. If the medicine was successful, the pot containing the disease would be "killed" and left at this sacred site. The ritual placement of the disease in a container and then destroying it was part of the healing process that guaranteed the disease would not re-enter the body of the person. The pots were healing vessels, not deadly in and of themselves, but dangerous once the disease had been given to the pot. Destruction of the vessel destroyed the disease. The archaeology team had permission from the royal family and the Queen Mother to explore the cache of pots only because Dr. Shinnie had married Ama, the Queen Mother's daughter.

I was there with the archaeology crew on the first day they explored the deeper, more ancient layers of the site. I began removing the debris from a large pot, carefully brushing away a hard-packed clump clinging to the side and base, uncovering a set of three tiny, perfect medicine pots, each one smaller than the last and set snug one inside the other. There were many sizes of pots in the place of pots, but these were so perfectly nestled and so perfectly made that they held a kind of beauty lacking in the rest. Also, this set of pots, unlike the others previously uncovered by the archaeologists, had not been "killed," indicating that it possibly possessed a "power" the other pots had relinquished. They were still whole and unused, pots ready to accept ritual magic, pots ready to be used for healing. Osei, an Asante worker, stood behind me watching intently as I brushed away debris from the nested pots. "The dwarves," he said, "continue to make pots and this place, the place of change, continues to grow." "The place of change?" I asked. "Nothing, no one, ever remains the same in this place. The healing pots," he said, pointing to my pots, "appear nightly, coming up from the earth or down from the sky."

He spoke softly so that no one else would hear him. He stopped speaking as the archaeologists moved closer with cameras and notepads. "*Meda-a-say*," I whispered — a special word for a heartfelt thank-you.

That night I remembered my first dream since arriving in Africa:

The Gift of the Ashanti Child

I sat up in the bed where I lay and lifted a small black child with large inquisitive eyes from the foot of the bed, where it had been placed by a young woman as a gift for me. The table beside my bed and the small items on it were moved aside so that the baby would not roll over and hurt itself. I asked everyone in the village about the child, but they all said that the child was a special gift for me. "Meda-a-say," I said in a soft whisper.

When I thought about the dream the next morning, I understood the gift to be a dream presentation of new life and a new way of receiving nurturing from a culture far removed from my own. During my three weeks in Africa, I received many gifts from the village people, all of which could be symbolized by this gift of a child. Children often came and sat beside me, and several of them whispered incredible words about my dreaming. In a dream-telling one morning in the hallway of the place I stayed in Esumeja, a child came up quietly behind me and said in a singsong whisper "Wan-da dreams well; Wan-da will dream for all of you." Sometimes a child would walk through the hallway with a small banana or an egg and ask me to take the food gift for telling dreams with them. An egg was expensive and was a special gift for a dream. The words — or perhaps the cadence of the speech — were gifts that seemed to come from a magical place. All the people gave me gifts of love and healing that remained with me into the next year and beyond.

In the evenings, after we came back from working at our site, we ate native food — monkfish and various dishes of yams and spinach. We were asked to eat with our right hands, our left hands folded in our laps. The reason was a bit unsavory: the left hand was considered unclean because it was used to wipe oneself after defecation in the old days. At least I hoped it was in the old days. We pulled the yams apart with the fingers of our right hand.

We were also invited to experience the ceremonies of the Asante people, and to dance to the new "high life" music of the young. Late in the evenings, after a ceremony or dance, we would pile into the back of the crew pickup truck to return to our village, the dark night engulfing us and the warm air blowing on our faces. Impromptu street dancing involved drumming, dancing to beats as ancient as the village itself, sometimes giving way to trances as young women swirled and waved small, white handkerchief-like cloths in the air. The dances of the young, the teenagers, was "high life," a kind of disco sound with gyrating bodies, arms waving in the air, packed into small dance bars, usually in Kumasi or one of the slightly larger villages. The nights were beautiful, the stars oppressively close, and the songs, even the new ones, evocative and haunting in the night air:

> *"We all come to papa's land;*
> *Ghana is the papa's land."*

The tune was an ancient chant; the words soft and inviting. In the evenings, no matter how late we returned when we walked back to Esumeja, the Esumejahene would sometimes come out, take our hands, and offer prayers for our health and aid.

ONE EVENING I sat in the pickup truck as we returned from a ceremony in another village, listening to the songs and feeling content. I was so far away from home in the back of a truck in West Africa, yet I felt as though I had been there for a lifetime. I thought for just a moment about the illness I would have to battle when I returned home, but I had already found words of healing in this country: "No one remains the same here," Osei had said, "no one leaves the same from the place of change." I was the only member of the crew who had found — or perhaps received — "healing pots."

the royal family and the sacred forest

To AVOID THE HEAT of midday, we worked in the early morning, usually walking to our sites at about 6 A.M. each morning. We would have one break and then head back to Esumeja at noon. It was impossible to work beyond noon in the intense heat. In the afternoons we would sit and record or label the archaeological material, and Peter Shinnie would sit in a chair, preparing his written material, and give us a brief history lesson, adding layer upon layer of information as the days went by.

He told us that traditionally, many settlements in Ghana have relied on ancestral spirits for protection. These community gods or guardian spirits inhabit trees, stones, or even man-made objects. Many are associated with special dwelling places (streams, lagoons, forests) that are left undisturbed and only occasionally visited for important ceremonies, religious rituals, or meetings of secret societies.

Religion, taboos, norms, culture, and local rules and regulations govern who comes and goes in the sacred forest. Entry into the sacred forest is strictly limited to certain categories of people within the community at specific times and for specific purposes. One of the people forbidden to go into the sacred forest, or even to look upon it, is the *Asantehene*, the king of all the Asante people. He is not even allowed to set   foot in Asantemanso; if he sees the forest, something terrible will come to the Asante people. Like the Terrible Wednesdays, no one seemed clear on what terrible thing would occur, but it would be larger than the thing that could happen on a Terrible Wednesday. When the *Asantehene* passes through the area, he is blindfolded so that he cannot see the forest in any direction.

In Ghana, the suffix *hene* (pronounced "hee'nee") indicates the title of King. Each village has royalty (for example, the *Esumejahene* is the ruling authority of Esumeja), but the *Asantehene* is head authority of all of the villages. All of the kings may live in their villages except the Asantehene, who must not live in Asantemanso. Living there would be impossible with the forbidden forest always in view.

We usually walked together as a group between Esumeja and Asantemanso. On one morning we were invited to gather in a circle around the Queen Mother. She told us before we left Africa she would escort us within the boundaries of the sacred forest. There, she would pour libations for our safe return home and bless the pots representing the seven Asante tribes. The opening sentences of the parting ceremony would take place within a small, round building with thatched roof, the sacred shrine. The Queen Mother walked me to the shrine, locked at that time, and pointed to the areas outside the forest, but still within the village, where some of the sacred trees grew. These smaller individual trees, seemingly unconnected to the larger forest across the road, were marked with white cloth tied around their trunks, and sometimes with bundles of *suman* — objects endowed with power and wrapped in white cloth —

tied in their branches. No one is allowed to approach these trees or the sacred ground upon which they grow except in her presence. Disobeying this request would place one in grave danger. It was considered taboo for anyone other than Ama and other invited members of the royal family to enter the boundaries of the sacred forest unless permission and an invitation were given. Uninvited visitors could contaminate the sacred ground, and breaking the taboo was considered especially serious. In extreme cases, such as a person running from danger, the boundaries of the forest could be broached. If the fleeing person could touch one of the sacred trees before something terrible happened, then he would be safe.

The royal family sat on "stools," often beautifully carved, sometimes simple. They were sacred stools carved in a particular form: low, with a curved seat, and bearing the motifs of the Asante culture. These stools were brought together for special ceremonies. Guests and those not of royal blood sat in ordinary chairs or, in some cases, stood. It was said that Anokye (pronounced *A-noh-chay*), a great shaman and advisor who had originally brought a golden stool from the sky, rested it on the original ruler's shoulders and endowed it with the collective soul of the Asante people. Anokye was known to the Asante people as the most powerful and clever shaman of the Asante — a man who created, alongside Tutu, the initial power of the great Asante kingdom.

This background information and brief history prepared us for meeting the Esumejahene. At an appointed time, about a week into our stay, our group walked to his palace on the outskirts of the village to an enormous old cocoa tree, where large white armchairs were arranged in a semicircle facing the seated Esumejahene. Because the Esumejahene's feet are never allowed to touch the bare ground, he is required to rest his feet on a stool when he sits for an audience. The Esumejahene was dressed in the *Kente* cloth of his royal clan, which is characterized by large black-and-white patterns. He wore enormous gold rings, one on each hand, in the shape of flying birds that opened to reveal cavities for gunpowder storage. Large golden frogs — another ancient clan symbol — adorned the king's shiny black sandals. Each of us shook right hands with him, made our greeting — a simple bow from the waist — and sat down in the circle. The chairs were so large that my feet dangled like a child's, but crossing one's legs or feet would be insulting.

The Esumejahene now spoke. Ordinarily an interpreter from his court would perform the initial greeting, but today he asked Ama, as a member of the royal Aroko clan from Asantemanso, to do the honor of greeting us. Ama gave the lengthy greeting in Twi. Then, in both Twi and English, the Esumejahene narrated the story of the origins of his clan. His clan came from the hole in the forest, bringing with it a frog (who brought water), a dog (who brought fire), and a leopard (who brought food). Symbolic representations of the frog, the dog, and the leopard appeared on the tiled court floor, on the royal Kente cloth weavings of the Esumejahene's garments, and on staffs, rings, and other representations of royal power. The Esumejahene spoke of the first leader of his people, whom he called "grandfather" and from whom he claimed descent. He referred to the "grandfather" as though they were one and the same. In his lengthy retelling of his people's history, he described the bitter Asante war with the *Denkyra*. In the battle, the Denkyra leader was killed and his head removed. Body parts were distributed among the tribes, the Esumejahene receiving the left leg. This gave his tribe the right to always march in the left flank in battle or in ceremony. Other village rulers were given other body parts, which defined their physical placement in lines of battle or in ceremonies.

After the audience with the Esumejahene we walked back to the village, going first to the house of a man who worked in gold. I purchased small gold figurines of animals originally used as weights to balance scales.

Our guide was a small boy named Kwame, who led the way home by an unfamiliar path through dense undergrowth. He cut through the brush with his machete, exposing the root systems of vines and small trees that created a difficult path home. One of the crew joked about tripping because he was left-handed in a right-handed society. Our guide did not respond to the joke but marched on. Farther down the path, when passage was easy, the boy dropped back, took my hand in his, and said, grinning, "right-handed people are spiritual people." We walked on. The conversation turned to a young woman in our group who had been left behind in the village because she was ill. The young boy, Kwame, still listening to our conversation, interrupted, "Let Wan-da dream; she will dream for her." Everyone laughed. I was startled, but I said nothing. I was never sure how the boys knew about my dreaming — intuition, a shared empowerment, or a kind of destined response. I chose to believe that remarks such as the boy's were part of the reason for my journey.

She Who *Dreams*

a visit to kumasi

THE ARCHAEOLOGY GROUP took several field trips into the larger cities, including one to the cultural center in Kumasi. A guide at the center talked to us about the significance of the drums. He demonstrated the small drums first, then the powerful "talking" drums, which bore no resemblance to those sold in American music and craft catalogs. These enormous drums were covered with leopard skin and beaten with a crooked branch. The guide beat out the syllables of words from the Twi language, the drumbeat becoming the syllables. We watched ceremonial dances and were invited to share a meal with the royal family.

WE WILL MEET ON THE PATH OF DREAMS

THE NEXT DAY we returned to Kumasi for a special ceremony in which we would meet the Asantehene and the entire royal family of the Asante people. While we were waiting to be invited into the main ceremonial court, a pleasant old man dressed in royal white cloth walked up to me and invited me to follow him. I looked around anxiously, and Dr. Shinnie told me that it was suitable to follow him if I wished. The old man motioned once again for me to follow and led me to a large inner courtyard where he introduced me to his "senior" wife, her sister, and his son. He looked around for a piece of paper and a pencil, then carefully printed his name, folded the piece of paper, and tucked it into my hand. He led me to a large alcove off the courtyard and pulled back a curtain, revealing a number of large old drums like the ancient ones in the cultural center. He told me in halting English that he had been the drummer for the Asante ceremonies before he became too old to make the drums "talk" properly. He asked if I would take a photograph of him among the drums. I carefully framed him standing among the large drums in the deep shadows of the alcove. He stepped down and came close to me and held my hands in the same way my grandmother had held them when I was a child.

"We will meet again many years from now and we will remember one another. I will die to this earth soon and my body will pass away. I will wait for you on a path you will see in your dreams, and I will aid you however you wish. You will know on the day I leave this earth, and I will be ready then to help and assist you, to be your guide in your dreaming. You do not need to remember or even recall my name; you will hear the drums talking and know me and know what to do."

He held my hands tighter. I felt my eyes filling with tears, and I could say nothing. He continued: "You have great love and must never allow anyone to change your predestined path. It is a quiet path of great power, the power of peace, more powerful than words." I felt weak. He dropped my hands and then took one hand and led me into the groups of people gathering for the ceremony, then seated me behind the drummers in the courtyard where the ceremony would take place. He'd placed me in the first row of seats on the platform to the right side of the king's seat. I was a bit awed. I was sitting onstage in a small semi-circle of seats between the royal family and the line of men who would chant the recitative of their peoples' historic origins. Mine was the only white face on the platform, but that seemed not to disturb anyone.

One of the lessons of being in West Africa centered on the people as a dreaming culture. I didn't need to explain that I dreamed or what I dreamed. Dreaming and mystery were tied to the taboos and ceremonies and defined their life. They "knew" who I was and "knew" about my dreams. I didn't have to tell them or share anything about my reasons for a spiritual journey within their country. I drank in the culture, the ceremonies, their peculiar intuitive responses to things I said or did not say, and the gift of themselves when I needed it.

The ceremony began. Sacred objects covered with ancient leopard skins had been placed in the spaces between members of the royal families and their impressive retinue. Drummers and elephant-horn blowers introduced the endless lines of people bringing offerings and presenting problems to the Asantehene. Hypnotic recitation of history progressed with soft drumming and an occasional horn, one narrator reciting in a loud, high voice and the second repeating what he said in a low singing voice. Sometimes I recognized phrases or names of historical figures — *Osei Tutu, Anoke,* and *Poku Ware.*

Some of us were presented to the king. The old man in white approached me, took my hand, and led me to the aisle, where I was gently instructed to bow, looking always toward the king. He smiled and nodded, and I returned to my seat. After the ceremonies were over, the old man in white led me among his people, introducing me to everyone as the person he would be assisting when he passed on to the path beyond earth. Peter Shinnie told me later that this peculiar insistence by the old man to introduce himself as an after-death guide would not be an unusual practice, but why he singled me out from among our group puzzled Peter.

Several years after my trip to Africa, I had a dream that may or may not have related to the old man. The man in the dream told me his name, but I had long before lost the piece of paper given to me by the old man in white who lived in Kumasi.

A VISIT FROM UNA BEKWAI

I am at a file drawer, labeling file folders with the names of all the teachers and guides who were important in my life, in alphabetical order. I am placing markers on the folders of those who might still be helpful to me. A tall, very black, extremely good-humored individual suddenly appears at my shoulder and tells me I have overlooked him. He is young. I am impressed with his voice and his attitude. I ask him his name. He laughs and says I know him. He says his name is Una Bekwai. He flashes an enormous grin and instructs me to place his folder in the front part of the file box so that it will be handy when I need it. I do, and he places in the folder a portrait of himself, pieces of jewelry from his hand and neck, and data about himself so that I will remember who he is and what he looks like when he appears again. He says that information in the folder will enable me to recognize him because each piece is unique to him. He has placed in the folder an Asante-style ring worn by the royal family. On it is an enormous gold leopard, sitting in a crouching position. He also places in the folder a picture of himself standing among drums. I think I hear drums. Una Bekwai flamboyantly throws his robe across his shoulder and leaves the room.

When I dreamed about the visit of Una Bekwai, I was long past the year of my healing journey. He appeared to me as a young man, which probably worked best for most people he visited in dreams. I would not have recognized him in the dream if he hadn't said that I knew him. Also, I didn't know many men who were that shade of black. His color was pure ebony. All the objects in the dream — a royal Asante leopard ring, gold, and the drum itself — also pointed toward my promised guide. The men in West Africa always laughed like Una Bekwai — loud and with sounds that came from deep within their chests — and they loved to laugh. Una Bekwai made sure his folder was pulled forward to the front in the dream so that I would no longer neglect him. I believed, upon waking, that the old man in white had passed on and would be available for me whenever I needed him.

Back in my room in Esumeja that night, after meeting the man in white, I fell asleep listening to the village drums. It was February 6. I dreamed the most specific, most terrifying dream of my illness yet:

MY DEPARTED FATHER NAMES MY DISEASE

My father appears and seems to be checking on me. Someone else is also in the dream: a man dressed in a medical coat. He tells me, almost shouting, that I have a malignant lump in my breast and that I must have my breast removed. He continues to shout, telling me that, no matter what I hear, it is not benign. He is now leading me out the door to the Mayo Clinic, where a doctor is shouting to me that I have a malignancy and I must act immediately.

I woke up from the dream and wrote it down, almost mechanically. I was no longer denying to myself that there was a problem, but I could do nothing about it here — at least nothing medical. I lay back on the bed and began doing some breathing exercises: I concentrated on pulling the malignancy into a single space and then expelling it mentally from my body, breathing in light in deep breaths, expelling dark waves of air in deep breaths. The pain seemed to abate just a bit. I slept fitfully the rest of the night.

a new excavation site, kente weavings, and the celebration of funerals

WHILE WE WERE WORKING at the place of pots, part of the archaeology team had opened two new sites, one the ancient foundations of one of the earliest dwellings in Asantemanso and one a small site trenched to determine the boundaries of the dwelling site. Dr. Shinnie wanted all of us to experience more than one site so a week and a half into the project he asked us to switch sites. I was now working closer to the main village at a place thought to be a house-site of a member of the royal family. We found beautiful objects: whole pots with line-and-ridge decorations, sacred adzes, finials, and lids, some a deep blue color. The objects were so amazing that we began to speculate that we might have found a shrine within a house. It didn't seem to be a burial pit.

We took breaks near the house of Crazy John, the seer, who lived slightly away from the village houses. As in many cultures, the Asante believed that "crazy" people had special powers and could see in ways that others could not. Crazy John wandered the cocoa groves all day with an empty basket on his head, singing and laughing aloud. He was an old man, and people came to him from villages miles away. He wasn't shut away, as he would be in America, but he was embraced and sought out for his words. He accepted gifts of food and clothing. He had been called Crazy John for as long as the village people could remember. He chose his own dwelling place; he liked being away from other people and he had his own garden.

One afternoon we walked several miles beyond Esumeja to Sebedie, where the men weave the Asante Kente strips. Kente is an Asante ceremonial cloth, woven by hand on treadle looms. Multicolored strips four inches wide are woven and then sewn together into larger pieces of cloth, which are worn during important social and religious ceremonies. Like the wampum belts of the Iroquois in America, Kente cloth is more than just cloth; the patterns woven into it represent West African history, religious beliefs, and social customs. Sebedie was the weaving village for the cloth of Esumeja and Asantemanso. There are certain patterns that are only worn by the Esumejahene and the Asantehene. Other patterns can be worn by villagers and purchased by visitors.

The Sebedie master weaver was an elderly man named Kwaku Buoaki. He was working on a strip on the loom and had sewn together a large piece, about twelve yards long and four feet wide. He removed the piece from the loom and asked us to follow him. We followed, along with most of the village adults and children, probably about fifty people of assorted ages, through a cocoa grove, through a mud-brick fence, and into a courtyard. The house was enclosed on three sides and the back was open to a courtyard, which was mostly taken up by a large, freestanding, outdoor baking hearth with beehive-shaped mud ovens shaded with a thatched roof. The weaver folded the cloth and placed it on a hammock hung in one of the house's two rooms. Most of the household possessions — pots, pans, clothing — were also in the hammock. In the small space between the house and the hearth, the weaver placed stools for the three of us who had come to buy cloth. We sat down and waited while Kwaku left, then returned with the cloth.

The villagers hovered behind and around us — some of the children sitting on the shoulders of adults — while we bargained. Each time the bid came close to Kwaku's acceptable price, he made an elaborate pantomime of pretending to cut the cloth apart with a razor in order to raise the prospect of a higher bid. The final bid brought happy smiles to the faces of the villagers. Bargaining was the basis for any purchase, from eggs in the market to the Kente cloth in Sebedie. It was also an art — one I never fully adopted. As the bargaining progressed, I watched the women gathered at the hearth preparing vegetables and yams for dinner. They sat, probably as their ancestors had sat, either on small stools or squatting balanced on their feet, gossiping and watching their pots.

As I watched the women cooking under the shelter of the bamboo roof, I felt an odd sense of nostalgia for a culture that had changed so little for so many centuries — a culture that, by its lack of change, permitted its people the intimate knowledge of the mind and soul of its ancestors. How could you not feel the presence of your ancestors, of your grandmother, when you stirred the same pot on the same hearth and wore the same pattern in your clothing that had been worn for thousands of years? The simple addition of your personal history to hers, the addition of a few names to the endless list of quoted ancestors, was all that would be required to bind your history to hers.

As the weekend before our final week began, we joined the processions moving from village to village, celebrating funerals. Bryan, one of the archaeologists, told us that certain weeks of the year were reserved for ceremonies for the dead. People would take the opportunity of these ceremonies to visit relatives in other villages. Hundreds of people moved between the villages, dancing, playing music, and whirling in the streets to the rhythmic beating of the drums, then slowing, swaying back and forth in trance, moaning, and talking. Men carrying staffs led the processions, moving through the village streets, pounding the ground, pounding the souls of the spirits of the dead to their appointed places, pounding life into the village people. We passed an old English cemetery graced by enormous stone angels with outstretched wings, carved by some colonial hand. I felt safe beneath those wings so far from home, "shadowed by" those wings, yet so close "to home" in this foreign land. As we neared our village in the late evening, the mourners were offered beer and the

children gathered singing songs, surrounding us with beautiful harmonies that followed us back into the hallway of our lodging house and
sifted into the village. The children sang into the morning.

On Sunday of that final weekend, one of the Earthwatch volunteers
asked if I would like to attend church. Initially I declined, then walked
upstairs to the roof and sat in the hot morning sun. I heard drums and
watched a procession of young women coming from the northwest side
of the village, winding their way down the side of a long hill. A small
girl, dressed in white, watched me from below, disappeared, then re-
appeared on the stairs. She told me that her name was Sarah and that she
would take me to her church. I walked with her to a bamboo-thatched
pavilion where women had gathered on one side and men on the opposite side, drums still beating. I joined the women. A male leader chanted
a sermon, every few moments shouting in English, "Hallelujah, Amen!"
The congregation would respond "Hallelujah, Amen!" and begin
dancing to the rhythm of the drums.

Sarah took my hand and we moved in a line with the chanting
women, who waved white scarves. The line of women moved first in a
circle inside the pavilion, then wove back in an S formation outside,
then back inside again where the chant reached a loud, hypnotic
crescendo of humming sounds. Inside the room the women whirled,
wove, and danced, some in trance at the center of the circle. The men
drummed, shouted, and sang.

Everyone's breathing accelerated with the music, and the hypnotic
humming seemed to permeate the air inside and around the pavilion.
The air vibrated with sound and color. The movement slowed, and the
women in the center drifted back into the circle. The circle moved
slowly out of the pavilion, and the women began to move away and proceed up the hill to their homes. The ceremony had lasted a little more
than an hour. Sarah and I parted company, and she went on her way
toward home.

I walked back to my lodging and sat on a ledge in the hallway. I
took a grapefruit out of a basket, peeled it, and reflected on the wonderful ceremony in the pavilion and how I was led there by little Sarah.
Kojo, a child from the village, sat down beside me and took his own
grapefruit from the basket, peeling it and moving closer to me. Finally
he was next to me. "Children working alone in the farm fields must be
watchful and very careful, lest the dwarves steal them. Those stolen are

taken into the sacred forest and kept there for twenty years. When they come back out of the sacred forest, they are clothed in the forest as fetish [or shaman] priests." I nodded, and we both ate our grapefruits.

The fetish priests or shamans were both revered and feared. Their lives were different; they carried the ability to inflict damage if taboos were broken, or to bring joy if their messages were heeded properly. There were shamans who did not wear the fetish skirts or appear quite so obviously in the village ceremonies. They seemed to be less involved in games of jealousy and rivalry that sprung up in petty village quarrels. These shamans were known to the people and were more revered than feared. People feared that their children might be snatched away by some trickster in the night and turned into fetish priests. The priests lived lonely lives and, in my view, spent a great deal of time nurturing petty jealousies and creating peculiar little problems for people — like making car keys disappear if they felt slighted. At other times they would appear in more dramatic fashion, dressed in sacred grass skirts and wielding symbols of Asante power in spiritual ceremonies; in trances, women danced before them and men were possessed by power animals. The power of the fetish priest seemed to range dramatically from the petty to the sacred, but perhaps that is true of all spiritual leadership.

a farewell blessing

THE DAYS PASSED QUICKLY, punctuated by more ceremonies and other wonderful experiences with the people of Esumeja and Asantemanso. Finally the time came to close the archaeology sites. We volunteers felt a special intimacy with one another, born of living and working together for three weeks. Nana, the Queen Mother, had asked us to gather at the village shrine for a ceremony, which would conclude within the sacred forest. It would be a ceremony of blessing for our good health and for a safe journey home.

We walked together to the small, round, white shrine covered with thatch in the center of the village common at Asantemanso. Strings of bones hung by the door. Nana opened the door and entered with her family. We removed our shoes and followed, forming a small circle inside against the curved wall of the shrine. At the altar opposite the door was a raised floor with a chair in the middle. On either side of the chair were fetish bowls — simple iron bowls for potions and divination, topped with lids. Underneath the chair were fetish bundles, grasses, and symbolic objects that were tied together. The fetish bundles were endowed with spiritual power; the bowls represented the spirits of the village and the sacred beginnings of the village clans. A large round pan sat on the chair. The pan was filled with a clay-like substance, and a white animal skin hung over the back of the chair. A sacred linguist sword, a large, curved sword with handles covered with gold leaf, the insignia of the linguists who serve as spokespersons for those in authority, leaned to the right of the chair, and a fetish priest's skirt hung on the wall.

Kwasi stepped forward and spoke the prayers, poured libations on the ground, then turned and bent slightly toward the chair, still speaking softly. His eyes widened; his voice rose and fell in cadence as he directed loud questions and soft statements toward the chair. As he spoke, the swirling cadence of his voice once again filled my insides as it had on our first day near the sacred forest. The air felt tight and close, almost as if the people he called upon had walked into the tiny room and filled the space. An intense blue-green light seemed to glow around the chair. Kwasi stopped talking and waited. The light seemed to change to yellow, then white. Kwasi poured libations into the pan on the chair. In a very soft, almost inaudible voice, Kwasi spoke to the smaller pots and performed a similar but much shorter ceremony to these "lesser" spirits. I realized that it was Kwasi, not the fetish priests, who held the real spiritual power in this village.

We left the shrine in a single silent procession, following Nana into the forest, to a clearing in a circle of trees that were marked with white cloth. My breathing almost stopped in the presence of the magnificent trees. No one could stand in that circle without feeling the awe that must have seized every person who had stood there since the beginning of time. I had never visited a place in America where I could say that I believed the world's creation story began. When the Asante people stand in this forest, they are in the very place where they believe creation began for the entire world. At that moment, I could not say that they were wrong. We all moved closer to a special "sanctuary" tree, where we formed another circle in this great forest, and Nana performed a ceremonial blessing over the fetish pots of the seven clans who made up the origins of the African people.

In this place, it was the trees, not the ceremony, that produced the magic. The essence of the enormous trees reached around me and through my soul — trees so large that all of us holding hands would not have been able to stretch around them, trees so tall that the tops could no longer be seen from the ground. There were palm trees, hardwoods with exotic names like *Cese* and *Aduro*, and enormous old kola-nut trees, all with twelve-inch-diameter vines tangled among them. The feeling, the magic took my breath away. White rays of sunlight found their way through the tops of the trees and streaked down the gigantic, smooth-as-silk gray trunks, painting dramatic patterns of shade across the sandy earth swept free of leaves and branches around the circle of pots. Birds chattered, warbled, swept low, and soared high among the branches. Sunbirds flew high above our heads, their magnificent colors vibrant in the rays of white light. I heard drums that weren't there. I heard the roar of the leopard in the soft circling of branch against drum skin. As she intoned her blessing, Nana's voice was the voice of generations of her people, the voice of the first man and first woman, the voice of the first blessing, the voice of the leopard and the bird.

In the late evening back in Esumeja, some of the young women of Asantemanso joined us and sang their favorite songs for our departure: *Su-la-blu-blu* (the "weatherbird") and other slow, swaying, sensuous little songs. In a small ceremony, the children gave me my birth name, *Adjua*, meaning "born on a Monday." A birth name is literally the name of the day of the week on which one was born. Some of the archaeologists didn't know the weekday of their birth, and the children were amazed. They each had two names, but their birth name was the name most frequently used. There were seven boys' names and seven girls' names, which explained why so many names, such as Kwame (a boy's name) or Akua (a girl's name), were heard throughout the country.

We were in the last of the three weeks and in that week we traveled to the sacred lake of Bosomchi. There, animal sacrifices are still made and libations poured to appease angry spirits who caused periodic "explosions" that heated the water and killed the fish. I was astonished; the water was so hot that one could hardly touch it. In some places it bubbled, as though we were sitting on top of a volcano covered with water.

After visiting the lake, we went to the nearby market village of Bequai. There we gathered food supplies for a village feast. Bryan, an assistant to Dr. Shinnie, and I walked down the street to a shop that sold coffee and chocolate.

Outside the shop sat an old woman wearing a dark, ragged, brown dress sewn all over with fetish bundles. Her head hung sideways against her shoulder, and her eyes were closed. Bracelets and necklaces of herbs hung from her arms and neck — amulets of power to ward off evil, cast spells, uncast spells, and perform all kinds of small practical magic. I had seen no one else like her. Seers and fetish priests were male. She was a bit frightening and seemed possessed by something unsavory. She moved her hands toward me, and Bryan told me that she wanted to talk to me. She moved her head slightly up and back, her mouth opened, and her eyes rolled back beyond her eyelids with only the whites showing. I moved back from her slightly. Bryan whispered that she was the village prophet, and that people sought her advice about their future. He pushed me back toward her. I started to draw back again, but she grabbed my hands and closed her eyes. I pulled away as far as I could. Her head rolled from side to side on her shoulders, then she became very still for what seemed like minutes. Then she opened her eyes wide and looked at me startled, as if she had seen me for the first time. "You have your own light," she said, "you don't need me." Her eyes closed and she dropped my hand. I scurried away, content with my own light.

The night before we left Asantemanso, children gathered and sang to us late into the night. People walked in from the surrounding villages to bring us presents of chickens and eggs, which we discreetly gave to the kitchen staff.

The next morning, I left Asantemanso on the same long, dusty road I had traveled to get there. Some of the main archaeology team from Calgary stayed on with Dr. Shinnie; one person left the group to explore more of Africa. Several of us were placed in a van to Kumasi where we then caught a bus to Accra. The public bus was crowded, my body squeezed between two village travelers, one of whom fell asleep in my lap. Privacy was never a particularly useful concept in West Africa, and strangers, black or white, were treated with familiarity in public places. I was mildly curious about the person who fell asleep in my lap, but I no longer considered what he did peculiar. There were so many people on the bus that even breathing was difficult. Some people were squeezed against the windows so hard that I thought they would burst through.

A Journey into the Sacred Forest

I had many reveries on my way back across the miles to Accra, several of them about the ceremonies, the magic, and a healing that perhaps was already taking place. I thought about the village child who said that I was one who dreamed. I thought about my dream of the clinic in which I was told that I had breast cancer. I had purposely set aside my dreams and intuitive feelings of illness, and I'd attempted to leave the pain behind, but I was only mildly successful in that. I needed the space in which to think and begin to heal even before beginning the battle. The journey home was long and exhausting. My ultrasound was scheduled for only days away. The closer I came to home, the more my confidence and optimism waned.

Part 2

Rewriting My Sacred Contract

The Road to the
Healing Pool

*O*n the long flight home, I drifted between sleep and waking, squashed against the wall of the plane by the bulk of a businessman who typed incessantly on his laptop computer. I felt doubly squeezed by his weight and the burden of the illness I knew was growing in my body.

"What time is it?" the man asked, and I realized that my watch had stopped. Many restless hours later, the pilot's voice announced that Boston was twenty minutes away. I looked at my watch and found that it had started again — at exactly the correct time in the new time zone, not a moment off. Construction was underway at Logan Airport, requiring tedious hikes through debris; gates were changed and exits and entrances were blocked and reconfigured with red cones and yellow tape. Exhaustion overcame me.

After more flying, I finally arrived back in Albany, New York, late at night. I was almost home — near the conclusion of my first journey. In the dull winter light of the airport waiting room stood my husband and son, the last two people waiting for the last deplaning of the evening. This was my first contact with my family in three weeks. Concern showed on their faces. Ron said that I was ghostly white from exhaustion. I was also beginning to feel crushed by the enormity of the medical tests and decisions that lay ahead.

I had visited places in Africa that had been sacred to its people for thousands of years, places of healing and places of refuge, places that brought me comfort and peace of mind because they were so far removed in time and place from my own home. I had shared the culture of a generous people, and I hoped I had gained the emotional strength to prepare myself for the battle ahead. Many of the living symbols of the Asante culture embodied the people's past within their present and future, providing good lessons for their children and keeping their cultural and spiritual memory present in all their actions. As I worked with my dreams in the weeks and months ahead, in healing my mind and body, I found myself drawing on an even deeper well of memory. My dreams were my spiritual memory and my way of scanning the future to choose the right paths.

The hour was late when I arrived home, but nervous energy kept me awake. Back at our house in the hamlet of Glen, I sat down and began to tell stories, almost unable to stop. I talked into the early morning and gave gifts to Ron and Evan: pieces of Kente cloth, gold weights, carved Akuaba dolls (wooden fertility dolls), gold dust boxes (small brass boxes decorated with birds and other cultural symbols used to hold valuable gold dust used for trade and commerce), and carved staffs, the carving on one representing the proverb "two heads are better than one."

don't take the bridge

THE NEXT MORNING I opened my appointment book and looked at the circled date: February 20. I steeled myself for the ultrasound scheduled for that day, now only hours away. The hours felt like weeks. I couldn't sit still. I paced, almost on the verge of tears — shaky one moment, calm the next. I asked Ron not to come with me. Although I was terrified, I felt that I needed to keep this appointment alone. I arrived at the medical office, completed forms, and barely heard the staff conversation, mostly assuring me that I had nothing to fear, that women with fibrocystic breast disease frequently felt lumps, that lumps such as mine were usually benign. I was white with fear. A nurse handed me a sheet of paper filled with optimistic statistics on the percentage of breast lumps that were benign. But I knew I had a malignant lump. I had my dreams, but I had no idea how I would convince the medical staff of their validity if the ultrasound showed nothing of concern. I was almost more terrified of the possible battle with the technicians than I was of the malignancy itself — almost.

The examination room was cold. The jellies and the nurse's hands were even colder. I began to shake violently from a combination of cold and fear. The nurse wrapped me in a blanket and tried to calm me. Why was I so terrified of a confirmation of what I already knew? The answer was easy: I still hoped that I was wrong and they were right. They moved the pads of the machine over my breast, trying to keep me warm as they performed the ultrasound exam. They disappeared and returned. They said they needed to do part of the exam over again; there was something, something far beneath the thick central tissue that had not been picked up by the mammogram. I breathed deeply and felt an unnatural calm settle over my body; they had found the malignancy, the source of the pain. I would at least be spared one battle. The radiologist continued to work on the second film, assuring me once again that I had nothing to worry about. The second film was completed.

I dressed and found the radiologist's office, where I was directed to take a seat. He walked in and sat down, carefully placing a pad of paper in front of me. He drew a breast on the pad and began drawing a diagram of a small mass within the breast. His voice rambled softly. He was saying that he saw this kind of mass every day and that it was nothing to worry about. It was a dark mass just behind the main tissue with some radiating spots, a little "like stars spinning away from the main body." Like stars! Like my dreams of orbs and globes of stars! Like my dreams of radiating stars that were dangerous spinning shooting cells from a malignant mass!! Like my dreams of nebulae! In that moment, I was sure my dreams had given me an accurate diagnosis, and that it was very serious. I barely heard the radiologist's assurance that nothing was really wrong. I was calm and terrified at the same time. I wanted to begin now, right this moment, to get rid of this horrible mass of malignant cells!

"I see this all the time," he said. "Ninety percent of the time this is a benign mass."

"What about the other ten percent?" I asked. He didn't answer immediately. He turned the pad around and said, "It's really nothing. Don't do something stupid. Don't take the bridge."

I knew what he was saying, and I was stunned when he repeated it, again using a flippant analogy to suicide: "It's nothing. Don't take the bridge."

He was telling me not to kill myself. This time, in an attempt to be empathetic, he smiled. I was outraged by his words; how dare he be so cavalier, so cruel, after I had spent four months pursuing doctors because I knew from my dreams and my intuition that I was carrying a deadly passenger in my body that needed to be unseated with as much mental and physical force as possible!

Don't take the bridge. In my mind, I raged at this stranger for daring to suppose, even with the best of intentions, that I had fought my way through the often patronizing conversations of well-meaning but unbelieving doctors — who scoffed at my intuitive certainty — to simply come to the point where I would consider suicide, would endanger my life just when they were cautiously acknowledging that something might be wrong because they had confirmation from a machine!

I walked to the car in a daze. I slid into the seat and stared at the building next door for what seemed like hours. I gripped the steering wheel, almost ripping it out of its post. I screamed as loud as I could, but nobody heard me. Nobody was there to hear me. I had known for months, but none of their tests, until now, would confirm my knowledge. I had known for months, and finally they were coming to the place of my knowledge. I desperately wanted what I had known deep inside to be wrong. I wasn't wrong. I had to do something now.

Don't take the bridge. I drove home in a rage, pounding my fists on the steering wheel. Four wasted months fighting with doctors, four months that might have made some difference in the size of the tumor or the treatment, four months of fighting with people and not fighting for my life! No, I told myself, they were not wasted months. I had acknowledged the problem those four long months ago, and I had already been fighting for my life. I had not allowed them to tell me that I was wrong. My mind and my body were already pulling the disease back to where it could be dealt with and controlled.

GUIDANCE FROM A WAKING DREAM

THERE ARE MANY KINDS of bridges. I would not take the bridge the radiologist had mentioned, but there was another crossing I must take, and I needed clear guidance. When I got home, the place felt strange and empty. I lay down on the sofa. I had to think. I had to not think. My mind flew into a thousand corners of my subconscious. Exhausted thoughts sent my head spinning. My dreams had warned me of my illness, months — almost a year — before, but I had not understood as long ago as that. My eyes closed. I drifted into a dream:

THE CONE BREAST

I was standing over a bowl of water, holding a sponge shaped like a wide, flat cone — like a breast. There were two voices in the room, but I could not identify them. They were men. I paid no attention to them. I held the breast-shaped cone under the water, convex side up, and I could see a dark spot. I squeezed the water from the cone, and the voices of the men became more pronounced, saying to each other that I had the cone upside-down. I looked up, then back down at the cone. I turned the cone over with the flat side facing me, and I squeezed the water from it again. This time, a small cylinder filled with dark material flushed into the water, leaving the cone clear. Then the cylinder disappeared, and the material closed over itself.

My waking dream gave me a powerful and specific image that I was soon able to use for healing, in concert with my medical treatments. Previous dreams had been warnings, precognitive messages foreshadowing my illness. This was the first of many dreams that marked the transition between the messages of danger and messages that provided images I could use for my recovery. I wrote the dream in my journal and found nearby a paragraph I had copied from an essay on Paracelsus, a Renaissance physician. I had paraphrased his words to say:

The doctor is within each of us; we are our own physician and within ourselves we find all we need for healing. The power of the imagination is incomparable. It can both cause diesase and cure disease.

Peracelsus defined what later became for me a healing cocktail — healing the body using medical knowledge in combination with dreaming.

This cone breast was the first dream in a new experiment, a new beginning for my mind and body. It launched my journey through a multitude of internal and external emotions — a long process during which I would take those emotions one at a time, turn each of them inside out, investigate each one, embrace and retain some, and cast off others. Through it all, I would be shadowed by the support of friends and family and lectured and consoled, chastened and healed by my dreams, the "language of the soul."

I had found the bridge I would take.

healing imagery in the cone breast

THE WAKING DREAM showed me the exact location of the malignancy and presented me with an image I could use in meditation between then and my first visit with my surgeon. I had never experimented with actively using my dreams for healing. I had not realized, until that moment, how vitally useful and important a dream image can be in one's healing process. I sat down and considered all the possibilities for using the image — a strong, exact image that showed me the problem and the beginning of a solution. The most obvious use of the image was in meditation, which I decided to do as often as possible. I wrote out the content of the dream as a paragraph. The simplicity of the dream image of squeezing a cone and clearing it of the dark liquid provided an easy meditation for the evening.

Quiet music always had a soothing effect for me, so I chose a light classical piece and played it as background music while I recited the dream, both aloud and in my mind. I recited it before I went to bed, then I began to recite it during the day with and without the background music — a simple recall mechanism that turned the dream into useful imagery and brought it to mind instantly throughout the day. This last exercise gave the dream a functional purpose; it played again and again in my mind during the busiest part of my day. I imagined myself pulling the radiating cells back toward the mass and then taking the breast, cells now contained within a single mass, and squeezing the dark fluid into a bowl. Meditation, I determined, needed to be active, not passive. Active use gave the dream energy and placed it within reach of everything I did throughout the day. "Active" meant working with the images wherever I was — in the car, walking down the street, at work — not just sitting quietly in a room with soft music. I continued to go to work. I needed to keep busy and I needed to be around all the familiar places of my life, which included work as well as home.

rushing of the waters

Two DAYS LATER my gynecologist called, still exasperated with what she believed to be my unrealistic obsession with a malignancy that wasn't there. She began a sentence, stopped, started again, and finally, almost sighing, asked if I would like to proceed with a needle biopsy. I told her I would like to do that. She recommended an older surgeon, Dr. Bart, whom she respected, and noted that she felt he would always have my best interests in mind. I called the surgeon's office and made an appointment for the next day. The next morning I moved like a robot, trying not to think about the biopsy. I didn't know if a needle biopsy was performed in the office or if it required surgery. When I met with Dr. Bart, he told me that a needle biopsy could be performed in his office, but that it could indicate a surgical biopsy. He wasn't condescending; I already liked him. He was very gentle and talked to me constantly. During the needle biopsy, there was resistance within the breast; this was not good. Dr. Bart moved the needle cautiously around the small mass, but he could not extract fluid. A nonmalignant mass would have yielded cells more easily.

Dr. Bart stepped back and spoke directly to me: "Go home and do something about this. Take your time, maybe a few days," implying I had the ability to somehow use my mind to begin working toward dissolving the lump, "and then call me for a surgical biopsy. You can make a difference in this lump. You might even be able to make it disappear. You can do this."

I left the office. I was stunned. I had not mentioned my "cone breast" dream or the dreams that had brought me to the medical community. He seemed to have an innate sense of the mind's ability to heal, and I appreciated his giving me the time to use mind/body resources. "A few days" wasn't a very long time. I thought I might be able to begin to make a difference. I admired a surgeon who believed, along with me, that I could make a difference — could, in fact, make the lump disappear. However, I knew from my dreaming that my situation was much more dangerous than even he imagined at this point. I knew intuitively that I was dealing with something more significant than a simple lump.

I determined that I would continue to use my first healing image — the image of the cone — and work with it. I was a novice at using imagery; perhaps, I thought, if I had more experience using images and imagery I could make even more of a difference. Perhaps if I had more confidence in my ability to make myself well, I could make a complete difference and bring myself back to a perfect state of health in a few days. I did know that the "radiating cells" could continue spreading (the implied nature of "radiating"), and that my dream image, if used properly, could stop the spreading cells and pull them back to a single place where the doctor could work with them. I spent several days working continuously with the image of the cone and the basin of water, working with mind-pictures to move the malignant cells back toward the parent lump and squeeze them into the basin of water, then disposing of the dark water.

New dreams assisted me, presenting me with simple pictures of healing. I had made my appointment for the surgical biopsy, and I concentrated on my new dreams, carefully recording them and using them as active meditations. In one dream, I was given a necklace containing healing amulets from another culture. An old adversary tried to snatch the necklace away from me, but I turned on her with uncharacteristic strength. When I reached to grab the necklace, it leaped from her hands back into mine and she disappeared. I placed the healing necklace in a soft leather pouch where the amulets would be safe, then put the pouch in a locked drawer where I could find it if I needed it. I was also aware that the amulet necklace was a gift of healing that I could pass on to others if I wished. I was even more aware that, in this dream, I was given the opportunity to divest myself of old hurts and anger — an opportunity to move forward with my life, to shed the past with all its attendant anxiety, frustration, and petty hatreds, and to move on to a place where I could find healing.

In the days before my biopsy, I was gifted with a big dream — what Robert calls a "dream of power" — whose gifts I am still unfolding in my life and in my work with others. I suspect that this dream marked the true beginning of my journey into healing.

In the dream, I was transported into an ancient place of healing and into the presence of sacred healers. Robert was my companion and helper in this dream.

THE HEALING POOL

I walk with Robert to the pool at Bethesda. There is a long row of steps with a columned arcade above, and I meet an angel who says its name is Eliseus. I ask the angel for help. I hold Robert's hand as a child would, and

The Road to the Healing Pool

I move cautiously into the edge of the pool. An angel moves forward — I am not sure if it is the same one — and stands beside me. This angel tells me that I will find healing in the "rushes" or "rushing."

Suddenly I move into a village landscape and an enormous spider appears. I do not like spiders, and I really do not like this spider. I don't know what to do about the spider, so I decide to make it less frightening. I turn it into a wind-up toy and send it away.

I move away from the now-harmless spider and become a cowherd. A large, soft-eyed cow — a real cow — is looking at me. I gently place my hands on either side of her head and easily remove her head. I move to a place where a door is being erected or re-erected among ruins, and I place it above the door. I move my hands over her head, turning it into the head of a ram. As my hands move over the horns of the ram's head, a word appears: YEHOUSE.

I needed to understand the references in this dream. I went to the local library and found a nineteenth-century Bible with an extensive concordance. I looked up the words "Bethesda" and "Eliseus" and began with the biblical verses themselves:

Now there is at Jerusalem by the sheep market a pool, which is called in the Hebrew tongue Bethesda, having five porches.

In these lay a great multitude of impotent folk, of blind, halt, withered, waiting for the moving of the water.

For an angel went down at a certain season into the pool, and troubled the water: whosoever then first after the troubling of the water stepped in was made whole of whatever disease he had.[3]

The Pool of Bethesda was an ancient place that boasted remarkable healing powers. The Hebrew word *Bethesda* means "the house of mercy." Those who were sick or diseased came in large numbers to this pool for healing, but not all of them were healed. In the area around the pool were five porches, cloisters, piazzas, or roofed walks, described much like the arcade I had seen in my dream.

In the stories of the miraculous healings at the Pool of Bethesda, an angel of the Lord would "trouble" the water and whoever stepped first into the pool after the troubling, or "rushing," of the water would be

---

[3] John 5: 2–4, King James Version.

healed. The wisdom of the angel would determine when the waters would be "troubled," thus determining who would be healed and who would not. However, the responsibility for healing was shared by the person with the disease. That person had to step forward at the right moment and aggressively pursue his or her own healing. Healing, when it occurred, was instantaneous.

Archaeologists have investigated what they believe to be the Pool of Bethesda, and they theorize that the reference to a "certain season" concerns intermittent springs that only "rushed" into the now-arid pool at intervals of several hours during specific times of the year. There is now a story associated with the pool in which a sleeping dragon, when awake, swallows or stops the water and, when asleep, allows the water to flow from its mouth back into the pool. Other Bible verses in the book of Nehemiah (Nehemiah 2) described the rebuilding of the temple of Jerusalem and further defined the location of the Pool of Bethesda.

The Pool of Bethesda was located in the Sheep Market near the temple, just to the north of the temple court. The Sheep Gate of the city was also near the temple. The Sheep Market of Jerusalem was not far from the general area of an even older market. In the book of Nehemiah were long descriptions of the families who rebuilt the temple, including the rebuilding of the Sheep Gate near the Pool of Bethesda. The latter provided a link to a portion of the dream I'd originally thought of as disconnected from the images of the pool and the troubling of the water: the placing of a ram's head above a door that was being re-erected. In the dream, I was not only participating in my healing by walking first into the pool as the waters were "troubled" by the angel, but also by assisting in the restoration of the gate which led to the body of the temple.

My search for Eliseus was no less intriguing. I discovered that "Eliseus" was the Greek word for the name of the prophet Elisha, who both prophesied and healed in the time of Elijah. He was given a special blessing and was allowed to perform miracles of healing. Both the story of the Pool of Bethesda and the information about Eliseus were previously unfamiliar to me, which made their presence in my dream even more powerful.

In the year after my chemotherapy, I returned to this dream and realized that it was universal to anyone facing an illness, a crisis, or even a major turning point. I began to share this dream with others and invite them to either use my dream or discover their own sacred pool within a meditative reentry into my dream where they could return often in their own personal meditations to find healing and comfort.

This dream was a powerful antidote to my fears of death and dying; it offered direct, spontaneous healing and cleansing, and presented me with dream imagery I could use to create my own miracle. The spider as a message of disease had already appeared several times in my dreams and could easily be identified with the malignancy. In this dream, I had turned the harmful poisonous spider into a harmless child's toy. The expression "YeHouse," though still mysterious to me, suggested the possibility that the magic of the dream could come home into the house of my body and live. I was not yet ready to trust myself entirely to the power of this amazing dream and the angel of the rushing waters, but I knew that it was an extraordinary gift, already a miracle of healing.

talking to my body

IN THE LITTLE TIME I had left before the next biopsy, I worked tirelessly to do something, as directed, about the possibly malignant breast lump. I continued working with the first dream of the cone and basin, but added to it the powerful dream of cleansing and healing at the Pool of Bethesda. I rewrote the new dream into a meditation called "Into the Pool of Healing." As with the cone dream, I used music as a background for my meditation, but this time I recorded it onto a tape and listened to it before I went to sleep and throughout the day.

Recording these meditations in my own voice was another significant step. I decided that my body needed to hear my voice, not a taped meditation from a bookstore. It needed to hear the dreams that came to me in the night. I knew that my body would listen best to a familiar voice, the voice it was accustomed to hearing every day.

Other dreams offered an abundant supply of new imagery. In one, I was pushing a barge laden with debris down a small canal. The water in the canal began to swirl, assisting me with moving the barge. Waves came in, offering further assistance; I was able to push the barge under a rock ledge, and finally into the open sea where it floated away beyond view. One of the doctors had described the cancer mass as being "under a ledge of tissue" and then as "stars radiating from a mass" — images that had appeared in two separate dreams. The dream of the barge and the rock ledge became another active meditation for working with the cancer mass.

I created another tape using the barge-and-debris dream. In it, I described the "debris" — the malignancy — being dissolved as the barge moved away from the ledge. My first step was to rewrite the dream as a simple visualization, in which the debris under the ledge dissolved and moved out to sea where it vanished harmlessly into the larger universe of the sea. Then I read it into a tape recorder and carried the tape with me. I played it everywhere I had access to a tape player, and finally it became so much a part of my memory that I no longer needed the tape.

I also noticed that my dreams began to change rapidly, offering what I needed immediately, night after night. The dreams that defined and foreshadowed my disease had come slowly over a period of two years, but the new dreams were rushing in. Defining my intention to work toward healing triggered nightly dreams of healing that were easy to work with by day. I traveled ten miles between my house and my job, which was about twenty minutes of travel time — ample opportunity to play taped dream messages. At work, I set up a small tape player near my desk and kept the tapes with me, popping them in periodically to remind my body of its personal daily task: healing. This cancer didn't arrive in a quiet room. Therefore, it had to be dislodged and destroyed with as much force and activity as possible.

shooting stars

MY BIRTHDAY PASSED. I was forty-three years old, living in the year of my Dance Hall dream of death. Dr. Bart had made appointments for blood tests and other routine preadmission tests to be performed before my surgical biopsy. I was nervous during the tests. My blood pressure soared.

Nine days later, on March 1, Ron brought me to the hospital for the surgical biopsy. I was frightened and cold, and my blood pressure was once again unusually high. Ron wrapped blankets around me and stood nervously by the bed. He looked almost as frightened as I felt. I had only been in hospitals to visit other people and to give birth. I had never been sick enough to be inside a hospital for any other reason.

Nurses came in and out of my room trying to calm me. They talked to me and asked questions about my family as they wheeled me into the operating room. I had never been in an operating room; it looked like a movie set. The anesthesiologist had a sense of humor, a comforting attribute at the moment. He also had a gentle touch, an even more comforting attribute since I had almost invisible veins. I watched him insert the needle into my arm, then the room seemed to fold into quarters toward me.

My next memory was of waking in what seemed like only seconds later. I wondered if death were the same: large sections of time passing in fractions of seconds, a blurred continuum of feelings and emotions. I tried to move, but could not; I was strapped into a bed. I listened for a moment; nurses were moving from patient to patient, all of us strapped into beds in the recovery room. Two nurses closest to my bed were talking and joking with an elderly man who was waking up. He had apparently laughed throughout his surgery; the nurses were asking him if he recalled the source of his laughter — a story, a joke. They talked for a few moments, their affirmation of his unremembered joy working its own magic on his awakening. I, too, was completely awake now, but the nurses had moved away and I could not call them. I wanted to ask about the biopsy. I was clinging to one final hope that either I had been wrong or I had indeed managed to "do something" about the lump and it had disappeared. I wanted to hear them say that what they found was benign. Nurses came to my side, unstrapped me, and talked to me slowly, still believing that I was groggy. I startled them when I responded in complete sentences, and they seemed surprised that I had come awake with so much ease.

They rolled the bed back down the hall, and Dr. Bart, Ron beside him, joined me just as I was being pushed into my room. He, too, was unaware of the extent of my alertness. His voice was soft, but he was speaking rapidly, as though he needed to get the words out as quickly as possible. He explained that I probably was not yet awake enough to fully understand him, but that the news was not what he had hoped it would be. I was awake. I heard and understood every word he said, and I felt that the words would suffocate me. I wanted a surprise, the surprise of good health. I did not want to hear what he was saying. I still wanted my dreams of warning to be wrong. His words crushed me, draining the energy from my body. Every muscle tightened, and all the feeling and emotion seemed to drain away. I couldn't breathe. I felt that my mind, my body, and the guardians of my spirit had betrayed me. I always thought

I'd taken good care of all of them, and they had betrayed me in an instant; how would I ever be able to trust those vital parts of me again?

Nurses seemed to come from every direction, giving me juice, telling me they would help me with the next appointments, giving me brochures, telling me to read everything. I was transferred into a stationary bed and given piles of literature to take home. I began to stand up, looking for my clothing. I told the nurses I needed to go home. They were concerned; I should still be under the influence of the anesthesia. They tried to push me back down, telling me to spend several hours in the room until I was able to wake up and move around better. There seemed to be some concern that I would come unhinged if I left too soon. I stood, picked up my clothes, and told them I was going home. The nurses backed away. "Okay," one of them said, "you can leave."

Ron helped me find my clothing, get dressed, and get to the car. I felt a bit like a child who had lost the ability to put herself together properly, but I didn't want to stay in a hospital. Ron then drove me home, a trip of about thirty-five minutes. I asked him over and over to tell and retell me every detail of every word of the conversation he'd had with Dr. Bart. He patiently told me the words over and over again: my case was extremely unusual; there were only a few like mine every year, and he didn't like to see them. The cells had split away from the mass and were traveling, not as a mass, but as individual cells. The cells had radiated beyond the tumor, like an array of stars, creating a situation that made it difficult — in fact almost impossible — to pick them up on a mammogram or even an ultrasound. The parent mass had been picked up on the ultrasound along with some of the radiating cells, but certainly not all of them. Dr. Bart, like the radiologist, used the image of a group of stars — like the image in my earlier dreams of stars shooting away from a cellular mass. Dr. Bart had also told Ron that he had taken out as much of the tumor as he possibly could during the biopsy, but that he hadn't been successful in removing all of the tumor mass.

reaching out

WHEN WE ARRIVED HOME and I was back in familiar, comfortable surroundings where I could think about the day's events, I realized how confused and frightened I was. I was frightened by the unfamiliar path I was to travel. I knew nothing about the treatment of breast cancer, particularly a difficult breast cancer. Would they take part of a breast, all of it? Was chemotherapy always necessary? I knew the basic words for the treatments, but I already knew that each cancer was unique and had its own treatment pattern. What would they suggest for me? My particular cancer was apparently worse than the doctor anticipated, or certainly "different."

Then I wondered if I knew people within my own community who had breast cancer. If so, none of them had ever said so. Most were my age or my mother's age, surely an age when something like breast cancer would have surfaced in conversation. But people often hid cancer. I had grown up in a time when cancer was referred to as "The Big C," and even mention of The Big C meant that the person would soon die. Cobalt treatments would be mentioned next, and then the people were dead. People my age had grown up with a fear of The Big C, and more than likely wouldn't have discussed it even if they'd survived it. I had barely acknowledged to my family that I feared for my life, but now that I had taken on the second journey and armed myself with new dreams, I needed to find out everything I possibly could about the disease I was preparing to confront. I needed to know what other people had felt and what the surgery had been like for them. I needed to find people who would talk about cancer. Mark Twain once said that he didn't want to find out about the moon from people who hadn't been there; I needed to find those who had been there.

I called close friends and told them what had happened over the past few weeks. Talking to my friends helped me through the first few days, and I talked to everyone — my friends, my family, even people I didn't know whose names friends had given me. I sat down with my son and told him what was happening. He had known, but the confirmation of the biopsy frightened him. He went into the woods beyond our house to think, assuring me that I was going to get through this in fine condition. His assurance comforted me and gave me hope because I trusted his instincts. We'd always seemed tied to each other in a special way, probably no different than any mother and child. He seemed to know if I was okay, and I seemed to know the same about him.

I spent more time than usual sleeping, perhaps as an escape from waking fear. Hospital staff called me for two days, checking on my emotional state and making arrangements for my next surgery, which was scheduled for March 29.

reality check

DR. BART CALLED with the results of the biopsy, which had removed a portion of study tissue. I had small breasts, and he removed as much for study as possible in the biopsy, hoping actually to snare the entire tumor section. He was now somewhat evasive and aloof, leading me to believe he saw something much more serious than he had anticipated. He recommended a modified radical mastectomy followed by chemotherapy. Mastectomies were a last resort for Dr. Bart, so his recommendation of such radical surgery was further confirmation that I had a dangerous tumor. I asked him to explain his recommendation. He told me that if the biopsy had shown a simple tumor with no radiating cells, then a lumpectomy (the biopsy plus some tissue) would have been sufficient. Since I had small breasts, even a lumpectomy would have been disfiguring for me. However, my cancer showed evidence of more extensive involvement, which was why he recommended a modified radical mastectomy: removing the entire breast and the lymph nodes in my left arm. A radical mastectomy would have taken even more of the chest tissue, which he felt he could leave.

Dr. Bart recommended that I see Dr. Jay, an oncologist he trusted. Dr. Bart would be my surgeon and would work as a team with Dr. Jay, who would be my oncologist. Dr. Jay would work solely with the chemotherapy treatments in a state of the art research center near Schenectady (about forty minutes from my home), where new treatments were constantly monitored and tracked. As more information came to light with the biopsy, chemotherapy treatment suggestions might change until the full palette of information was revealed. Almost as soon as Dr. Bart hung up, Dr. Jay called. He immediately set up an appointment for several days later. I was in a whirl of calls and appointments — blood tests, X rays, and then more blood tests — surprised at the rapidity of movement toward the surgery and subsequent chemotherapy after months of snail-like responses from physicians who chose not to believe that anything was wrong with me. Apparently this responsiveness was normal after a cancer diagnosis — if anything about this process could be considered normal. Later I spoke with women who said they barely had time to think once their diagnosis was confirmed. It's as if the doctors thought something in the body was going to explode if immediate action wasn't taken once they decided immediate action should be taken.

Ron took me to my first meeting with Dr. Jay and sat beside me, holding my hand. Dr. Jay seemed impressed that my husband was there and was listening. He said that many women with cancer felt abandoned by their immediate family members, particularly with a diagnosis of breast cancer, and that a surprising number of men filed for divorce before the treatments were completed. I had no fear of abandonment, and I felt comforted by Dr. Jay. I liked his attitude, his voice, everything about him. He radiated well-being and hope.

In our first meeting, Dr. Jay told me that my surgery would probably dictate my having the less harsh dose of chemotherapy, which would include eight sessions spread over most of a year. He also told me that this recommendation could change once the surgery was performed. The less harsh dose of chemotherapy was based on the assumption of no lymph node involvement. We would know more after the results of the mastectomy, bone scans, and other tests I would have over the next few days. I would be given an "ice cap," a blue cone-shaped hat with a kind of chilled filling, to wear during chemotherapy treatments, which might prevent most of my hair from falling out. The cap looked like an ice pack sculpted into a cone. My hair would thin, he said, but the lower chemical dose would keep the loss to a minimum. This visit was encouraging. He told me that my attitude would affect my recovery and survival — a belief I shared. I also felt comforted in Dr. Jay's presence; cancer seemed less threatening than it had been even that morning, perhaps because this doctor dealt with cancer every day and saw as many miracles as he saw deaths from this disease. He described cancers, including breast cancers, that were now statistically in the "complete cure" category, whereas there had been no cures several years ago.

Dr. Jay walked with me through the rooms where I would receive the chemotherapy treatments. We even discussed the design of the building. The architect, it turned out, lived in my small hamlet, and the doctors had worked closely with him to ensure the best environment for someone undergoing cancer treatments. Glass walls faced a large grove of trees on a hillside, and the filtered light and shadows from the woods mingled with the patterns on the floor in the treatment room, creating a feeling of wellness, not illness. Green plants and flowering baskets filled every corner of the room.

I had believed that I didn't know anyone who had experienced breast cancer, but I was wrong. At work, I attended a monthly staff meeting that included staff from the historic sites and parks in the region. I told them briefly what was happening in my life. Afterward, a man my age told me that he admired my courage for telling the group that I had breast cancer. He was a twenty-five-year lymphoma survivor who had originally been told that he had weeks to live. Not only had he survived, but now he helped children who had cancer. He credited his intuition and a power greater than himself with saving his life. He had never discussed his illness at work.

During the next few weeks, people began to call and tell me about their mastectomies, or about those of their sisters, mothers, or even daughters. I had read the discouraging statistics: one in eight people get breast cancer during their lifetime. I had no idea how many people I saw each day who had lived through this disease. Lived through! That was an important thought to keep in mind. The numbers of people I knew who'd had breast cancer made the question "why me?" seem much less dramatic. Some of the people I talked with had not one, but two, breasts removed. Some had stories of reoccurrence, but they had survived — many of them for at least twenty years thus far. It felt good to talk with these people.

I was almost feeling that I would have no problem dealing with breast cancer when a neighbor called. She wanted to offer me some scarves that her sister had used during chemotherapy nine years earlier. I had heard so many success stories, so many incredible stories of survival that I was ready to finish the sentence for her "...and she is still alive today." "No," the neighbor replied somberly, "she died a year after the diagnosis." My heart sank. I had been spared this side of the story.

I now listened to this woman, who needed to talk as much as I had needed to both talk and listen. Her sister had gone to the doctor with a breast lump but had been told, as I had been, that it was nothing to be concerned about — that it was part of her fibrocystic breast disease. She was told to "watch" the lump for a year, and to return if she were still concerned. The beginning of this story sounded much too familiar. They told her the kind of lump she had would be benign, that the pain she was feeling simply indicated that it would not be a malignant tumor. In that year during which she "watched" her breast lump, the cancer spread into her organs and then into her brain. She died in excruciating agony. In a soft voice, my neighbor told me that the scarves and head coverings were made for people undergoing chemotherapy. She said they were beautiful; her sister always chose pretty fabrics, loved exotic cottons, and had a flair for color and design.

Then my neighbor's tone of voice changed, and she became angry. She said that her sister had eaten no fats or preservatives, and that there was nothing artificial in her food, her home, or her life. My heart went out to this woman who was filled with resentment because nothing her sister had done had prevented this disease from finding her and destroying her. Doctors, when approached, had not recognized her intuitive sense of danger. My neighbor wept bitterly. I told her that I would accept the scarves, and that I would pass them on to others who might need them, and who could then pass them on again. That way, in a sense, the scarves would help those who could perhaps be the first of a larger and larger group of survivors. I told her that the scarves could have a positive influence; they could be a gift from a sister whose voice, although not heard in time to save her own life, would remind people that this was a disease that one could survive.

Then the emotional highs and lows began. They were to be part of my life for a year. Days and nights passed — some comfortable, some not. On some days I felt that all would turn out well. On others I wept, terrified that my life might be ending, that it might have been shortened needlessly. I made mental lists of all the things I wanted to do, all the things I had not yet done, the places I wanted to go, the people I loved and cared about and might never see again, the people I wanted to spend time with. I wanted to see my son graduate. I wanted to have grandchildren someday. On the good days, I was confident that everything I wanted to see and do would take place because I would survive this disease; on other days I felt that all of it was being snatched away from me. By the end of the first week after my biopsy, my emotions were out of control. I sobbed and trembled; my mind raced through the details of conversations with doctors and nurses. I replayed every thought, every sentence, every imagined glance, looking for every implied meaning in every sentence that I could recall.

Ron tried to cheer me up. He even took a few days off from work to sit with me, but nothing seemed to help. The biopsy surgery had created a small wound. It healed fast, but it reminded me that I would soon have an even more difficult surgery.

Clara, the wife of a colleague, called. I had never met her, but she was my age and she had gone through breast cancer surgery and chemotherapy the year before. She was pleasant, and her voice was even and calm. She told me the things I needed to hear: what the surgery felt like (she described waking from surgery and feeling like a hot iron was on her chest), the numbness I might feel that might go away, the return of sensations and when that might happen, the pain and how she dealt with it, what her chemotherapy was like. She had reacted poorly to the chemotherapy. She told me that I probably wouldn't react as badly, but that if I did there were drugs to relieve nausea. I calmed when she told me her story. She provided a road map of the surgery and the kind of post-surgical pain I might or might not feel. She made it bearable. She told me humorous stories about her surgery and chemotherapy. I was able to laugh with her, and each story brought more questions to mind. I asked what seemed like hundreds of questions, and she gave me answers that meant something to me because they were coming from someone who had been there. She told me about Reach for Recovery, a support group for breast cancer patients that had helped her a great deal.

This was the conversation I needed at that moment: practical advice, answers, and statements from someone my age who'd had breast cancer and was still very much alive. I found myself laughing when she described the inopportune moments when her hair would choose to fall out — sometimes in enormous clumps, including once when she was driving down the street. She advised me to have my long hair cut short so that the subsequent loss would appear to be gradual and less traumatic. As she talked, my muscles relaxed, my anxiety eased, and my tears dried. I would be able to sleep that night. I would not feel so alone and frightened, at least not for that night. Someone had done this before me — someone with a name and a voice, someone my age, someone who knew the road map, someone who knew the way in and the way out. I had needed to know, on a very practical level, what someone else had experienced when they went through this journey that lay before me.

resuming my dreamwork

ROBERT WAS DEEPLY WORRIED about me, and urged me to continue to work with my dream of the healing pool at Bethesda. He believed — as I came to believe myself through a subsequent big dream — that direct healing can occur inside the dreamspace in the presence of a sacred power. He urged me not to give up on miracles.

I longed for a miracle. But I knew, both from my dream warnings and from my gut instincts and emotions, that I would need all the tools of modern medicine to deal with my disease.

Robert asked me to dream on the chemotherapy, meaning I should go to sleep with a statement of intent. The statement could be in my mind and could be presented as a question, such as: "I need a dream for healing." Robert even suggested that I might want to write the statement on a piece of paper and place it under my pillow. As suggested, I made a statement of intent and sought guidance for healing before falling asleep. I received the following dream:

KILLING THE BATS

I walk into a large room — a bedroom, except the bed has sides like a crib. Robert and my family come into the room with me. Under the bed lies a large bat. I rush for the bat, pick it up by the head, and break the head in my hands. Then I throw the bat down a flight of stairs, where it is impaled on a knife-like tool protruding from the wall. I look up. The ceiling is covered with smaller bats. I ask for help. We begin exterminating the bats with poison until the room is clear. Then I curl up peacefully in the bed and go to sleep.

I shared this dream with Robert at once. He listened with deep attention, and agreed that the dream confirmed that I'd chosen the right medical treatments. The first bat — the cancer, the parent tumor — was surgically removed (impaling the large bat on the knife-like tool), and then the cancer cells radiating from the parent tumor that had escaped surgery (the smaller bats) were destroyed with poison (chemotherapy). It was only after the final bats had been destroyed with poison that the room (my body) was clear and healed, and I could curl up peacefully in sleep.

Robert and I agreed that, while I would undergo surgery and chemotherapy, I would draw on the power of my dreams to support rapid healing and recovery.

Then the tests from the surgical biopsy came back; they showed that the cancer had spread beyond the breast tumor. Dr. Jay told me that this new information altered the recommended chemotherapy treatment. He felt that the best way to approach my unusually aggressive cancer was to proceed with the suggested modified radical mastectomy, and follow it with aggressive chemotherapy. This meant that I would lose my hair in chemotherapy; it wouldn't just thin. I thought about the dream of the bats and accepted the revised format for my healing. I wanted to use every resource available to me, and I firmly believed that I could combine my dreams with the harsh treatment suggested, possibly even eliminating some of the worst side effects.

reprise

AT FIRST BLINK, ILLNESS — especially cancer — does not look like a spiritual exercise. In the face of a serious illness, we can become paralyzed, suspend judgment and intuition, and accept an environment where options no longer seem to exist. When the body is dealt a serious physical blow, doctors often take advantage of the situation, providing healing "options" that define healing within the narrowest of definitions. It is up to the individual to turn illness into a spiritual exercise and to bring dreams — and other alternative healing methods of choice — into the healing process.

I made my choices: surgery and chemotherapy, with a heavy syrup of dreaming stirred in — a recipe for healing. I still dreaded the process and awaited the date of my surgery — March 29, 1990 — with some fear, some unexpected calm, and a strong desire to simply have it be over.

THE HEALING COCKTAIL

*I*n the dream of killing the bats, I throw the bat down a flight of stairs where it is impaled on a knife-like tool, but I use poison — chemotherapy — to destroy the remaining bats. This mix of surgery and chemotherapy, given to me in my dreams, became my "healing cocktail" — a lethal syrup of dreams and medicine to battle the cancer, a prescription for a return to health. The dreams for that cocktail came long before I first walked into a doctor's office. They were already providing me with the ingredients for the alternative and natural methods that would allow me to safely proceed with both the brutal surgical removal of the cancer and the subsequent attack on the remaining cancer cells with chemotherapy.

On the day of the surgery, I moved through the morning's activities like a robot. Coincidentally, the morning news commentator spoke of events in one's life that become reference points against which every subsequent event is measured: "That happened three years before or two years after…" After what? Breast cancer? Would this process be such a big part of my life that it would become a reference point? Almost eleven years later, I reflected on that notion when I participated in a sophisticated National Breast Cancer workshop. One of the facilitators stated emphatically and repeatedly that having breast cancer would and should be the theme against which every event in a breast cancer survivor's life would be measured. Her statements took on a life of their own; they became a mantra of sorts. Following her lead, several participants began and ended their sentences with "before I had breast cancer" or "after I had breast cancer," and the impressionable survivors who filled the room applauded those statements. I was appalled. I had been briefly tempted in those early moments to make breast cancer a definition for my life, but thirteen years of subsequent living and personal growth have taught me how important it is to do otherwise.

However, on this day in March of 1990, my concentration didn't extend much farther than the reality of having breast cancer. I took a shower. I stared at my breasts in the mirror — two of them — for perhaps the last time. Then I dressed. I first dressed in a blouse with a somewhat plunging neckline — just one last time. Then I found a T-shirt and jeans. My body and mind were tense, jittery, on edge. I tried to remind myself to breathe deeply. I tried to remind myself to take any kind of breath, to stay alive for one more moment that might turn into another moment and another until days and months and years, perhaps even decades, passed and having breast cancer became a dim memory, just a moment of my life long ago. Ron was packing a small bag for my hospital stay, readying the car, and playing timekeeper. My surgery was early; in fact it was still dark outside, and there was a dreary, cold rain. The hospital was almost an hour away. I was dawdling, holding onto old memories of who I was and how I looked with two breasts, just for a few more hours, as long as possible.

The telephone rang. The voice was one I hadn't heard for a long time: an old friend, Oren Lyons, who was faith-keeper for the Onondaga Nation. My years in the Mohawk Valley had brought a few enduring friendships among the people of the Six Nations. I had shared those friendships with Robert when he first came to Johnson Hall to research Six Nations history and culture. My best friendships were always intuitively based, and Oren was calling this particular morning because he felt that something was wrong. He had dreamed about me and found the dream disturbing: a dream in which I was very ill. I told him as much as I could in the few moments I had to talk. He asked the exact time of my surgery, and told me that he would gather the chiefs of the Onondaga Nation to smoke for me. In this ancient traditional ceremony, the tobacco smoke would take his prayers of healing to the heavens. This offer of prayers deeply touched me; it was a blessing that would stir the spirits of the heavens, woods, and rivers where I now made my home.

Then I made one last telephone call before leaving: I called my mother. I had not told her anything about my diagnosis of cancer. She was experiencing early stages of dementia and would have turned her limited understanding of my illness into a worrisome reflection of her own health problems. The new problems we were both experiencing with my mother's increasing dementia had been mirrored in my dream of her falling from a second-story window. In the dream I couldn't stop her fall. I had originally associated that dream with her difficulty in dealing with my father's illness and subsequent death. Now the dream seemed more relevant to her current situation. My mother's dementia hampered her ability to see positive directions in many situations she was facing. She would have dwelled on my illness and would have begun to weep and call me repeatedly, believing I was dying. She had no basis for believing that someone could survive cancer. I didn't need that added burden, nor did she. But at the last moment, Ron insisted that I tell her something. I told her that I was ill and needed surgery. She was concerned and wanted to know if she should come and stay with me. "No," I said, "I will be fine. I will be home in a few days, and I'll keep you informed of how I'm doing." That brief conversation seemed to work for her, and I was glad I had called.

It was time to go. On the way to the hospital, I sat in the back seat of the car while Ron and Evan sat in front. I wanted to be apart from my family so that I could think, so that I could wrap myself in my aloneness and find out if there was anything I had overlooked that could help me. In the darkness of the new morning, there was a light drizzle and a few wet snowflakes fell on the car windshield. The light was just appearing in patches in the sky. It all gave me a feeling of loneliness so deep that I couldn't reach out beyond it — not just yet.

We arrived at the hospital and I was shown my room. In a small anteroom, I undressed and redressed in the hospital gown. I stared one last time at my breasts and wept. I pulled the skimpy hospital gown tighter. I couldn't bear these feelings. Shivering from either cold or nerves, I crawled into the bed, hugging my knees and feeling very small and vulnerable. I had difficulty speaking with Ron and Evan. My voice shook, and I was trembling uncontrollably. They sat on the side of the bed holding me tight until I stopped shaking. A nurse stopped in briefly and then disappeared. After almost an hour, I felt calm and resigned. Then I felt nervous and afraid again, and these feelings alternated for quite a while. I had an odd sense of unreality. So many fears: What would I look like without a breast? I couldn't even imagine. I knew there were prostheses, but how could they ever look like a real breast? They certainly couldn't feel like one. Would I truly survive this? My dreams confused me. Some had been vibrant and healing like the Healing Pool at Bethesda, but the Dance Hall dream predicted my death that year. Was I destined to die no matter what I did, or would I be able to use all of those wonderful healing dreams and advance toward my next birthday with new dreams and a glorious future? Why did the answers seem so bright one moment and so dark the next? Ron and Evan stood nearby saying comforting things that I barely heard. Their voices sounded far away, like distant echoes.

Then the gurney arrived, and I tried to choke back the tears as I said good-bye to my family. Strapped down and headed for the operating room through a maze of hallways, I listened to the nurses talking as they pushed the gurney through the corridors and onto the elevator. I couldn't see their faces, only the backs of their heads. They were talking about a dramatic automobile crash that had caused a number of deaths; the family had not been wearing seat belts. The details of the multiple deaths seized me, and I began to shake violently. Then I began sobbing, still strapped to the bed. The startled nurses apologized profusely; they hadn't realized that I was awake and cognizant during their conversation.

In fact, I should have been nearly unconscious at that point. The nurse who had briefly appeared and then disappeared from my room had neglected to give me the sedative that would have prepared me for the journey to the operating room. Instead, I was alert and awake as I entered the operating room where Dr. Bart and his staff were preparing for my surgery. Dr. Bart was stunned. Not only had I arrived unsedated, but no one had discussed the surgery with me or prepared me for the operation. An attendant had been assigned all of those duties. Dr. Bart tried to hide his anger to avoid causing me further upset. He calmed himself, shooting angry glances at the attendants on either side of the gurney, and began to answer my questions and tell me as much as he could about the recovery process. Then he called for the anesthesiologist.

My veins would not cooperate; the anesthesiologist couldn't find a vein for the needle. The torture seemed endless, but finally the room began to turn and spiral into a dizzying blackness. Once again, it seemed only seconds before I awoke. However, this time I did not simply awaken feeling groggy. I awoke in the hospital recovery room gagging and choking on the tubes in my throat, not understanding where I was or what was happening. I instinctively began pulling at the tubes, trying to extricate them from my throat. My actions brought nurses scurrying to my side, trapping my hands at my sides, trying to control me while they carefully removed the apparatus attached to me. I was awake, completely awake.

Then I felt the pain from the mastectomy: the intense, searing-hot pain on my left side. It was just as Clara, the woman who'd told me about her own surgery, had described it to me; it indeed felt like a hot iron sitting on my chest. I had never felt such pain. I couldn't remove it or make it go away, and my throat ached from the tubes. I lost consciousness again and awoke in a different room, a semi-private room in the hospital. I saw Ron, Evan, and a few friends beside the bed, but they moved in and out of focus. I would awaken for seconds at a time and be aware of people moving in and out of the room. As I drifted in and out of awareness, I went on fantasy adventures in which I visited kings and queens and great events in history, all moving through my subconscious like a panorama on a movie reel — a visit to world ancestors in the spiritual plane. In my foggy mental state, I was barely able to recall these dream journeys through time and space.

A few hours later, I awoke again and this time remained conscious. I was attached to a tree of bags and paraphernalia, and I felt the tension of a bandage around my chest. I was afraid to touch it or even look at it yet. My arm was stinging, and there were tubes taped to it that led to small pouches on my chest. I moved my arm into a slightly more comfortable position then noticed that the tightness had created some swelling in my arm and hand. I assumed the tightness and swelling would disappear when the tubes and pouches were removed. I slept again, this time more normally. I had paper and pens with me. When I awoke again for a few moments, I tried to write in my journal. But my hand shook and my fingers couldn't control the pen. A doctor arrived to give me the wonderful news: The bone scan was clear! I was a little perplexed; I hadn't realized they'd expected anything less. The nurse came in and needed to change all the bedding and said that I also needed to begin moving about. After a struggle to stand and walk a bit, I was led to a wheelchair in the hallway where Dr. Bart joined me. He kneeled close to me, no longer aloof or evasive. He confessed that he'd been extremely worried about my surgery. The radiating cells coming from the mass might have easily spelled a more disastrous situation. He was still concerned; there were more test results due from the material sent to the lab, but he was visibly relieved about the bone scan results. I had lost a tremendous amount of blood — much more than he had anticipated — so I would have to stay in the hospital longer than expected. My heart sank; I wanted to go home. I was wheeled back into the room and helped into the bed, where nurses took my blood pressure, asked questions, and changed various pouches attached to my body. As I listened to the litany of instructions, I determined that I needed to dream myself out of the hospital. I could not get well if I stayed there. Also, Robert had a new baby girl whose christening was scheduled two weeks from that day. I needed to be present and wearing a normal dress. Dr. Bart, coming and going, still avoided some of my questions about my prognosis. He was awaiting further test results — still, in my opinion, convinced that the final news about my tumor would not be good.

Dream visitors in the operating room

THE DAY PASSED slowly into evening. Images faded in and out of my mind, still in a fog from the drugs. My eyes finally settled clearly on my son, who sat on the edge of the bed.

"Do you remember your surgery?" he asked. I pulled myself upright; he was really there beside me; I wasn't dreaming. He was picking at my uneaten dessert from a truly boring dinner. "What is this supposed to be?" he asked, pointing with the fork toward a shapeless blob on a small plate.

"Lemon meringue pie."

"Hmmm." Even he put the fork down and pushed the tray away. He asked again: "You really don't remember anything that happened during your surgery?"

"No," I said.

"Then I have something to tell you. I left your room and followed Dad into the waiting room, where we were told to stay until the doctor came out again. I found a large reclining chair where I could listen to the TV, but I was really sleepy. Then I began to wonder if I could purposely state an intention to enter your subconscious, since we often dream into each other's dreams at night. I said over and over to myself that I knew my mom was afraid; that I needed to help my mom; that I needed to help

my mom think about something that would make her happy or something that would help her during the surgery. Then I fell into a really
deep sleep; I don't even remember falling asleep. I only remember saying
those things to myself over and over. Immediately upon falling asleep, I
was there: right beside you, right there in the operating room. I was
really uncomfortable about being there. At first I thought it was because
I don't like operating rooms, but then I realized it was because someone
else was there with me — maybe several people, all in the same dream.

"I focused on the other people in the room, and I recognized my
grandfather, who appeared to be hovering up near the ceiling making
sure that all went well. My grandfather nodded to me and disappeared.
Then I was aware of another presence — a presence greater than me that
seemed to have no body, just presence. This presence made me feel
instantly comfortable and relaxed. Then I remembered why I was there,
and I decided to try to enter your dreams and see where you were or
bring something to you.

"I was immediately taken to Robert's house, where I saw Robert and
his wife Marcia dressed for a party. I spoke to them, and they insisted
that we needed to make you laugh. I was feeling disoriented and I could
think of nothing, so Robert asked me to think about his fortieth birthday
party. I had not attended that party, but I concentrated on the evening as
Robert began to describe it. Then I was there, and I saw you standing in
the doorway between the kitchen and the den. You were laughing and
enjoying yourself. Robert stood behind you, and a tall, very thin woman
dressed in a slinky black dress stood beside you. Her mouth was the most
dominant feature on her face; as she talked, she fingered a small dia-
mond you were wearing on a chain around your neck. You were laughing and continued to laugh as she related some story about herself."

My son paused in his narrative. "You don't remember any of that as
a dream in the operating room?" he asked.

I didn't recall anything from the operating room, but I had no doubt
that it had all happened as Evan described it. I did recall the party Evan
referred to, and he'd left out an important detail about the woman.
"What color was the woman's skin?" I asked.

"Oh," he said, "it was black — really, really black and smooth as
silk; there seemed to be no pores in her skin. People at the party thought
she was beautiful, but I just thought she was interesting."

I remembered the scene at Robert's birthday party, and Evan had described in precise detail not only the scene, but also Lorraine, a New York City model whom he'd never met. The important thing he remembered was my laughter.

I closed my eyes, trying to bring back anything I might have experienced in a dreamscape during the surgery, but anesthesia had apparently destroyed any waking memory of a dream or vision. I recalled nothing about Evan's visit in the dreamspace, nor a journey to Robert's birthday party, but I had no doubt that Evan had been there with me through the surgery, helping me find a good place to be in my darkness.

Evan picked a bit more at the dull food and finally pushed it away. He had just turned seventeen and was learning to drive, so we talked about school, friends, girls, and adventures in driving. As he left the room, he glanced back at me: "You will be okay, you know."

"I know."

Robert came to visit next, arriving during a block of hours reserved for close family members. When the nurses had attempted to stop him, he'd told them he was my brother. I chuckled; of course he was my brother. I shared Evan's dream vision with him, and he said that he, too, had visited me in my subconscious state and recounted stories from our adventures together in both physical and dream reality. He'd hoped the stories would make me smile. I smiled; how could I have not seen so many people there in the operating room with me? Robert, Evan, my father, and a house full of party-goers had all been there — as well as a friendly presence, a guardian or guide.

That night I was uncomfortable. I awoke frequently, believing each time that I was well and back home in my own bed. Then the pain would pull me sharply back to the hospital bed. The next morning, Dr. Bart visited and spent some time talking, pacing around the bed, and looking at charts. The nurses appeared again, insisting that I needed to continue to move around. I laboriously heaved myself up from the bed and, with my ever-present tree of pouches, walked up and down the hall, finally sitting down again in a wheelchair in the hallway where Dr. Bart joined me. I always seemed to be in the hallway in a wheelchair when he appeared.

"Absolutely amazing," he said.

"Amazing? Why?"

"Your body has completely rallied — overnight, as a matter of fact."

Still sounding stunned, he continued, "Your blood count is normal; everything is normal." I was thrilled. I wondered, not aloud, if willing myself well enough to go home had worked. I had recalled no dreams, but I had stated to myself that I needed to dream myself home. Something had worked. "In fact," he said, "I can sign the paperwork for you to go home a day early if you wish." Wow — not only was I going home; I was going home earlier than normally allowed.

"Yes," I said, "of course I want to go home. Are you saying I can go home tomorrow?"

He smiled, "You can go home tomorrow."

Yes! Going home would help me sleep. Who could heal in such a place: constant noise, glaring lights that reminded one of old train stations or badly lit barrooms, pain medication that simply masked the heated pain with an overlay of fog, and the chatter of nurses coming and going on endless shift changes.

Dr. Bart was leaving that day for a brief vacation. He told me that his office colleague would come in before I left the next day to do a few necessary things and give me the results of any further tests. He felt that most of the tests were coming back with good results now, so he was no longer evasive about them. I felt a more positive spin in his attitude.

A few hours later, Dr. Bart's colleague arrived. I didn't like him. He was self-centered, abrupt, and arrogant. He asked me to sit up, then abruptly removed one of the tubes from my chest, barely announcing what he was going to do. I gasped and felt slightly faint.

He had turned away with the tube apparatus and then turned back to face me. "You're much too young to have this happen," he said. "How old are you anyway?"

"Exactly how old should I be to have breast cancer?" I asked. "Is there an age manual or do you just make it up as you go along?"

He changed his tone slightly. "I'm sorry, how old are you?"

"I'm forty-three."

"Oh," he said, "I would have thought you were much younger than that."

"Well," I said, "then it is okay to have breast cancer at forty-three but it wouldn't have been okay if I were younger; how much younger?"

He blanched but didn't answer. Instead he picked up a pile of brochures and handed them to me, then asked when I might like to have reconstructive surgery. I was appalled. I stared at him in total disbelief. I could barely piece together the next five minutes of my life and he was behaving as if I were taking a cruise.

"Never, certainly not in your care," I replied.

"You'll change your mind," he snapped.

Weeks later, when Dr. Bart returned from vacation, I reported this conversation to him. He was stunned and disappointed. His colleague had been sent to my room to share good test results with me; those he had finally shared, but in an offhand manner as though they were not the reason for his visit. As it turns out, Dr. Bart left that practice the following year and joined a small practice that included alternative health-care providers. I like to believe that his experience with my using dreams to diagnose my illness solidified his decision to join an alternative health-care group.

The only good thing about my exchange with Dr. Bart's colleague was that my final test results were very good and complemented my mercifully brief hospital stay — not even three days. The tests, in fact, brought wonderful news: The cancer had not metastasized. Nurses escorted me to the door buzzing among themselves about my recovery, which was rapid and apparently surprising given the intensity of the process and the unexpected loss of large amounts of blood.

the normal house

WHEN I ARRIVED HOME, I was met with a flurry of activity from my neighbors. They had cleaned my house, filled the parlor with fruit and flowers, and formed an incredible network of families assigned to provide all my meals for the next two weeks. I wasn't sure whether to tell them that I was relatively mobile and could function; I rather enjoyed all the attention, at least for the first few days. Part of their extensive planning included sitting with me. I managed to convince them, without hurt feelings, that I was not an invalid and that I had come home early because I wanted and needed some time alone.

My first day at home progressed slowly. The pain came and went in intense bursts, but I delighted in the spotlessly clean house. The evening was the first real challenge; I tried to go upstairs and sleep in a bed, but the discomfort was constant and the pain returned with a vengeance when I attempted to lie down. I still had a small drainage tube and a small bag attached to me, which added to my discomfort and required my regular attention.

I was also experiencing more of the tingling and swelling in my arm. My concern grew about the arm, and I reminded myself to ask about it in my follow-up visits to Dr. Bart.

When I spent my first night back at home, I engineered an elaborate pile of pillows on the bed. They put me in a partially sitting position, and provided some comfort for both my arm and the searing pain on the left side of my chest. I slept and dreamed the first remembered dream since my surgery. The dream, which mirrored my tension, confusion, fear, and pain, placed me within a normal house, but I was not normal.

THE NORMAL HOUSE

In the dream I am larger than everything around me. I walk to a tiny shelf, pick up tiny forks, and stack them neatly. Then I take the forks to a sink for washing and place them to dry on a porcelain ledge above the sink. However, there is a crack behind the ledge, and the forks fall. I grab them just before they disappear and pull them to safety. Then I take them to a tiny bookshelf and place them carefully in velvet bags. Then I walk to a window, but I am still larger than my surroundings. I am confused and frightened. I hold the end of a tightrope, which is stretched across to a window directly across from mine. Someone else holds the other end of the rope. A yellow velvet blanket or robe hangs from the rope, and I reach for it.

Although I could not see my father in the dream, I knew that he, or someone like him, was returning my gift of the yellow robe to help me in my recovery — or to simply remind me that my father was present and would be available when I needed him. Like the person in the dream, I felt out of scale with my surroundings. My body was no longer the same; it had seriously malfunctioned. I wanted the world, however briefly, to pay attention to me, to solve the larger problem of breast cancer, to cure "my" disease, to save me from a disease I had hardly considered before the diagnosis. Now this disease was personal; I resented everyone else's normality, and I would resent it until I found a way to "fit" again. The image of my being abnormal accurately reflected my feelings and, in my current state of mind, my reality. I was no longer the person I had been — even just days ago — physically or mentally. Over the next few days, other dreams left me with only brief memories of "dark" imagery: dark objects, darkness, and even dark people.

Spring was approaching. As the days became warmer, I found myself often going through an elaborate ritual of convincing myself that I needed to be upbeat and positive. Sunshine would accentuate real feelings of wellness and give me confidence in my ability to recover completely. Cloudy days would find me feeling the darkness in my dreams. Evenings often brought depression, tears, and terrible bouts of feeling sorry for myself. The physical reality of what had happened to me seemed to be worse in the evening. As in my dream of the normal house, I became increasingly aware of how focused the world was on the "normal" human being: commercials, catalogs, newspaper ads, clothing, and underwear ads. I felt that I was desperately trying to re-fit into a culture obsessed with being "normal." Or perhaps it was simply me; I was obsessed with the comparison of myself as once "normal" and now somehow so obviously "less than normal." Ron was home with me for a week, and I was unable to go to work in the first weeks after surgery. I read and moved about as much as possible, trying to regain my place in my home and surroundings. I enjoyed just being home for a week with Ron, reading and writing. Neighbors came and went, but I found chatty company almost intolerable, so I found busy wok to do to keep myself occupied. I also slept more than normal.

Some dreams just after the surgery played catch-up with waking reality, or at least helped me define it. Prior dreams had warned me of coming illness, the Dance Hall dream having done so for twenty years. Dreams just before surgery offered me information I could use for healing before and after surgery. The big dream of the Healing Pool at Bethesda presented a sacred healing space that I would later be able to share with others and return to for the rest of my life. The dream of the normal house was a mirror — a reflection of where I was at that time, like taking stock of who I was and my frightening, not very flattering, image of myself and how I fit in the world. What would I learn from this dream? Maybe simply that abnormality had now become normal for me, and that I needed to learn how to work that into my life and create a positive image of myself from it.

On April 5, I took my first complete shower since returning home. A real shower was an event, an occasion, another example of normal behavior becoming extraordinary. It never occurred to me how important everyday activity — activity one usually took for granted — could be when pitted against a temporary or permanent disability. That first shower took most of an hour, the bulk of the time spent in removing layer after layer of bandages and emotionally preparing myself to face the scar. Ron was in the house, but I preferred to be alone in the bathroom for the initial unveiling. He was nearby in case I found the sight more than I could handle.

I showered with my face to the water, not ready to look just yet. I stepped out of the shower and stood in front of the mirror, my eyes closed. Then I took a deep breath and opened my eyes. There it was, and it wasn't nearly as horrible as I had imagined. In fact, I managed to laugh at myself. I looked a bit like Frankenstein, a bit unreal: large black staples held the surgical wound together in a meandering path across the left side of my chest. I had small breasts, so I only looked a little lopsided. Ron carefully crept into the bathroom and laughed too. He said I looked a bit like a stitched toy. How flattering!

Then I had a strange thought: I wondered if other women who had lost a breast to cancer thought about the whereabouts of their missing breast. I wondered where the hospital disposed of breasts and other body parts that had been lopped away. I had, of course, signed documents authorizing its disposal, but I'd never thought about where it might be. Was it placed in one of those hazardous-waste containers and taken to a toxic medical waste dump? Was it buried somewhere? It was difficult to imagine my left breast as toxic medical waste, but what else could it be?

The pain where my left breast once lived was a little less constant, but definitely still present. I threw the bandages away. I sat in the bathroom for quite some time, thinking about "normal" versus "abnormal." I thought about "loss," not just the loss of a physical part of myself but the indefinable loss of some deeper emotional part. I thought about my sexuality, about the problems of wearing once-favorite clothing, about bathing suits, about nightgowns and all those parts of a woman's day that define it as "normal" — and which perhaps would never again be normal for me.

helpers on the path to recovery

ONLY DAYS HAD PASSED since my surgery. In some ways it seemed a lifetime. My entire life had changed in that week. However, my recovery from major surgery was astonishing. I was certain that using the dream of the cone breast after the biopsy and the dream of the healing pool as active meditations plus using the strong intent to leave the hospital early had been responsible.

A week after the surgery, Ron drove me to my first follow-up visit at Dr. Bart's office. Dr. Bart was still away, so attendants removed the final tube and bag from me. As soon as the bag disappeared, my clothing fit more comfortably and my arm fell more naturally at my side. The surgery wound was still too tender for me to wear a bra or a prosthesis, so I wore loose clothing and still moved a bit slowly to accommodate the remaining pain. The tests on my lymph nodes, all of which had been removed in a modified radical mastectomy, showed cancer involvement in only one. This was good news. No lymph node involvement would have been better, but one was still good news. The pain had gradually lessened, each day better than the last. Most of the pain now was centered around the area with the stitches, probably caused by the stitches themselves. I did not like taking unnecessary medication, so I was weaning myself away from the prescribed pain medications.

Robert's new baby daughter was scheduled for christening, and I would be her godmother. The christening was only days away. I was happy to have the last bag and tube removed so that I would look somewhat normal at the christening.

Robert had asked Ron to play for his daughter's christening. Classically trained in the piano, music was not his career; but it was his great love. Ron agreed to play the organ for the hamlet church after the elderly organist could no longer play, because he felt that playing an instrument on a regular basis would allow him practice time that he might neglect in his busy schedule. His parents had recently transferred the large Steinway he had grown up playing from Memphis to our house in Glen. It was placed in the parlor with other musical instruments, which included an early nineteenth-century pianoforte, a small square instrument with a sound like a harpsichord; dulcimers, an English guitar with a belly shaped like a lute; numerous recorders; and two guitars. I had no musical talents but loved to sit in the living room on the sofa and listen to Ron playing in the parlor. The slightly muted sounds of music one room away haunted and soothed me. Robert assigned me the task of helping Ron find music for the christening. Ron was at work, and Robert thought my quest for music might keep me busy and less focused on the surgery. He requested "Jerusalem," which, for a few days, seemed impossible to find. Keeping busy during those early days at home was good for me; it placed me back in a normal world of activity and of doing things for and with people. We located the music, and Ron began rehearsing the piece in the late afternoon or evening on the large Steinway in our front parlor.

I particularly enjoyed listening to Ron play late at night. He played the christening pieces and others from the popular film *Chariots of Fire*, as well as pieces by Chopin. When he played, I would close my eyes and use my dreams for meditation. Both the music and the dream meditation calmed me, at least for those moments. Occasionally I would fall asleep, one of my grandmother's quilts pulled snug around me, and allow the music to weave its melodies into my dreams.

On one of those evenings, drifting in and out of sleep, I thought about Millie Coutant, a friend and popular psychic from Lake George, New York, who had died several years earlier. Before she died, she often visited me and sometimes told me what she foresaw about my life. Once she told me that something would happen to me — that I would become very ill, and that in recovering from that illness I would learn valuable lessons about healing and about myself. In the process of illness and recovery, I would learn to teach others to heal, because I possessed the gift of healing that we all have within ourselves but tend to forget or tend to never use. A teacher's main task is to release what already dwells within us. She wanted me to take that gift and teach others about the magic we all have within for creating our own miracles. Millie also told me that I would not die from that illness. I was comforted now by that memory. I drifted asleep, lost in the music and the warmth of the quilt, thinking about Millie:

WALKING THE PLANK

I am looking everywhere for Millie. I want to tell her that I have had my illness. I want to ask her if she knows whether I will live. Instead I see Robert and I am disappointed because I am not looking for Robert. There are dark colors in the sky, and I try to use an enormous eraser to wash them away. Then I try to reach Robert, but he has gone farther away. In trying to reach him, I am walking on a narrow plank, and several times I almost slip into soft sand. A person comes up beside me and places wider boards on either side of the narrow boards until I have a safe place for walking. As I reach out, I realize that I have tubes attached to my arms and energy food is being fed into my body through the tubes.

I awoke still in pain, but comforted and excited. My new dream offered additional guidance on my journey: a presence who would continue to make sure I would have safe passage across the shifting, uncertain sand. And I was again assured that my healing cocktail of spiritual and medical resources would provide healing energy. The dream tubes looked remarkably similar to the chemotherapy tubes I'd been shown on the tour of Dr. Jay's chemotherapy treatment facility. The contents — the chemicals, also referred to as a "cocktail" by his nurses — would be conduits for healing energy, not toxins that would make me even more ill.

the christening

APRIL 8, PALM SUNDAY, I put on a pink suit and sat with Marcia, Robert, and their child in the pews of St. John's Episcopal Church, in Johnstown, New York, and listened as the sounds of "Jerusalem" from organ and pipes filled the church under Ron's loving guidance. I liked to watch him play as well as listen to his music. His entire body moved into the music and he seemed to be swept into it; one couldn't help but follow. The rite of christening proceeded, and I felt joy and peace in being present at the spiritual beginning of a life. I moved a bit stiffly but fairly comfortably. The stitches tugged a bit, but the pain had lessened. So much still lay ahead, but my body was mending well from the surgery.

Dream themes

EACH TIME I progressed to a new point in my recovery, the themes of my dreams changed. The themes manifested themselves in similar but different images in groups of dreams that drifted into patterns night after night. The dreams bombarded me with the part of my recovery I needed at a particular point in time, providing me with a goal until I passed successfully to the next stage of my recovery. Then my dreams would change themes again. This was probably not unusual, but I had nothing for comparison.

Following the dream of the unseen hand providing planks for my safe passage, I dreamed of a broken bridge that repaired itself before I crossed, a ladder with broken rungs mended by an invisible hand so that I could safely climb upward, and a swinging bridge over a gorge, broken and once again repaired by an invisible hand. I gleaned guidance and safe passage for the coming journey from simple, short dreams. They provided imagery that was easy to use in my meditation exercises and easy to recall as healing snapshots. They were simple dreams with simple pictures: a ladder with broken rungs being repaired or planks being offered for safe passage. I could keep them in my mind to remember the dream message like one keeps a photograph of a person in their wallet to remind them of the person.

following my dream compass

THE DAY FOLLOWING the christening, the oncology office secretary called and asked me to get my calendar. The dates were set for the chemotherapy. I felt armored for the process by two of my dreams: the confirming dream of destroying the remaining bats with poison, and the new dream of energy being delivered to me through tubes. I would use these dreams during the long hour of sitting in a chair waiting for the dripping toxins to travel from the bag on the metal tree down the tubes and into my veins. I could use these dreams to turn poisons into "energy food." My mind could pull the healing energy from both dreams. My intention to heal would provide power to the images in the dreams.

The next day, April 10, a volunteer from Reach for Recovery called and asked if she could visit me. Reach for Recovery is an organization whose members, breast-cancer survivors themselves, visit new breast-cancer patients in the hospital within the first few days of their surgery. Since I left the hospital early I had missed the usual visit, so they called to ask permission to visit my home. My assigned volunteer arrived at my door several hours later, carrying a bag of information and items to help with my recovery.

My son and several of his friends, out of school for spring break, were watching videos in the living room, so I brought the volunteer into the parlor where we could talk. She was quite elderly and very kind, and she spoke softly about her own experience with breast cancer. She showed me the contents of the Reach for Recovery bag: a small pillow, a foam breast filled with cotton, a special bra — a mastectomy bra — with a pouch for the foam breast, and a small rubber ball. I never understood the purpose of the small pillow. The ball was for strengthening exercises; I had been instructed to work with a series of arm exercises, so the ball would be useful. However, I hoped that the "breast" might be the most useful gift from the bag. The volunteer asked if I found the information shared with me in the hospital useful when I was visited by the Reach for Recovery volunteer on the third day. I told her I had left on the second day and had no visit. She was visibly upset — she had been in the hospital for eight days.

The volunteer told me about the meeting times for the support group (once a month) and told me that the members of the group were available to help me readjust at home since I no longer had hospital staff to watch over me. She then lowered her voice even further and told me that the support group was also available to help me talk with the men in my life — my husband and son — about my new "life changes." I was startled by this sentence and tried not to laugh. I couldn't imagine having reached this point without confiding in the "men in my life." My "men" had been with me mentally and physically from the very beginning. How could I have shared the intimate details of my illness with strangers if I couldn't share them with my family and friends?

At this point, as if on cue, my teenage son bounded into the room and sat down opposite me. He grinned, introduced himself to the volunteer, and asked if he could see my fake "boob." I handed him the special bra and the "breast." He hooted!

"Wow, this is supposed to be a small one? It's way too big for you!"

I glanced in the direction of the sweet elderly lady, who was visibly shaken. She quickly piled at my feet a small stack of brochures and a helpful list of sales representatives for wigs and prostheses. She then gathered up her things and made a quick exit, probably thinking that this was the most embarrassing visit she had ever made.

Later that evening I dismantled the fake breast, pulling out most of the cotton in hopes of making it fit, and tried on the new bra. Ron, Evan, and I howled with laughter; it was still way too big for me, and the soft little bra crawled up beneath my armpit. After the laughter died down, I gathered all my old bras into my lap and cried for a while. Ron sat down with me quietly and rocked me in his arms like a baby. When I regained my composure, I sewed a pocket into one of my old bras and stuffed it with an old shoulder pad. It worked.

The remainder of the week was difficult. My son went back to school, and Ron had already returned to work. He had only been able to take a week off from work. Now that Evan, too, was away during the day, I assured him that I would be fine alone. I was not. I was lonely and depressed, and I thought too much about the negative aspects of my situation. I did what I'd promised myself I wouldn't do: I rehearsed scenarios of what could have happened had I not pressed the doctors for further tests. I dwelled on the uncertain future I was creating for myself, and I got myself into an almost frantic state of mind thinking about the nature of the cells that had floated away from the smaller mass and the possible places in my body where they might have traveled. Tests showed that only one lymph node had been invaded by the cancer cells, but I now exaggerated the importance of this piece of knowledge. I asked myself whether I had the courage I needed for this battle, for this second "journey." Of course, I did, but I didn't feel courageous at the moment. I alternately created terrible outcomes for this journey and then despised my self-pity, my lack of confidence in myself, my lack of faith in my family and friends, and my lack of spiritual strength.

Only ten years earlier, magazines had published statistics on breast cancer survival rates in terms of years, not in terms of cures. But technology was changing. People still died, but many now survived. There were stories daily on television, in newspapers, and in magazines of people who survived against incredible odds. These were the real success stories. I had to reach deep inside myself now, on these long days alone, and see myself as one of the people who would be healed, who would be one of those success stories. I would use the dreams of bats and tubes to make the chemotherapy work to my advantage; I would wait for the next dreams that would give me further guidance on my healing journey. But my mind still fluctuated from humor and confidence to frustration and sadness.

looking back in order to go forward

I USED SOME OF THIS "alone time" to read back through my journals. I pulled out all my dream journals, my day journals, and the journal of my expedition to West Africa. I finished writing my West African journal, using the notes I had scribbled on pads and loose pieces of paper, writing and rewriting until I had recorded all the scattered and jumbled information. In the dream journals, I selected and recopied dreams that seemed directly related to my diagnosis and pored over them, finally understanding the once-clouded messages.

I had already worked with one of these past dreams, the dream of the globe of stars that accurately described my breast cancer. What I had not remembered was the date: May 1989, almost a year before my surgery. The details were even more incredible than I had recalled: an almost exact picture of the location of the breast cancer and the description — a globe of stars — that had already been echoed by several doctors in language almost identical to the dream language. However, there was more information in this dream than I'd previously paid attention to; it also held a message of a hopeful future:

THE COMPASS GLOBE OR ORB OF STARS

I am traveling with Robert and my grandfather in an old car. There is an orb-like compass on the dashboard with celestial directions clearly marked. I am intently watching the orb. As I watch, the orb turns and changes into a black crystal ball filled with stars. My grandfather, long dead, carefully asks me to remember the image of the stars and tells me that we can leave now, that my spirit will be the compass I need for my journey; my memory will be my map. After he gives me this advice, I find myself in a glade; the trees cast shadows, filtering the light from the sun. The glade is framed, like a photograph, with the word LEBANON printed beneath the frame. I take a pear from a tree in the glade. I hold it in my hand, break it in half, and remove the seeds. I plant the seeds, and they immediately grow, producing an elegant pear tree. As they are growing, I carefully arrange the branches of the tree into an elegant espaliered form. There are words in the leaves, like in an old Shaker spirit or "gift" drawing, but I have difficulty reading them.

In an early reading of the dream, before I became ill, I had recognized the familiar Shaker symbolism as a common theme in upstate New York communities. In looking back through my journals after the surgery, I made additional associations with the elements of this dream. When Robert was researching material for his novels, I had accompanied him to workshops held at a Sufi community in an area called Mount Lebanon, which had once been a Shaker community. The Shakers used simple drawings of trees, called Spirit Drawings, with words of hope and encouragement printed in the branches and among the leaves of the tree where fruit would appear on a living tree. With this personal connection, the Tree of Life blossomed; it offered affirmation, hope, and healing. In the dream, I had been unable to read the words in the leaves — a strong reference to my unawareness of the message in the dream. In my new awareness, I remembered that the words in Shaker spirit drawings were always single words invoking love, hope, healing, and affirmation. My participation in the dream was positive and active in my planting seeds and arranging branches, a promise of new growth and new life. Just before I was guided to the tree, my grandfather took the message of the compass of stars one step farther: He told me that my spirit would be the compass for my journey; my memory — my intuition, my dreams — would be my map.

I turned the pages of my journal and moved forward a month. I came across a dream that had preceded the dream of bats and energy tubes. This dream foreshadowed my "healing cocktail" — the mixture of alternative and natural methods that would help me through surgery and chemotherapy. Once again, I had focused on only part of this dream, a Bible verse that referenced the Ashanti people in their ancient "land shadowing with wings." I had overlooked the important elements of my second journey, a healing journey. Robert once again played a pivotal role in this dream:

Robert arranged our dream meeting in a sophisticated classroom, where he appeared as a much older guide and teacher. He asked me to do something important: to seek guidance within myself for an important journey. He then led me into a classroom we had built together, an elaborate energy plant that produced both synthetic and natural energy — a complementary blend wherein the elements worked in complete harmony with each other. I asked Robert how we would use this marvelous machine, and he told me that I would operate it and he would provide guidance.

Although this dream referenced the healing cocktail of spirit, surgery, and chemicals, it also presented Robert's incomparable support and friendship during my illness.

In a dream that followed closely behind the Globe of Stars, Robert established a "dream study" where we could talk in my dreams — a comfortable space with book-lined shelves, a desk, cozy old chairs, and a quiet place for discussion, not unlike Robert's study in his house. In the dream:

Robert pulled philosophy texts from the bookshelves and told me that I had to learn how to ask questions. As I listened to him, I began to sculpt a vessel in clay. I stopped briefly, turned to Robert, and asked, "Who would really ask the questions, you or me?" Robert replied that it was important for me to ask the questions because the questions I would ask would be important to my healing, but that he would lend his voice so that the questions and the answers would be strong, one voice together.

This dream accurately described interactions Robert and I were to have later. As Robert developed teaching techniques for working with dreams, we had long discussions in which he would read to me from philosophical or religious texts, quote dream stories from other cultures, and share aloud his thoughts on dreaming and intuition — a direct fulfillment of the "dream study."

Then I came upon a disturbing dream that forcefully announced a health problem that I had not then understood. In the dream, I walked again and again from a plateau to the top of a high windblown hill. The dream contained three segments, and in each segment I battled and destroyed an enormous, devouring, poisonous snake. I was not afraid in the dream, but there was an urgent need to completely destroy the snake so that it would not reform itself into another snake. In the third segment of the dream, I sewed the skins of the three snakes together, wrapping them around each other into a cross-like form, very much like a caduceus. I received assistance from an unseen hand in picking up the enormous snake/cross and hurling it over the top of the high hill, where it appeared to vanish. At the conclusion of the dream, I recorded a sense of victory. Over what? I didn't know at the time.

There had been smaller dreams in which I was losing my way, losing my footing — one a dream of myself on a block of ice floating in a river. In that dream, I was slipping and sliding, having a difficult time gaining a firm footing. I progressed across the ice to firm ground, but the journey to safety was slow and uncertain. This dream occurred six months before the diagnosis of breast cancer, at a time when I experienced the first physical pain. I recorded the pain in my journal, but I still made no direct association with breast cancer.

Some of my dreams during that six-month period were disjointed and strange, murky and disturbing. One was filled with assorted images of faces, one of them kind with no particular gender, stretching into a full image with a body, and finally stretching its arms toward me, its hands holding an old wooden box. It voicelessly indicated that I should open the box and follow. I shook my head "no" and pushed back away from the face and body, telling it that it was not time for me to go. I walked away from the peculiar amoeba-like body. I continued walking, then I walked through a stream. I noticed flat rocks in the stream with messages inscribed in an unrecognizable language. Like the words in the leaves of the tree of life, I couldn't read the message. I shared this dream with my son the next morning, and he reported a similar dream. In his dream, he dove deep into a stream. A large fish helped him pull an enormous boulder to the surface of the water and then onto the land. On the boulder was an inscription in a language he couldn't read. These shared dreams had disturbed me, and I had written a note about having an inner voice that bore a message I couldn't comprehend. The body had beckoned toward me. Was it time for me to leave? Was it my death that the genderless being had offered and that I had so offhandedly rejected? The inner voice was becoming stronger in my journals. The dreams were becoming clear. The warnings had been there, just waiting for my awakening.

This journey back into my old dreams offered new insight and brought forward messages I had barely acknowledged when I'd recorded them. Even though these dreams had been partially fulfilled, there were still useful elements waiting for further digestion. However, I had also been humbled and chastised by this visit into my journals; I needed to become more adept at reading and understanding my dreams. I had to learn how to use the information available in the "dream study" offered by Robert in my dreams. But I was learning; I was now using my dreams when they were presented, destroying bats and turning poisons into positive healing energy.

returning to the "normal" world

A FEW MORE DAYS PASSED, not quite two weeks from the surgery. The pain from the surgery lessened still more, in fact was almost gone unless I moved my body too quickly. When I was able to drive, I visited my staff at work and spent the day sharing stories. These activities were part of my physical and spiritual recovery — the re-creation of my once-normal world and a path for healing.

I had many appropriate small dreams during these days: dreams of landscaping my lawn and putting things in order in my house. The ordering of my house did not seem to be in preparation for death, but rather in preparation for living.

By Easter, I felt better physically. I could move my arm in any direc-tion without pain and without tightness from the disturbed muscles, veins, and nerves, but the swelling did not go away. The tingling in my arm, which had now produced chronic swelling, concerned me. I still received no satisfactory answer when I approached my physicians with the problem; no one was willing to tell me I had lymphedema. I was told that "this" sometimes happened; that it was a rare condition, and that it might go back to normal after the chemotherapy. I was prescribed diuretics, which accomplished nothing.

I went to a library, looked up *edema* in a medical dictionary, and followed the colored engravings until I found an arm and hand that looked like mine. The arm and hand were labeled examples of lymphedema. Research from there led to the discovery of several lym-phedema organizations. In phone calls to them, I discovered I was not alone in my frustration. When I confronted both Dr. Bart and Dr. Jay, each by phone, with my own simple research, they acknowledged that my condition was called lymphedema and that very little was known about the lymph system. In some people, blockage occurs and the lymph system ceases to function normally after surgery and chemotherapy, especially when multiple lymph nodes are removed. In others, it does not, yet a slight trauma any time, even years later, can trigger the condi-tion. Once triggered it does not return to normal.

Later, I discovered in talking with other breast cancer survivors that lymphedema was rarely discussed with any of them. Nowadays, at last, it is presented as a possible side effect of breast-cancer surgery, along with the options for managing and controlling it if it develops. Resources for managing also now exist throughout the country. Those options did not exist near the area where I lived at that time, but Dr. Jay continued the research I began and located one of the few clinics in the New York City area that taught patients and a helper (Ron, in my case) how to work with the lymphedema with massage and how to manage it with the wearing of special sleeves. Lymphedema, to date, has no cure.

The swelling in my arm increased and decreased for weeks, and then the arm finally settled into a chronically swollen state. The chronic swelling in my arm could be managed through massage, wrapping with bandages, and elastic sleeves, but it could never — or so they said — be healed. I met someone whose lymphedema went away and her arm had returned to its normal size. I continue to believe, in spite of the statistics, that it is possible for lymphedema to be healed. But the lessons I learned through dealing with lymphedema came slowly, and dealing with lymphedema became as emotional a battle as the one I encountered while dealing with breast cancer, surgery, chemotherapy, and the accompanying depression.

Although I was having difficulty with my arm, my body was recovering and repairing itself. My appetite turned toward carbohydrates and diary foods. I found that I craved "white" food, a traditional "comfort" food for me when I was ill. This craving intensified when I began chemotherapy treatments. I yearned for potatoes, yogurt, cottage cheese, pasta, cauliflower — anything white! The doctors seemed surprised by this craving, so I assumed it was a peculiar response after surgery.

The day after Easter, things began to move forward. I scheduled my first appointment with my oncologist, Dr. Jay, to initiate chemotherapy, and an appointment for the next follow-up visit with Dr. Bart. I also asked for permission to return to work. Being at home provided too much time for me to dwell on made-up scenarios that brought on depression and a pathetic self-image.

Visits to my surgeon were positive. Dr. Bart removed the staples. I made terrible grimacing faces expecting pain, but there was no pain. He was impressed with the healing around my scar and told me that it was quite beautiful as scars went. He also told me, grinning, that I was "no longer behind the eight-ball." I was healing more rapidly than he imagined; most people, he said, were not at this point in their healing even after two months. I had only been home from the hospital for two weeks. He was ecstatic about my prognosis. He confessed that everything he'd seen just after the biopsy had led him to expect the worst. He had feared that most of my lymph system would be involved, and that there might be involvement beyond the lymph system. He asked if I had consciously done something during that period to reverse what he felt had been certain death for me. After telling him about my dreams — the breast cone dream, the dream of bats, the sacred healing pool, and then the dream of the energy tubes — he said, "It was you who brought yourself to this amazing state." He then placed his hands on my shoulders: "The rest is still up to you; it always has been."

I went home. Chemotherapy was next. I had several dreams to work with. But I asked for a new dream, and went to sleep that night with that intention. I walked into a marvelous, refreshing dream that presented a picture of me successfully coming through my ordeal:

I am walking toward a beautiful blue sea. There are two paths, both difficult. One is over treacherous rocks, slippery, high, and jagged, with no even walking surfaces. The second is almost straight up, steep, with narrow steps. I push through a mass of people, all moving in the opposite direction. I must squeeze through tight spaces, forcing myself against the people so that I will not be dragged back to the starting place. I arrive with others at the end of my ordeal, to the edge of the beautiful sea, feeling exhilaration and a sense of great accomplishment.

The dream confirmed that there were no easy solutions to my health problem — that any healing path I chose would be difficult. However, both paths shown in the dream led to spiritual and physical healing (the beautiful sea), and I had company: my family, my friends, and others who had been on this same path before me.

All of the dreams were confirming elements in my magic healing cocktail, stirred carefully in a syrup of surgery and chemotherapy, working their magic under the guiding star of my spirit and intuition.

Turning Poison
into Medicine

*M*onday morning, April 16, brought the beginning of a new phase in my healing — an incredible challenge, difficult to digest, difficult to face: the destruction of the bats with poison. Chemotherapy, even mixed with dreams, was hard medicine to swallow. I would have to look back again and again at my journals to remind myself that this was not only the path I chose, but the path my dreams offered as a safe option.

Anxious and nervous, my body tensed at the torturous thought of the number of times needles would have to penetrate my elusive veins. Fortunately, the nurses at the cancer research center proved to be well trained in locating veins. After a blood test to determine the readiness of my body for chemotherapy, I settled into a large chair in Dr. Jay's office, prepared at last to discuss the details of my treatment. The nature of my particular kind of breast cancer and the additional information regarding lymph node involvement had changed the treatment plan, as he stated again, from mild to aggressive chemotherapy, from little hair loss to total hair loss. However, he emphasized the choice was still mine if I determined I did not want to go with the more aggressive chemotherapy. The range of options was outlined as follows:

1. **No chemotherapy,** with a 40-percent cancer return rate.
2. **Mild chemotherapy** — the option discussed before surgery — with return-rate odds that were still unacceptable to me.
3. **Aggressive chemotherapy,** which would cause total hair loss but produce the probability of a complete cure.

Lengthy discussion with Ron and Dr. Jay accompanied the description of each potential choice. My cancer was aggressive. Dr. Jay strongly recommended the third choice. I elected to proceed with the most aggressive chemotherapy — "exterminating the bats with poison," a choice already presented in my dream. Ron knew about my dream and supported me completely in my choice. Once begun, I would need to stay on course with the selected option; each choice dictated a specific level of chemotherapy and specific combinations of drugs.

Once I stated my choice aloud, I felt more in control. An odd sensation filled my insides, as if a silken lotion were poured through the top of my head, coating the insides of my organs and the inner layer of my skin, forming a protective barrier that would prevent harm and assist my body in dealing with the dangerous drugs. My second chemotherapy dream came to mind: turning toxins into healing energy. I had prepared myself mentally and physically to choose all the medical options available to me in my battle to destroy the remaining cancer cells; dreams of bats and energy tubes, along with intuition, had assisted me in that preparation.

My hair was very long. A nurse talked with me about my hair and suggested that I cut it as short as possible before beginning the treatments. Stress would be reduced on the hair follicles, and I might be able to retain some hair a little longer if I shortened my hair now. I was introduced to the research center staff, who would be available to answer my questions and help me locate wigs or anything else I needed. We discussed diet and the medications available to reduce the chances of vomiting and nausea. I received my first prescriptions for the oral drugs I would need to take before each visit, and for a drug called Compazine, an anti-nausea suppository that I would also need during the prep period — the three-week spans between each of the six treatments.

Dr. Jay, impressed with my rapid healing after the surgery, decided that I should begin the chemotherapy treatments immediately. We discussed changes that had occurred in attitudes and treatment within the medical community during the last decade. Ten years ago, he said, most doctors would have said that there was no cure for breast cancer. There had always been cures — sizable numbers of them — but these cures were always viewed as extraordinary. Now the extraordinary was considered ordinary, normal. He emphasized the importance of not denying that I had cancer. In fact, he felt that it was important for me to say to myself, aloud, however I wished to say it, "I have cancer, and I will be cured." It was important to both acknowledge the existence of the disease and the ability of my body and mind, working together, to accomplish complete healing. He said that, as an intelligent, optimistic, educated woman, I was within the realm of the statistics of those who were cured.

Dr. Jay firmly believed that men and women who educated themselves — about the unlimited possibilities of their healing capabilities, about the reality of their particular disease, and about the amazing potential of the body and mind working in unison to heal — were the ones who lived. Those who did not were the ones who died unnecessary deaths. All deaths from breast cancer, he said, were unnecessary. "The reality," he stated, "is that you have a disease that is curable, you can participate fully in its cure, and you alone will know the point at which you can say: 'I no longer have cancer; I am cured.'"

the wig on the rabbit

ON TUESDAY, April 17, I went to a hair salon — a rare visit for me — and asked a young woman to cut my hair short so that the drama of losing it would be somewhat less shocking, or so I hoped. I told the hairdresser the reason for the dramatic cut. As she worked, she told me about her sister who worked with young cancer patients at St. Jude's Research Hospital in Memphis, Tennessee, where I grew up. As she continued to talk, her conversation seemed to move in a different direction. She was bored with cutting hair for all the normal reasons and thought perhaps she could offer something more positive to people. Before she had completed my haircut, she'd decided to call her sister and discuss the possibility of opening a special salon near the hospital. There she would work with people facing either total hair loss or thinning hair as a result of disease or treatments for disease. By the time I left the salon, she was ecstatic about her decision and was pulling telephone numbers out of her pocketbook.

Back at home, I once again faced the mirror and tried to recall the last time I'd had short hair, sometime around when I'd begun college in 1965. The change in my hairstyle was not objectionable — at least not for the moment — and reviewing my past, even reviewing something as shallow as what I looked like in 1965, offered me an opportunity to reflect on who I was and what I had become. Facing the mirror became a ritual that provided snapshots of myself and a chance to review memories that would provide strength when needed. Some of the memories were inconsequential, but they gave me gifts of time — time past, time present, and time future. Reviewing my life in terms of time became both friend and enemy. I cherished the past, felt grateful for being alive in the present, and alternately shuddered at and embraced the unknown — the future. Now time would be calculated in terms of the three-week periods between chemotherapy treatments.

As I stood facing the mirror on that April day, looking at my image still with long hair, and reviewing memories, mid-August — the scheduled date for the final chemotherapy treatment — seemed a long way off. But the first scheduled chemotherapy treatment — April 19 — seemed so close that I felt as if it was right there in the mirror, waiting to change me in ways that frightened and repelled me.

Friends and acquaintances called me over the next couple of days, sharing articles, news items, anything that seemed to fall into the category of helpful hints for surviving chemotherapy treatments. I was amazed at the synchronicity of magazine and newspaper articles that seemed to blossom in answer to my queries about my illness. Suggestions often contradicted each other: chemo treatments should be in the afternoon because the diurnal rhythms would cause less severe side effects from the drugs; chemo treatments should be in the morning because morning treatments caused fewer side effects. My first scheduled appointment was for a morning treatment. I arrived laden with articles and new questions. Dr. Jay encouraged my bringing in articles, but discouraged my believing everything I read until he had the opportunity to give me more material — some of it considerably more technical. I sorted through all of it, working out answers to my questions.

I would not permit the challenge of cancer to confine me to my house, so I returned to work the Monday before the first chemotherapy treatment. I had healed so rapidly that both my surgeon and my oncologist wrote permission slips for an early return to my job. Working placed me in close contact with people, which was good for me, and my staff shared their energy and enthusiasm for my recovery. My "weekends" were Fridays and Saturdays, and I helped with tours on Sundays at the historic site. I even arranged my chemotherapy treatments so that the injections would be given on Friday mornings. Then I would have all that day and the next to pull myself back together. I refused to stay home and be "ill." In fact, it never occurred to me that the treatments might cause fatigue or keep me in a state of illness. Not allowing myself to be handicapped by my illness was an unintentional benefit of working with my dreams — a fulfilled intention that I had not even considered.

My staff and colleagues had made an obvious pact to stay upbeat in my presence, commenting on a "glow" I seemed to have, joking about wigs and scarves, and humorously attempting to gauge their behavior on my reactions. They were concerned that they might offend me with humor, but they didn't want to walk around with long faces in my presence. They relaxed when I joked about cancer allowing me to express a bit of eccentricity. I told them I could wear wigs and large colorful hats like storybook southern belles.

In fact talking about hats and wigs and southern belles recalled to mind a story told by my father-in-law, a pharmaceutical chemicals salesman in the South. One of his frequent sales stops had been in a small southern town, where a Delta beauty from days long gone sat in the window of a hot, dusty diner facing onto a boardwalk. She was always there, near the train station, smoking cigarettes and staring out the window, her face framed by an over-large, slightly cocked picture hat decked with flowers and held tight on the side by a wide, soft, pastel ribbon. She claimed a relationship to Rosemary Clooney, and men would buy her breakfast and listen to her tales of lost love — a "Delta Dawn" character, aging and lost in her own past. I would look at my reflection in my bedroom mirror and imagine myself becoming a southern "character," wearing bizarre hats to hide my vanishing tresses. I could blame my descent into oddness on my breast cancer and chemotherapy. Probably not, but I welcomed the opportunity to remember family stories and to face my fears openly and freely. I welcomed the humor. I needed the humor. I rented funny videos — even videos my son thought were funny — and forced myself to see opportunity in the unfolding event of my illness. I needed people, stories, humor, and my dreams to ward off my tendency to descend rapidly into depression.

April 18, the night before I took the first pre-chemotherapy drugs, I dreamed about the actual process of using imagery:

THE DREAM LIBRARY

I had asked Ron to help me with my research on dream imagery. We were on the upper floor of a library, looking through texts on how to use imagery and looking for dream images that might assist me in my recovery. I didn't actually see any of the images referred to in the dream; the focus of the dream was on the definition of the word "imagery" as the ability of the mind to see its pathway to healing the body. (That pathway was different for everyone, but one needed a clear picture combined with a clear healing goal or intention. Seeing the body as healthy and whole was a useful intention if none other presented itself in a dream.) I also saw myself viewing my own body as a separate object: a small version of my body separated itself and turned in a spiral so that I could view it both inside and out.

I was excited about the possibilities of this method of viewing the body. Upon awakening, I began to use this technique for checking on my body's health when a new pain or area of discomfort presented itself. It also became a useful technique for checking on the progress of my healing during the chemotherapy. If a new symptom or a dream frightened me I would, in my mind's eye, place my body where I could view it in its entirety and mentally spin it around. If I saw nothing disturbing, I would immediately be calmed.

I wanted to learn more about how to use my dreams to create healing imagery. I pulled a few popular books from the library shelves. I found information on visualization and on the use of creative meditations or prepared meditations. Those were good but rarely, if ever, did they mention dreams as a source for meditation and active participation in healing. I expanded their meditation techniques into an active process whereby I wrote my dreams into what I called a "prescription" — a few succinct sentences summarizing the dream message like a physician writing a directive on a piece of paper with type of "pill" (dream in this case) and dosage, which I then turned into "medicine" or a "thought image," a short meditation that could be held in the mind like a statement of intent for a dream, said aloud before sleep. The thought image was the expansion of a statement of intent. A prescription (the dream) doesn't become medicine until it is actively used in some manner.

For example, I worked with the dream of turning toxins into healing energy. The statement of intent was: I am sitting in the treatment chair turning toxins into healing energy. I would write that statement in my journal and read it aloud, fixing the image from the dream in my mind. Like a doctor's prescription written for a medication, I could now take it into my mind as an image to use consistently until a new dream presented a new image or until the process of my healing had moved beyond the image being used. Using a dream image as a prescription medication took it off the page of the journal and made it active. I could use it while I was pursuing my daily activities. I would use that particular dream prescription for as long as necessary. My dreams usually told me when it was time for a new prescription or to change the one I was using.

Sometimes I rewrote the statement of intent into a longer meditation, which I would use in the morning or before going to bed in a traditional quiet, meditative space. I might also tape-record it in my own voice and play it back throughout the day as a more active meditation — a technique I was using more and more often. Whether I used the meditations in an active context or in a quiet space, they provided a comprehensive but instant review of the dream, like watching a short movie of the toxins flowing down the chemo tubes and turning into life-giving energy.

the first treatment

THURSDAY MORNING, April 19, I ate breakfast, and, from a prepared schedule, ate regular meals and after dinner that evening swallowed Prednisone, my first pre-chemo oral drug. This drug was taken the evening before the day of the treatment and then again early in the morning of the day of the treatment and again in the evening, altogether three pills by the end of the day of the chemotherapy injections. It took effect rapidly, altering my vision and movement. The day seemed to progress in slow motion, but I was not fatigued; I had been warned that I might be. In fact, waves of energy seemed to surge through my body, but I was unable to react quickly. My mind responded more slowly than normal to my body, and I was unable to make them function at the same speed. I had to keep moving, pacing — but even moving didn't satisfy my need for activity. The energy was uncontrolled and felt jagged; it left me shaky, wired, and strung out.

On the other hand, the Compazine suppository, which was given to control the nausea and energy, left me feeling drugged, my head heavy, my eyes not completely focused. I felt like I was in a mental fog, yet still wired and out of control. I couldn't sleep at all. I felt like I had taken uppers and downers at the same time. I felt like I was going crazy; I would burst into tears because I could find no comfort, no place to rest, nor could I focus on anything constructive. The lack of sleep wore on my body and mind. Also, the Compazine was supposed to be an anti-nausea drug, but the odor alone was so disgusting that I became nauseated as soon as I opened its foil-wrapped package.

On April 20, the morning of my first chemotherapy treatment, I awoke tense and nervous. I dreaded the experience, particularly the insertion of needles into my veins for the hour-long infusion of drugs. The process involved in locating my veins had always been torture for me. I could not imagine enduring it many more times — for the treatments themselves and for blood tests between treatments. My previous experience had been with the use of large needles before surgery; I was not familiar with the small needles used in chemotherapy. With a deep breath, I considered the new dream of imagery and body scanning. That dream helped me use my previous chemotherapy dreams to aid my healing, then do a body scan so that I would feel comfortable that the chemotherapy was working properly.

Ron drove me to the research center. We had brought along plastic bags so that I would be prepared for nausea, and I was still obsessed with thoughts of needles. The nurses led me to a large reclining chair facing the forest, sky, and spring flowers framed in the large windows of the treatment area. They gave me books and magazines and began hooking all the pouches of poisons to the metal tree. They described each step in the process, then one of the nurses — a cheerful, attractive young woman — sat down in front of me with the needle packet, a tiny piece of metal that was pricked into the top of my hand. In that instant, I recalled a colleague once telling me that "half of what we worry about never happens." The prick was painless.

The nurse sat beside me and described each drug, its purpose, and its target. Each description was accompanied by pamphlets giving more details about the drug, adding to my growing pile of reading material.

The nurse then described each step in the treatment process in terms of its healing potential. She answered questions and gently touched my hands and arms in a reassuring manner.

Thus far, the most debilitating part of chemotherapy had been the oral drugs I'd taken the evening and morning before the injected drugs. I told the nurses that I'd been unable to rest, sleep, or even sit still for more than a few moments. I tried to verbalize the experience of the Prednisone and the Compazine together, but it was so unusual that I had trouble describing my discomfort to the nurses. They sympathized with my feelings, but they were a little surprised. They expected me to share feelings of fatigue, not uncontrolled energy, although some people had reported similar reactions to the pretreatment drugs. They suggested that I find "busy" ways to work out the energy; the drugs were important to the treatment sequence. The nurses were also surprised that I'd found the Compazine itself nauseating. According to them, most patients asked for additional prescriptions to prevent nausea.

I was intrigued by the variations on the themes of "normal" and "abnormal." The dream of the Normal House, combined with the themes from the chemotherapy dreams, remained the backdrop for the treatment period. All of those dreams had rehearsed me for these events and prepared me for fitting or not fitting in previously "normal" situations. The dreams provided benchmarks for my mental and physical alternations between feeling okay about everything that was happening and feeling terrified by everything that was happening.

The treatment proceeded; I felt no nausea. A cone-shaped blue ice cap had been placed on my head for the hour's injections, making me look like one of *Saturday Night Live's* Coneheads. The purpose of the ice cap was to help me retain my hair for as long as possible. Apparently the cold sometimes delayed hair loss. As the drugs were injected into the IV tubes, the nurse explained that the red one — Andryamiacin — would completely destroy the duplicating cells, including those that allowed hair growth and attachment.

Ron sat across from me. Dr. Jay strolled in and out checking on my progress and trading jokes about my looking like Beldar or, even worse, the Smurfs with my conehead attachment. One drug after another, all poisons, were inserted into the tubes, the nurse continuing to explain each one as she inserted it. I was intrigued by the scientific description of the balance point at which a plant or drug could cause harm, and just how much poison a body could take for the destruction of cancer cells before the poisons destroyed too much. This balance point between harm and healing was determined by the oncologist, whose treatment pattern was based on age, sex, height, weight, type of cancer, and many other factors. I had asked Dr. Jay about the side effects of the chemotherapy in the weeks in between treatments. He responded: "You tell me. I won't set you up by describing what could happen. If I describe it, it will happen." In my dream of tubes connected to my arms, it was healthy energy, not toxins, that was being fed into my body. In my dream of poisoning the bats, I had relaxed when all the bats were destroyed. I wondered at what point my body would know that all the cancer cells were destroyed and I was healed. What dream would impart that information? Was there a point at which I would be harming my body if I continued, if I passed the point of "enough"? I had no doubt that my dreams would say "enough" if harm attended the treatments.

The first treatment was over. I did not suffer from nausea, but the jagged energy had increased. Ron and I decided that, since I felt no nausea and I had boundless nervous energy, this would be a good time to shop for a wig. I recalled how Clara, soon after my biopsy, had described clumps of hair falling in her lap while she was driving her car. This might or might not happen to me in such a dramatic fashion, but her story and her experience cemented my decision to purchase a wig as quickly as possible. Wig shopping might also help me feel that I was still in control of my appearance.

I walked into the wig salon and strolled down the aisle toward the back of the room, uncomfortably aware of the similarity between this experience and my Dance Hall dream. Hundreds of bodiless heads stared at me from both sides of the aisle, all sporting different colors, shapes, and sizes of "hair." I exited the aisle of heads and entered the small fitting room, where I was placed in front of a gaudy mirror, surrounded by towers of wig boxes of every imaginable size, shape, and color. An overenthusiastic sales person, oohing and aahing at the image change with each new hairpiece, bombarded me with hair: hundreds of wigs, long, short, curly, straight, red, black, brown, and blond. She squealed with glee each time I tried on a wig — all atrocious — and exclaimed about how much fun it would be to be someone different, someone else I'd always wanted to be. I had never even liked trying on shoes, much less hair. The short wigs reminded me of a particular curly-yarned hat of mine that my son hated; they also reminded me of curly permed hair dyed various shades of reddish-brown and often worn by elderly women — an age I would attain soon enough without being prematurely cast into the role. Most of the long wigs looked like tresses ripped from the scenes of grade-B Westerns or cast-offs from the Grand Ole Opry. Finally, after putting on and taking off piles of hair, I chose a medium-length bob that closely resembled the light brown of my own hair.

The next stop was the grocery store to follow up on an anti-nausea diet suggested by the nurses: ginger ale, jello, seltzer, tonic water, and other clear liquids. What I really craved were my "comfort" foods: pasta, potatoes, milk, and white vegetables. But I dutifully purchased the suggested items on the list — the items least likely to trigger stomach problems. Back at home, I poured a glass of ginger ale. I hated ginger ale. The taste was sweet, slimy, and unpalatable. My family had always joked about my cast-iron stomach, so I abandoned the ginger ale. I decided to give in to my craving; what was the worst thing that could happen? I would vomit! So what! I baked a huge potato and drank an enormous glass of milk. For dinner I made pasta and sauce and ate two plates because my appetite, not usually so hearty, was enormous. The only nausea so far was from the horrid Compazine, and even that had vanished over the last few hours; the pervasive odor seemed to disappear. I felt considerably more stable. I did not vomit; I would eat "white"; I felt good.

When I tried on my new hair for my son, he said, "You look like Hayley Mills in a sixties beach movie." I didn't realize he was even familiar with Hayley Mills. At least Hayley Mills suited me better than the Grand Ole Opry look! I walked upstairs to my bedroom and stood in front of the mirror again, holding the new wig. I sat down and stared at my image for a long time. I had lost a breast; I had seen my new breastless chest in the mirror. Now I would lose my hair, another piece of my identity. I stared at my face, framed by my own hair. This was the self I had always recognized in the mirror: my hair, my face, my body. And all of it was changing. I had grown to know the self in the mirror; I wasn't sure I could so easily accept the new person. Evan and Ron had brought me a stuffed white rabbit with long ears when I was in the hospital. That rabbit now sat on the dresser and stared back at me as I assessed my self. I adjusted the wig on the rabbit's head, pulling his floppy ears carefully down and in front of the hair, deciding, at least for the moment, that he looked much better in the role of Hayley Mills than I did. I didn't know how much longer I would have my own hair — a few days, a few weeks, perhaps a month. I looked at myself for a few moments more. I had been nineteen years old when I allowed my hair to grow long. Growing long hair had been a statement — one of many of my generation. What one did with one's hair had always provided an easy form of rebellion for every generation. Now I would lose that hair and I would have to redefine who I was in simple, subtle ways. The loss of hair that would grow back was such a simple thing, yet such a hard concept to face in a mirror.

Now I had to deal with the problem of sleep. I tried to sleep, but only tossed and turned. I gave up on sleep and tried to read. Unable to do that, I walked throughout the house and outside. Every hour or so a hot flash, set off by the drugs, drenched me in sweat. I was required to take the chemotherapy pills for three days after the research center injection treatments, and I could not imagine how I would get through those days. I tried to find some task that would require large amounts of jagged energy; I needed an outlet for the wired nervous energy I was experiencing and the disturbing sensation of going crazy. On Saturday following the treatment, Ron felt that going for rides in the car or running errands would help. Instead, I felt as though I were trapped in a box. We stopped at a restaurant for a late breakfast. Waiting for the food to arrive was torturous; each moment seemed an eternity. Eating helped; the actual chewing and swallowing of food relieved some of the wild energy as well as my insatiable appetite. I ate more food than I normally ate, but there was a void within my body that needed food. My body craved food, and there appeared to be no shutoff valve for my appetite.

Saturday night passed slightly more evenly. I slept without realizing it, but the drugs and my erratic sleeping disrupted and disturbed my dream memory. I was scheduled to work on Sunday, but I was still on a nervous-energy high, only slightly calmer than I had been Friday and Saturday. When Sunday came, I gave the tour of the historic house where I worked, but the experience of walking and talking with people was surreal. Objects seemed to have a visible aura, and people seemed to be physically farther away than they really were, like objects in a car's side mirror.

That evening, I relaxed long enough to try new imagery exercises using my dreams. I scanned my journal and made a list of brief scenarios and words from my dreams that I could use in meditation and other visualization exercises. Based on these, I created writing assignments, voice meditations, and statements of intent that I could mentally recite through the day and use as a "dream prescription" for healing medicine. I practiced traditional healing meditations, which involved breathing properly and bringing a white healing light through my body to cleanse it and remove residue, anxiety, agitation, and discomfort. I used the dream of a barge taking debris out to sea to create a series of healing statements. I also used the comforting dream in which an unseen hand placed planks over muck and mire so that I would be allowed to reach high ground safely. I used the Killing the Bats dream over and over, turning the chemo poisons into true weapons of destruction against the cancer cells while sparing all other cells. In this way, I mobilized the tools of self-healing from my dreams to support the healing cocktail that both my dreams and my doctors had suggested.

The surgical wound had not completely healed; I still had some minor, but annoying, pain. Sunday night I slept poorly, but I slept through the night.

healing imagery from dreams

MONDAY MORNING, April 23, I took the final Prednisone pill required for the first treatment. The morning was beautiful — sunny and seventy degrees — but I was still disoriented. The treatment plan involved one Prednisone the night before the injections, two the day of the injections and one the following three mornings. Each pill increased my level of supercharged energy. Problems with time, space, and distance continued most of the day, but finally began to ease later. Slowly the effects of the Prednisone wore away. I walked normally, performed my work, came home, cleaned the house, ate meals, and reflected on my body's response to the drugs.

That evening, Robert and I spoke on the phone about the different ways in which people dream. We had discussed dreams in which the dreamer is present and participates in many parts of the dream, and dreams in which the dreamer is simply watching the events of the dream unfold. That night I slept normally for the first time in days. The conversation with Robert continued in my night dreams, in which we discussed the avenues available in dreams for developing healing visualizations. In the dream, we focused on the ability of a dreamscape to target a specific body area or symptom — as in my dream of squeezing dark liquid from a breast-like cone — or to offer a larger template, as in my dream of hauling a barge filled with debris out to sea. A big dream might offer a vital space for healing, as in the dream of the sacred healing pool, and even a means for interacting directly with the body's cellular system to move it in the direction of wellness.

GIFTS OF HORUS

TUESDAY NIGHT, April 24, I recalled more of the landscape of my dreams. I still felt some discomfort from the scar on the left side of my chest and from the lymphedema in my left arm, but the discomfort decreased with each evening. That night brought my first big dream since the surgery:

SHOPPING FOR HORUS

I walk into an elegant shop, very much like the expensive gift shops attached to large urban museums. The shop is filled with large carvings of animals. I am carrying in my hands a small carving of a stylized bird. I have one bird carving and I want another one just like the one in my hand. The bird is a falcon. The shop-person tells me that there is only one left and that it is mounted. I am disappointed. I then find myself no longer in the shop but in the hallway of another building looking down into a kitchen, which is lower than the main floor, very much like the kitchen in my house. I recognize Ron in the kitchen, and he is busy cooking for me. I continue down the hall. I sit down in a chair and look at my legs, which are covered by thick, wax-like applied hieroglyphics. The designs are quite magnificent, many of them displaying the profile of the Egyptian falcon Horus. An old, dark-skinned man reads the hieroglyphic symbols and is pleased with the message. I do not understand what he has said, but I know that he likes the reading. I then carry my bird carving into a small store where I choose scented soaps and lace potpourri sachets. A salesperson places my purchases in a drawstring bag for me and says they are gifts — that I do not have to buy them. While pulling the bag shut, I puncture the end of a car key into the palm of my hand. When I remove the key, a hole remains in my hand and blood begins to spurt from my hand, but then the wound instantly seals and heals itself. I pick up the scented objects and take them back to a small apartment — not elegant, but cozy and feminine.

An elderly lady from a nearby apartment comes inside my apartment. I do not like her at all. I place my new things in the bedroom and the bathroom. The old lady follows me, picks them up, and puts them back down. She follows me into the front room and begins painting dark colors and symbols on the wall. I am furious. I physically toss her out of the apartment. Then I look at the symbols she has painted on the wall. I peel them off the wall like pieces of wallpaper and throw them away. Then I pull on the base of the walls and they raise like window shades, revealing beautiful new white walls, cleared of all disfiguration.

I was tremendously excited when I awoke from this powerful dream of loss and surgery, of darkness, cleansing, and healing. With my family I had visited friends in Egypt five years earlier. At that time, I had immersed myself in the history of the country and I recognized Horus and the dream hieroglyphics. I read further about Horus and found the story of Horus — the wounded healer who was stung by a scorpion and through divine intervention was restored to life — relevant to my own healing.

I shared the dream with Robert, who had extensive background in ancient and religious history. We used one of Robert's techniques of saying "if it were my dream," in which he would see the dream from his own perspective and state the elements of the dream from his own perspective. Then, using a technique which he called a "reality check" exercise, he would ask me which, if any, of the dream elements could be found either now or possibly in the future in my waking reality. Some of his "if it were my dream" associations were instant confirmations of my own; some were not. This was the purpose of the exercise: clarification of the dream for the dreamer. In the "reality check" exercise, I recognized some of the elements from my own waking reality: rooms in a dream reflected the condition of my life or body and kitchens were places of nurturing and nourishment: how well my mind and body were being fed — or not.

The dream opened with me "shopping" for healing. In asking for a second item, and being told that there was only one and that it was mounted, I relived my fear and disappointment over having a breast removed — a loss that I could not repair. However, the carving of the falcon that I held in the dream was the Egyptian god Horus. As a child, Horus was stung by a scorpion. The intervention of his mother, who prayed to the sun god Ra for help, restored his life. The poison from the scorpion bite flowed from Horus's body, and he was reborn and renewed — an incredible gift of healing for a chemotherapy patient.

Other scenes from the dream reflected the spaces in my house where healing could take place. The kitchen, where Ron was cooking for me, was a place for nurturing and support — and a place where, in waking reality, I was making conscious changes in my diet. My bedroom was a space where I spent time reflecting on my self. The bathroom was a place for cleansing. And the potpourri gifts of aromatic herbs and sachets combined natural healing with the possibility of experimenting with aromatherapy. The connecting hallway linked all the rooms together and provided access in and out of each space. In the dream I was also provided with the gift of healing, perhaps not only for myself but to pass on to others. The chemotherapy treatments were reflected in blood spurting from my hand, but healing was instant — an important message that referred to my rapid healing from surgery and the rapid cell recovery I experienced after my first chemotherapy treatment.

The key belonged to a vehicle — a common image in my dreams, usually representing the amount of control I had over a situation — in this case identified with the spurting blood in my hand (the chemotherapy treatments). Some of the healing message was passive: the old man was reading the message; I didn't understand it, but it was positive nonetheless. The message came from outside of me. The message was written in hieroglyphics in wax and covered my legs, some of the more prominent figures once again depicting Horus. The stelae of Horus, often used as charms in ancient Egypt, featured figures of the god Horus sculpted in relief. The backs, sides, and bases of these were usually covered with magical texts. The recitation of these texts — in my dream by an elderly man acting as my translator — made the poison go forth from the body and returned strength to the body. The engravings of magical motifs of gods, combined with words of power, was a powerful talisman that protected its owner from the attacks of hostile beings, both visible and invisible; the power of this talisman was believed to be invincible. The Egyptians believed that because these words had restored Horus to life, they would — when uttered in a suitable and respectful tone of voice, with appropriate gestures and ceremonies — never fail to produce the same effect again. The possessor of these texts — which was me, in my dream — had access to all the powers of heaven and earth.

In the last scene in the dream, I took final charge of my own healing. Houses, rooms, and apartments reflected my state of being. In my apartment in the dream, I flew into a rage, erased the dark symbols and colors, and threw the frightening old woman out of my apartment. Ridding myself of darkness and fear (represented by the old woman), I stood in a room with a new, clean, white wall — unblemished, cleared of darkness and disfiguration. There was also a connection between the white wall and my white blood cells, whose job was to cleanse and heal my body. This was a dream, like the sacred Healing Pool dream, in which healing occurred within the dream but I was also presented with gifts that must be shared with others — a role of the wounded healer not to be ignored or taken lightly. I had been presented with powerful gifts from the spirit of another culture, and I needed to use them and to treasure them.

Sometimes choosing something tangible in waking life to honor a dream is a delightful way to keep the dream active in one's memory. To honor this dream, I rescued a small toy falcon made of a chalk-like substance from a box of old childhood toys and placed it on the dresser near the white rabbit.

a reach for recovery

As the week progressed, the jagged, wired effect of the oral drugs wore off. I was not sure what else lay in store. My dreams dealt with survival and with showing others that I was alive. In one dream, I was sitting in a chair in a room filled with tables and chairs, but I had arranged the room so that I was "on view" sitting on a stage. The room was filled with light, and I announced to the audience that I had survived. I stood up and walked past friends and several recognizable celebrities out of the room and into a hallway. This hallway led, not to my death, but to a street festival where everyone was very much alive, dancing, singing, decked out in festive costumes and colorful jewelry.

However, a new problem arose when I awoke from this festive dream. I was seized physically with an intense, palpable feeling of despair and depression so deep that my insides ached and my breathing became short and tight. The problem intensified with the passing days, occurring instantly upon awakening each morning. No matter how positive the night's dreams, no matter how deep and restful the sleep, the despair was there with my first breath of waking. Some of my hair was beginning to fall out. Side effects, mimicking flu, began the Wednesday after my first treatment: sore, aching muscles and joints and painful mouth sores. I gargled with salt water and ate fresh vegetables. The flu-like symptoms lasted three days, the mouth sores a little longer. My skin felt odd: very dry and smooth, almost like plastic. I washed my hands frequently. The cool water felt wonderful on my hands and my hot, puffy face (another side effect of the Prednisone, I discovered). I even dreamed of splashing the cool water on my face and hands, and awoke with my hands clasped to my face. I was blessed with an oncologist who understood the power of the imagination and had not presented me with side effects, but, as the days progressed, here they were, appearing one at a time as a new experience. Dr. Jay had told me that as soon as my body began to return to normal the next treatment would begin.

Friends begged me to attend a Reach for Recovery support group meeting. In general, I didn't feel the solace many people found in support groups, probably because I had such a strong personal support group among my family and friends. However, the next scheduled meeting was close at hand. I promised to go to at least one meeting and vowed that I would attend with an open mind. I walked into the meeting room, which was a small conference room space provided by a local hospital. The room was filled with women who were probably all in their sixties and seventies. I felt out of place and depressed in a room filled with people who had apparently been much older when they had to face breast cancer. I envied their time without disease — almost two additional decades with intact breasts and sound arms. Then the women answered a roll call with the number of years they had survived, many of them answering with the numbers twenty, twenty-five, thirty, thirty-five. I was wrong. Subtracting backward, I realized that some of these women had been even younger than me when they got breast cancer. I felt a bit embarrassed. These women were among the "extraordinary" cures Dr. Jay had mentioned.

The speaker for the evening was a nurse who had information about inexpensive prostheses and sources for mastectomy bras. The ladies were excited. An elderly lady who sat beside me leaned over and told me that I had to be careful with pins.

"What?" I asked.

"With pins," she said. "I had a beau once who pinned a corsage on my breast — you know, the silicone one. It was Christmas and we were going to a dance. Well, all the 'jelly' filling leaked out, and I was very embarrassed."

We both laughed. Her breasts were quite large; mine were small, so that would not be my problem. I could get away with little pouches filled with cotton.

Most of the women in this group were from Italian-American neighborhoods. Most of them had large breasts, similar problems, and similar religious and community backgrounds; even their ages were similar. The conversation continued with discussions of "equalizers," a term describing some kind of insert that would balance any difference between a real breast and a prosthesis and make them look more equal, and other kinds of bra additions. I stayed until a motivational video was put on the monitor, and then I left. The support group was not the path I would choose, but I understood its value to the women who attended and had become friends.

All of the side effects, including the mouth sores and flu symptoms, disappeared by Wednesday, May 2, one and a half weeks after my first treatment. During that period, I had felt like the huge person in my Normal House dream, dealing with tiny objects — or at least objects that appeared smaller than they were. Distorted vision and unbalanced energy levels had visually and sensorially created an abnormal world within an otherwise normal day.

It was time to return to the research center for a blood count, which was scheduled to take place midway between injection treatments. Just as Dr. Jay had noted, I was beginning to feel normal and I was only another week and a half from the next treatment. My first interim blood count was slightly low in white cells but better than they had expected.

My hair was now falling out more rapidly, but I could still cover the thinning areas with a scarf. Sometimes my hair came out in small clumps, usually in my comb. My skin provided a warning for each period of hair loss; just before the hair came loose from my scalp, my head would become sensitive to the touch and extremely painful. The slightest touch of a scarf, a hand brushing over my head, or even a slight breeze over my tender skin would cause terrible pain. Then, after the next clump of hair fell out, my skin would return to normal. Sometimes I awakened with large sections of my hair so impossibly tangled and matted from its loosening during sleep that I couldn't comb it. I would take a clump in my fingers and pull it apart until it finally came loose from my head as a large mass. At first this process was terrifying. Then it was humorous. Then I just wanted all my old hair to come loose so that I could begin again. The nurses at the oncology lab had explained that my hair would actually begin to grow back before the treatments ended. The Andryamiacin only affected the attachment cells that were in place when the treatments began; new hair would not be affected. I delayed putting on the wig; I still had a fringe of hair. In fact I looked like a monk; my hair fell out first on top and at my neckline, leaving a circular tonsure of curls. I was waiting as long as possible before removing the wig from the rabbit's head.

Dr. Jay was extremely pleased with my body's response to the chemotherapy drugs. The healing cocktail was working. He asked if I had any side effects. I described the flu-like symptoms, the mouth sores, and the puffy redness in my face and hands. Sleeplessness, I told him, was one of the worst of the side effects, seconded by the jagged, wired feelings I experienced from the oral drugs. He gave me a prescription for just enough sleeping pills to carry me through the three worst nights around each treatment. I had five treatments remaining.

That evening and over the next few weeks, my dreams changed again. They focused on cleaning and positive change: cleaning houses, cleaning closets, rearranging closets. They were all simple, brief dreams — easy dreams to honor. In the evenings, I played "cleansing" tapes on the tape machine near my pillow and practiced breathing in light and breathing out darkness. One particular tape used sounds of ocean waves lapping back and forth. I imagined myself lying on the beach, with each incoming wave bringing healing and each outgoing wave washing away darkness and illness. I was pleasantly surprised at the intensity of feeling generated by the sound of the monotonous waves. I could feel tension leaving my body each time a wave lapped against the sandy beach.

The activities of my days spilled over into my night dreams. Just after a day in which matted clumps of hair fell out, I dreamed that I was trying on wigs and boldly experimenting with new hats. In one dream, while trying a new wig, I encountered a childhood friend who commented on my thinning hair. I explained that I needed a wig and told her that I had breast cancer. She then pointed to her own thinning dark hair and said that her chemotherapy treatments, although not as aggressive as mine, had caused such severe damage to her hair that she almost wished she had lost all of it instead of it just thinning. I hadn't noticed until she pointed to her hair.

Once again, as in the dream of Horus, using Robert's technique for working with a dream, I did a reality check with the dream material. I asked: Had my childhood friend, Diane, actually just experienced breast cancer and a slightly less aggressive dose of chemotherapy? I suspected so, but there was no easy way to verify that. I still trusted the possibility that a dream was describing a situation in waking reality; my personal experiences had verified my ability to track other people in my dreams. However, that element in the dream — verified or not — gave me nothing new for my healing. But it did provide a space for a brief dialogue with someone who was facing a similar problem, and it gave me a dream opportunity to review my own feelings about the problem.

My dreams continued to address my current needs. As I've mentioned, more than one dream attended my concern about whether or not I should pursue chemotherapy: one dream gave me an okay for chemotherapy; two dreams presented imagery for working positively with the chemotherapy. When I was selecting wigs, two dreams mirrored my search for the correct wig and addressed my interaction with people. When I felt insecure, groups of dreams — not just one dream — came to my rescue with multiple possibilities for visualizations of safe and unsafe passage, including the introduction of an unseen guide who repaired ladders and bridges so that I could safely pass. These dreams helped me establish a base for my own personal dream vocabulary, which I noted in the edges of my dream journal. I also wrote questions for my groups of dreams:

- *What were the unsafe passages — fear, anxiety, something I needed to watch for in the treatments?*
- *Who were my helpers — animals or people?*
- *How could I use my helpers in waking reality?*
- *How could I use my dream to create safe passage?*

The questions and the dream vocabulary — a house means what in my dream? a passage means what in my dream? — provided more rapid transit through the dreams. I could recognize familiar elements more and more swiftly, especially those that repeated themselves in dream after dream. I no longer simply woke up, recorded a dream, and walked away from it, waiting for some event in waking reality to kick me awake and say, "Hey, do you remember you dreamed about this?" I shared the dreams and I worked with them in the creation of tapes, meditations, and prescriptive dream medicine. I used my dreams now with understanding and advantage. There were still dreams that needed time to play out, but a personal dream vocabulary allowed me the advantage of recalling the dreams with more clarity when time and the dream caught up with one another. I also recognized the need to continue to go back and look at past dreams. I would find new meaning in them and discover dreams that I had forgotten or neglected that had played out later in either simple or meaningful ways.

During my illness I sought specific dreams. I would write a statement of intent or say one aloud before going to sleep. If I presented my dreaming self with a problem before I fell asleep, the "working-out" process would take place during the dreaming and diminish or even solve the problem. This "working-out" process within the dream was very effective in dealing with anxiety and depression; the solutions were always there in my dreams. Sometimes I experienced difficulty in bringing a dream forward into the day. Each day I trapped myself in some new fear or anxious thought, so whatever benefit came from the previous night's dream seemed to melt in the face of a new anxiety. Nevertheless, despite my obstinate habit of creating new fears and anxieties during the day, the healing in my dreams was translating into physical healing in my body. The night dreams were taking care of the day's depression, doubt, and anxiety in such subtle ways that I was often unaware of the extent of the healing process in waking reality.

On Sunday, May 6, I noted in my journal that I could no longer brush my hair. The remaining clumps had matted themselves together during the night, forming a thick mass of tangled dead hair. My scalp was tender and sore to the touch, as it was just before each time I experienced hair loss. I stood in front of the mirror that had become the visual raconteur of my disease, pulling out masses of unattached matted hair, suddenly furious, suddenly wishing all of it would come out at the same time. Chunks of hair would appear in odd places: in the sink, on my clothing, on the sofa — a sad, depressing end to my once-long tresses. I was angry at everyone, particularly myself. I stormed around the house creating arguments with my family. My son trailed along behind me one evening, undaunted by my moodiness, shouting at me: "Hey, you're my mom; you will always be my mom, and my mom makes it through tough things, okay! Okay? Okay!!" he shouted again.

"Okay," I said.

I would make it through. No one said that a healing cocktail came without side effects. I would have to learn how to manage them until the mixture had passed completely from my system and I could curl up, healed and safe.

FIELDS OF DREAMS

I once saw a joke greeting card that depicted a person out standing in his field. The cover of the card showed a small person, surrounded but not overwhelmed by the personal world he had created. I'm sure this was not the intended message of the greeting card, but the image I visualized turned that field into all the dreams of one's life, surrounding, guarding, assisting, warning, but never overwhelming. In my healing image, I was standing in a field of dreams.

Dreams were not my only refuge during my healing. In fact, sometimes dreams themselves reminded me of other resources by showing me scenes of studies and libraries where I could find books to provide reflection, knowledge, and maybe just relaxation. In books, I journeyed into the most private parts of my psyche. I read books relevant to my illness and digested the parts of each that spoke most personally to me. But I also took issue with many that seemed, in my opinion, to simply set one up for failure. I was willing to take responsibility for my illness, but I was not willing to completely rule out external circumstances, especially in lethal combinations: viruses, heredity, our fouled air and water, chemicals in food, my childhood diet (especially a southern diet of fried food), my current diet, and numerous other internal and external influences — possibly even including the mental picture of my death in the Dance

Hall dream. This dream might have begun as a simple warning dream, but may have become a dangerous mental picture in itself because I didn't understand how to challenge and change its outcome. These were questions I raised, not conclusions. Perhaps I would never fully understand why I was among the "one in eight" whose body would be susceptible to breast cancer, but I knew that I had a good chance to be one of the thousands who would survive.

other sources

I READ BOOKS BY WOMEN who told their own stories of surviving cancer, but their stories did not speak to me. Some simply catalogued their physical journeys and some explored their emotional journeys. Much of their writing was relevant to my journey and those of other people with life-threatening illnesses, but their stories lacked the most important element in my healing: my dreaming. One survivor recorded a dream dating to her initial diagnosis of cancer, but she casually tossed the experience aside as a common "scary" dream that anyone facing loss might have in a dark moment. The dream, as I saw it in the context of my own life, provided a warning (the loss of a body part), recapped the dreamer's anxiety in a frightening realization of loss, and provided several pertinent healing images (healing salves), but the dreamer had ignored both the precognitive value of the dream and the even more valuable healing opportunity within it.

I also explored books on healing imagery and dream imagery — closer in content to what I sought but still lacking the depth I needed. I looked for experiences that I could compare to my own and found samples. Each book contained a gift, but fell short of presenting a journey. Each book, particularly those written by cancer survivors, found its way to "living in the moment" and then stopped. In the best of circumstances, "living in the moment" can be a difficult concept, but I found myself resenting the assumption that I had been living in any other timeframe. Some writers spoke about changing their priorities. My priorities had not changed; they had become more precious, more valuable, more intensely real: a job I enjoyed, a family I loved, incomparable friends, a system of beliefs and values that worked for me and gave meaning to my life, and my home in a small hamlet full of diverse personalities.

I thought about people I had known who had survived cancer or other life-threatening diseases and I remembered they had set goals as well as priorities for their lives. I only recalled one situation in which a couple inadvertently set death as their goal. Their story was tragic. It took place in 1974. The man had a wife who was battling leukemia. In his premature mourning he wrote the date of her death, as predicted by her physician, on a calendar and marked it in black. He set for her a goal — her moment of death — and thereby presented her with a negative future: the living of each moment shadowed by a vision of death. She lost the ability to change that vision, and she died as predicted on the date marked on the calendar. In her husband's coat pocket, she had left a note and a tape recording of an old folk song, in which she'd substituted their names for those of the doomed lovers who created each other's deaths. Her husband found the tape after the funeral, played it, and wept. She left a song, her condemnation of his action and her inaction: "Dig my grave and make it narrow, cover my grave with your guilt and sorrow." This was a sad story of poor choices and lost opportunity. Her mind adapted and responded to a visual and mental message set by him (a predicted time and date of death), and she translated that message to her body — a tragic example of the suggestive power of imagery. Doctors sometimes give patients a survival date — five years, ten years, sometimes much less — without realizing the power of the imagination. They hand out death sentences and then write case histories of those who survive against the odds they have given them. The man whose wife died as scheduled thought he was offering love and support. Instead, he set a goal: a date for her death that she unwittingly accepted in her imagination and faithfully kept in waking reality.

A host of popular theories touted an equally damaging trend: a denial of all benefits offered by the medical profession. I had made a choice. I chose to use a cocktail of dreams, meditation, an improved diet, exercise, and all the current knowledge available to me from the medical profession. Resources should, in my opinion, be used to one's advantage, and the advantage could be boundless if all were used in harmony with one another.

While undergoing chemotherapy treatments, I attended two alternative healing seminars given by writers and popular presenters. Both presenters had written books exploring the ability of the imagination to heal — or to kill. One presenter was a physician whose arrogant control of his audience did more harm than good. The second presenter completely rejected medical technology (especially the use of chemotherapy) as a healing resource. "You will lose your will; you will die," he shouted at a young woman who was considering chemotherapy as treatment for her cancer. At lunch, I confronted the presenter, in the presence of the young woman, at the lunch table. I told him that I was receiving chemotherapy treatments and had not lost my "will." I talked about dreams and healing; he talked about his peculiar theory that the mind can create an environment in which the body never ages. He appeared to be at least ten years older than his actual age. I hoped the young woman was listening to her own counsel, not his.

I read about the world's inventors, mathematicians, and scientists — Einstein, Elias Howe, Dr. Salk, and others — whose dreams had revealed the keys to each of their individual discoveries, which eventually led to technology that changed peoples' lives. I asked myself: What about the source of medical discovery? — much of it was developed in night dreams.

I WAS BLESSED with physicians who did not present death sentences and who were willing to listen to my dreams. My surgeon and my oncologist listened to my dreams because I shared them; I made each person a partner in my healing. My oncologist told me that most of his patients never told him what they were thinking, much less what they were dreaming; he was expected to read minds and put together a treatment without input. Imagine what doors might open if patients opened their coffers of dreams and shared them! My doctors appreciated my dreams and modeled treatments for my illness on our shared dreaming. Together we stepped beyond science and discovered the right combination of medicine for the body and medicine for the mind.

the second treatment

MY SECOND CHEMOTHERAPY session began on Friday, May 11. The sleeping pills were a helpful addition; they eased my ordeal with the oral medication. I still felt wired and jagged, but I slept through the night and could use my excess energy more constructively: mowing the lawn, cleaning house, doing anything that required physical labor. The drugs created a feeling of hollowness in my stomach that left me famished within hours of eating, so I continued to give in to my odd craving for white vegetables, milk, and pasta. As before, the nausea caused by the Compazine vanished with the consumption of these white foods. Dr. Jay was surprised at my energy; fatigue was often a side effect of chemotherapy. He looked at my blood tests and interim checkup results and pronounced me the "healthiest sick person he had ever treated."

My emotional torment increased, not so much from the loss of a breast, but from the lymphedema. Once my lymphedema was acknowledged and named, it continued to create emotional problems. I could replace the missing breast with a prosthesis and look more or less normal when I wore clothes. But my arm was always visible — a constant reminder that I would never look completely normal.

After the second treatment injections, I began my weekend with a better understanding of my own peculiar set of side effects. This time, however, the side effects were more tenacious. The flu-like symptoms began earlier and stayed longer; the mouth sores were more painful. The side effects would just begin to subside or disappear about a week before the next treatment, then they would begin again with each new treatment. Both emotional pain and physical discomfort were reflected in a night dream:

THE DRUG HOUSE

I am back in my childhood home in Memphis, driving past houses on Berclair Road, an adjoining neighborhood street. The windows of all the houses are boarded up. I walk up to one of the houses and cautiously look inside. The rooms are dirty; wallpaper is peeling off the walls, and they are lit only by bare lightbulbs. Men are dispensing crack and other drugs. There are mangy dogs in the streets. I pick my way quietly away from the door and begin to move, almost in slow motion, away from the scene.

This was not a memory of my childhood home, but a "reality-check" view of my current physical condition — a mirror of my waking reality of drug-induced images. Houses or rooms in houses were familiar images in my dreams. Rooms usually reflected my spirit, my internal emotional life. This dream accurately reflected the havoc that chemical poisons — the "hard drugs" — were creating in my physical body and my emotions. Even my slow movements in the dream reflected my daytime physical movement, or at least the way I perceived my movement: out of focus, in slow motion, not quite part of the scene. This feeling lasted for several days after each treatment until the drugs moved through my body, and dissipated before the next treatment — and a new set of side effects — began.

The flu-like symptoms, although more intense in this treatment, abated somewhat by Wednesday. After the second treatment, Ron and I established a ritual to celebrate my coming back to a more focused world: we would go to my favorite local Italian restaurant and order pasta with garlic and olive oil. Wednesday became an important turning point after each treatment.

On each of the Wednesdays following a Friday treatment, I would notice a change in my dreams. The Wednesday dreams, as I came to call them, would present the problem I was facing or mirror my progress through the illness. An acknowledgment of the problem or the progress would trigger a dream response. If I posed a question in my imagination, it would be answered in the night with a dream. Usually the dream that followed a question offered healing imagery to address whatever problem surfaced in my query. If a mirror was offered rather than a direct healing response, as in the Drug House dream, I could create my own healing response. For example, in the case of the Drug House dream, I visualized a house cleaned, redecorated, and cleared of men dispensing crack. I took careful note of the new pictures in each dream and used them to create visualization exercises. The exercises would then become a vital technique for healing, cleansing, and revitalization after the harsh chemotherapy treatments.

In another example, after the second treatment I was thinking about the effect of the hard drugs on my body. My Wednesday dream then mirrored my thinking and presented "boxes" and "higher planes":

WORKING WITH BOXES

I am in a small room moving objects into boxes, some of them too large to take with me. Then I am in a new place — my "new home" — an area with sunlight and lush, green surroundings. I feel as though I have been in this place before. There are different sizes of brightly colored boxes stacked everywhere, with numbers and figures on them. Someone moves up beside me and points to a "higher plane," a new set of boxes stacked high against the backdrop of a steep hill. This person tells me that I must begin working with the boxes at the base and move up to the brighter, higher boxes.

Coincidentally, I picked up a medical book several days after this dream and noticed the similarity between the illustrations of cells in the book and the boxes in my dream. The illustrator had used color to distinguish between the T cells and macrophages, the powerful cancer-attacking cells. I had the eerie sensation of looking at my own dream: old cells and new cells, cells protected by fighting cells and saved from certain destruction by the invading cancer cells; old boxes and new boxes — changes in my body and mind as dramatic as the cell pictures in the book. The small boxes were the cells that made up my physical body, and they were undergoing tremendous change in a continuous wave of destruction and rebuilding. I was new; I was no longer the same person, mentally or physically, inside or out, as I had been a year before.

This was a wonderful dream to use for creating dream exercises — easy to use for a meditation and easy to recall for prescriptive healing. My intent: to replace damaged cells (old boxes) with new cancer-free cells (new boxes). I rewrote the dream using that simple statement: I am rebuilding my body, replacing damaged cells with new cells. I taped the simple sentence against the background of the ocean wave music and used it in the day in my car tape player. I also used it at night in a tape player which I placed near my bed and set for playing through just once. I was asleep by the time the tape ended, the mental image of replacing damaged cells with new cells firmly in place in my mind.

surviving Jill Ireland

SATURDAY, MAY 19: I was driving home from work when I heard the radio announcer casually say that actress Jill Ireland had died after a six-year battle with breast cancer. The news blasted bomb-like through my already fragile emotions. I raced home like a maniac and tore into the house, sobbing uncontrollably. I could not stop sobbing; I was going to die, too, and I was not ready to die.

My reaction was completely irrational. It dredged up fears and doubts of such magnitude that I completely crumbled beneath them. If I'd had a virus, this would be called a setback. I suppose that "setback" was an adequate description of the complete devastation the radio news caused to my image of myself and where I was in my healing. The facts of Jill Ireland's breast cancer did not matter to me at that moment. It didn't matter that she had discovered her cancer after it had invaded many of her lymph nodes and was too far advanced to control. It didn't matter that she had lived an abnormally long life given the details of her cancer. I knew all of those facts; I heard them on the radio, but they did not matter. Nothing mattered at that moment, except that she was a woman with breast cancer who had died. She had died only six years after discovering the same disease I had. She had breast cancer and she had died. I had breast cancer and, some insane illogic in my mind convinced me, I would die. At that moment, I identified completely with a woman I had never met, and I could not see how I would survive.

I had many sleepless nights. I could not stop thinking about Jill Ireland's death day or night. She had died, therefore I would die. Why couldn't anyone understand the depth of my fear? I would wake up trembling with fear, stabs of fear so deep they pierced my heart and held me for the entire day, intense strangling fear that knotted my stomach and seized my body and mind. I argued with myself: I was alive; what was wrong with me? Where did such terror, such fear, come from in an instant? Was I so afraid of death? Jill Ireland had died in pain. Was I afraid of the pain more than I was afraid of death itself? Was I afraid to be alive? Or was I angry because my seemingly healthy body had betrayed me, let me down, and I couldn't trust it now? I screamed back at myself: I had to stop the fear! I was certain that I was destroying myself.

The cancer was gone, but now — at this moment — the cancer was not the problem. These feelings that had me in their grip were the problem. These feelings had the power of death — more power than the cancer ever had in my body — but I could not shake myself free of the fear. Nothing I said to myself, nothing anyone else said to me, made any difference. I was, for this period of time, Jill Ireland, and she was me. I was every woman who had ever died from this disease, and I had to find a way to come back to the path I was on: a healing path.

There was a lesson in my reaction to Jill Ireland's death. Like the young woman who died dutifully on the date marked by her husband, I fell prey to self-suggestion and the incredible power of the imagination. The imagination — as in dreaming — could heal; it could also kill. We are all responsible for which images we take in as the guiding energy for healing or not healing. I began to realize that I had allowed myself to give all my energy to fear and defeat. We constantly choose which images to give credence and energy to. We can also choose which ones to diminish. This lesson was vital — a message for me to observe and monitor the contents of my mind, then choose how much energy each piece deserves.

With my imagination back on the right track, time created the distance I needed. The pain and fear associated with Jill Ireland's death gradually lessened, and the reality of the circumstances of her death slowly replaced my fear of my own death.

My night dreams also helped me move beyond my fears of death and settled back into problem-solving mode, dealing with my bald-ness and my imagined lack of desirability. The dreams were brief but very straightforward, and dealt quickly with minor problems. In one dream, I carried balloons to the top of a hill. I wrote the word "fear" on one balloon and "anxiety" on another, then I set the balloons free into the air. I had this dream more than once during my healing. In another dream, I wrote the words of my negative emotions on boxes, like Chinese lanterns, and launched them on a fast-moving stream. A sensu-ous dream placed me in a beach house with a young blond lover. I was whole — no missing parts — and I was much younger. I awoke mildly amused that I needed to go back to my younger self in order to recapture a sense of being sexually desirable. These simple dreams drew me for-ward, step by step, to where I was before Jill Ireland's death derailed me.

Fear abated, but bouts of depression came and went, weighing heavily when they occurred. Spring rains began and continued for days on end, bringing with them grayness and heaviness that pushed me far-ther into depression. A conversation with a friend from my high school days extended into a night dream. In the night dream, we discussed the spirit: the difference in individual spiritual paths, and the ability of the soul to participate in healing. There were several old friends and acquaintances in this philosophical dream-discussion of the soul, one of them a college history professor who had become a friend and spiritual correspondent through my years in graduate school.

Shortly after this dream discussion, I pulled out my old notes from college classes, searching for relevant information. I found my notes from a course on intellectual history — synopses of books and treatises that presented the philosophies of mystics, historians, and dreamers from many periods. I read long into the evening, surrounding myself with the stories of these individuals' searches for their spiritual paths; they ranged from mystics fasting in lonely cells to philosophers and poets such as Bergson and Rilke. Bergson identified so intensely with the spirit of people and objects that he practiced becoming the spirit of all that he looked upon in order to understand the internal and external structure of every animate and inanimate thing. Rilke's anguished search through the darkest places of his soul's night eventually brought him salvation and light.

The message for me was that these people found no easy path to spiritual growth; most of them entered the darkest parts of their own souls before finding repair and rebirth. Their stories brought me a comforting feeling of identifying with others who were on their own journeys of spirit and healing. Their descriptions of dramatic plunges into the depths of their darkest self and then equally dramatic soarings of soul to enlightenment and rebirth gave me consolation and hope. I discovered that I was in distinguished company in my exploration of the universe of emotion and spirit, which brought each of them to change, healing, and rebirth. On the surface, the dream in which I discussed philosophy with a professor from my past was simple and straightforward. In waking reality, the dream forced me to revisit a historical journey of healing, beginning with the mystical *Cloud of Unknowing,* a fourteenth-century work by an unknown cloistered monk devoted to the contemplative life, who spoke of blind intent leading to spiritual healing, and ending with Bergson's search for soul in all the elements of the universe.

My depression slowly moved away, like the changing set of a multi-act play. The sun came out and the warm spring days began to push the lingering cold away. My dreams also emerged from darkness and brought me healing and sensations of pleasure:

TRIP INTO A PERIWINKLE SHELL

I enter an enormous periwinkle shell, which seems to spiral upward into the sky. I begin to walk inside the shell, slowly at first, upward, but then faster. The climb becomes a joyous race, with me at first running and then riding a bicycle when the incline becomes too steep. I dismount and walk slowly again, sometimes running for a small distance, but always moving upward, proceeding past all the other contestants, until I, at last, win the race.

I awoke with joy from this dream: no pain, no fear, no grabbing of my insides by some invisible force deep within. I felt the joy of the dream itself, the joy of moving toward a goal and winning. I climbed my upward path both on my own feet and with the aid of my own vehicle — albeit a slow one, a bicycle that I was pedaling. Even when I dismounted from the vehicle, I continued, mostly walking slowly, sometimes running, but still progressing toward a goal. The sometimes slow and sometimes fast progression mirrored my daytime journey through the emotional turmoil and physical progress of my healing. I was approaching my third chemotherapy treatment, and I used this new dream to better prepare myself for the first three days of oral and injected drugs.

the third treatment

FRIDAY, JUNE 1, the third treatment began. The oral drugs produced a harsh, cumulative effect. I felt more drugged and sluggish after the first two days than I had felt during the first two treatments. Sleep was heavy, not pleasant, and my body ached. I continued to dream student/teacher dreams, indulging in further dream discussions. Robert appeared in two dreams in bookstores, guiding me through sections on philosophy and self-help, selecting books and then, back in a study, reading to me from the selected texts. I was not aware of specific titles in the dreams, only that I was learning how to move forward using self-help. This dream became increasingly relevant as Robert developed highly useful techniques for working with dreams, targeting important elements within a dream, bringing them forward, and presenting them for further use and exploration. These invaluable techniques included exploring feelings upon awakening, asking questions of the dream, doing reality checks, exploring "if it were my dream" with a partner, and finding ways to honor the dream after determining what knowledge was needed from it. I was able to use these techniques both in my dreaming and in sharing my dreams with Robert.

When I finally fell into sluggish sleep on the Sunday following the third treatment, I found myself, in a dream, sitting in another classroom discussing questions on the nature of humans. My dream teacher responded to the questions with examples: humans as the creative builders of their environment; humans as uncreative beings, simply serving time on earth; and humans as complete masters of their environment, often, but not always, to earth's detriment. The first person in the dream was building a beautifully balanced construction of wires and wood, an imaginative process that involved the mind sending information to the eye and hand for the creation and production of a balanced finished product. Healing, as a dream process, was active and creative, and could send messages via the mind to create a balanced, healthy body. The second person in my dream sat passively, allowing the environment to exist statically with no interaction. This person could effect no change, either internally or in the physical environment. There was a warning for the third person. The person with mastery of the environment was instructed to pay attention; responsibility came with the mastering — the responsibility of power to both create and destroy.

In this dream I took three lessons into waking reality:

1. **Dream healing** is an active creative process which uses mind pictures to effect body wellness.

2. **In order to be effective,** there must be interaction between the dreamer and his physical environment — bring the dream pictures into waking reality and use them to influence an outcome.

3. **Pay attention** and use the power of the imagination to create, not to destroy.

On June 13, during a mid-treatment blood-count checkup, Dr. Jay revealed that he had originally planned to cut my chemotherapy dose by the third treatment because most of his patients who were undergoing aggressive chemotherapy began to have more severe side effects at that point. He was surprised by the few side effects I had exhibited, and particularly by my lack of fatigue; my energy, in fact, continued to be wild and a bit crazed. My response to additional questions convinced him that he would be able to continue with the more aggressive drugs. My blood tests were normal; my cells were repairing themselves rapidly (recalling the dream of new boxes). The nervous energy continued through the weekend, but this side effect and the flu-like body aches were normal reactions to the abnormal level of poisons being pumped into my body. They were not dangerous and had no damaging effect on my heart or on cell repair, nor did they create any other serious problems, confirmed by the blood tests I had every three weeks.

rebuilding the body: healing and renewal

THE WEDNESDAY family pasta feast was now followed by the predictable Wednesday change in dreaming. The healing dream after my third treatment dealt with rebuilding and cleansing my body:

USING THE LOST WAX PROCESS
TO REBUILD MY BODY

A doctor comes into my room and says he has been sent to help. He takes my entire body apart; he pulls out all the dark, tired muscles, tendons, nerves, and so on, and begins to refill the body shell with new insides, using the "lost wax" process. The process is slow and tedious, but leaves me feeling rejuvenated.

My research into the lost wax process revealed an intriguing model for healing. The mold, made usually of plaster with a rubber material (for detail), is made from the original. Liquid wax is poured into this mold, cooled, and removed. The wax is then melted out (lost), leaving the space in which the bronze is poured. As a liquid, it flows into every tiny part of a mold and reproduces very fine details. After cooling, the mold is broken, leaving an exact reproduction of the original. After the raw bronze has cooled and been removed from the mold material, it is sandblasted and cleaned. It is now ready to receive its patina. After the patina is finished, a final wax is applied and the bronze piece is given a final polishing.

This dream lost wax process was, like healing in my waking reality, slow and tedious but the end result would be a perfect new sculpture (body), the new sculpture emerging from the rough casting of an original.

This set of images — the complete replacement of my old internal body parts — was interesting to work with. As noted before, I was convinced throughout my treatments that the best way to work with a dream picture and maintain its active influence over my body was to use it while actively pursuing the day's activities. The best time for listening in the day was either playing the taped dream in the car while driving or in a tape player near my desk. During meetings — there were many — I doodled on the side of my notes , so I began doodling pictures of my dreams — another way of keeping the healing dream active in my imagination. Doodling the earlier dream of cellular building blocks was great fun. I doodled the balloon dream and I doodled the more sophisticated scenes of replacing body parts. I doodled molds of rather primitive bodies, since accurate life drawing eluded me, and created little lost wax figures moving along the sides of my notes.

As I was reminded by my dream teacher in the dream of three men, healing was a creative process; healing was active. I had become ill while carrying on with my life, therefore I would become well while doing the same thing. My intention to become well could be manifested in endless creative exercises, from tapes to poems, writing, meditations, and even my doodling. All of these vehicles — and countless more — could carry the picture of healing to my brain. That process would take place no matter where I was, no matter what I was doing. The Lost Wax dream made an easy subject for work with a picture. In my imagination, I could see the replacement images: sculpting, washing, repouring, chemically treating, and reproducing the original parts of my body that had been damaged by illness, that had become tired from the chemotherapy treatments, that were exhausted from the bouts of depression.

This Lost Wax dream joined the ranks of the big dreams; for years, I used it for reentry and rejuvenation as a meditation, to share with others, and on recorded tapes using my own voice. In fact, to honor this dream, although I did not do this, it might be fun to actually make a simple sculpture using the lost wax process.

Dismembered and re-membered

THE FLU-LIKE SIDE EFFECTS began, as usual, a week after my third treatment, and I experienced the usual aching and soreness. The wig was hot and itchy and added to my discomfort during the mid-treatment side effects. Each night I replaced the wig on the white rabbit and, before going to bed, looked again into the mirror; I had a perfectly round head. The physical pain of losing my hair had vanished along with my hair, but now the skin on the rest of my body felt particularly sensitive and fragile.

The next Wednesday dream, a little more than a week after the third treatment, was similar to the Lost Wax dream and was filled with equally exciting images of healing. The dream was empowering and active in the same way as the Lost Wax dream. Together, the two dreams were my most powerful dream tools yet for working with the negative effects of the chemotherapy treatments and turning them into a healing process:

FIELD OF BODY PARTS

I am in a large field, plowed in rows but sown with body parts. The parts are all new; they have grown like plants from the earth. They are arranged by type, and each row of types is labeled. I am walking up and down the rows in the field, choosing new body parts to replace my old ones. I choose a mask (a face), bones, muscles, veins, and so on, until I have everything I need. Then I begin to put them all together. Pots of herb mixtures, including hyssop, are provided for me. I take the body parts, one at a time, and dip them into the herb mixtures, cleansing each one thoroughly before placing it in my new body. Once my body is back together, I go to a kitchen where Ron and some friends are preparing vegetables, including potatoes, sour cream, and meat, to nourish my new body. Ron and my friends pour the vegetables and meat over large plates of grains, and I eat them. Then I walk to the top of a hill, where there is a large gathering of people. Flyers are handed to the gathered people. I look down and see that there is a song printed on the flyer ("Brightest and best are the sons of the morning..."). We all begin to sing the song, and the words echo back and forth across the hillsides.

The day after I had this dream, in a moment of synchronicity while reading accounts of native dreaming and soul flight, I read an early account of the spontaneous initiation of a Samoyed shaman. The account described a man who was unconscious for three days, stricken with chicken pox, which was fatal for many of his people at that time. Nearly lifeless, he had a vision of descending into the bowels of the earth where he traveled to the island of the tree of the creator of the earth. The creator gave him a branch of the tree and instructed him to make a drum. He then traveled to a mountain where a confrontation with a naked man resulted in the loss of his head. The naked man chopped his body into bits and boiled the parts in a kettle. The spirit of the man pulled the body parts from the kettle, reassembled them, rejoined them with the head, and covered them with flesh. The man drummed himself back to life, awoke fully recovered, and discovered that he had the ability to heal others. In a slightly different format, this was my dream.

The experience of the "wounded healer" is not reserved for cultures distant from ours in time and place. The wounded healer can be found in each of us. In my dream of completely rebuilding my body with new parts, I experienced images remarkably similar to the vision of the Samoyed shaman: I went through a plowed field strewn with body parts, including tissue, ligaments, bones, organs, and flesh. I gathered all the necessary parts, washed them individually in a bucket of water and hyssop (a healing, rejuvenating herb), and reassembled them into my own healed body. Then I entered a kitchen — a service center for nourishment — and gave my new body its first meal, which included carbohydrates, proteins, dairy products, and vegetables — a personal recipe for dietary healing. In the final part of the dream, I joined a group of people in a popular song of festive praise. I used these images to create exercises in which the dream, combined with intention, became the key to the next phase of my healing.

When I shared this dream with Robert, he said, "Being dismembered and put together in a new way (re-membered) is a primal initiation into the healer's calling." He noted that this theme resonates throughout the literature on indigenous shamanism. Robert continued: "In my native Australia, the Aboriginal shaman-to-be might have the terrifying experience of being abducted by spirits, torn apart, and put back together with magical substances — often described as crystals — shot or inserted into his body. In gentler but no less authentic ways, this kind of imagery can also be used for self-healing."

Robert told me of a similar experience he'd had of being dismembered and re-membered. In a dream a bear he calls Bear appeared to him, cracked open his sternum, removed his heart, washed it thoroughly, and replaced it after lining the heart cavity with a soft, clean layer of green organic material that might have been, aptly, moss. Robert reminded me that our dreams are important tools for working with the energy body. In his own work, Robert's Bear sometimes comes to perform similar operations on other people's energy bodies, removing vital organs, cleansing them, and reinserting them. Robert explained that, whenever this happens, he offers the imagery to the people he is counseling so that they can work with it in their own way. This sometimes produces wonderfully positive and healing results.

Robert encouraged me to offer my dream of the Field of Body Parts to others for healing, just as he invited Bear to assist him in healing. We talked about using healing dreams to help others. We can dream for others, using the dream like a transplant. In transplanting or transferring a dream, we can take our own dream, rework it, if necessary, into language that speaks to the person who needs a healing dream and then offer the dream as a gift. In this way we transfer the energy of the dream — in the rich imagery of its message — to the other person. The dream might be told best as a story or as a poem.

Working with imagery is powerful because the body doesn't distinguish between a mental or emotional event and a physical event. If the images are experienced with sufficient intensity, the body will conform to our images. Our minds, as I had directly experienced, can conform to images in both negative and positive ways. By working with personal imagery — and changing the images in positive ways — we can actually create a new blueprint for the body. Our dreams give us fresh and authentic images that carry great energy, partly because they are specific to our immediate needs and partly because they draw on our deep subconscious. These are more powerful tools for self-healing than prefabricated visualizations.

Discussing my dreams with Robert not only helped me understand the relationship of my dreams to the healing process within my own body, but it helped me understand the powerful tools each of us carries in dreaming for others as well as ourselves. Every dream that opens a new personal healing dimension can open fresh perspectives to others in their own healing.

Dreaming with the organist

WITH RON'S ACTIVE SUPPORT, I used one of the key elements in the Field of Body Parts dream — music — in a way that proved to be deeply healing. As mentioned earlier, Ron played the organ for the local church, which was within walking distance of our home. He often practiced at the church in the evenings, and I would walk there with him. He would turn on a foyer light and the lights around the organ, leaving the main body of the church in soft darkness, lit only by the glow from the organ box. In the dark aisle of the church just below the organ box, I would lie down and close my eyes with my arms, legs, back, and head resting on the floor. As Ron played, the organ chords sent the music vibrating from the top of my head to the tips of my toes. I allowed current dream images to flow through my body, washing over and through every organ, through my blood, bone, tendons, muscles, nerves, lymph system, fibers — through every part of my body — washing and cleansing, with the deep vibrating tones serving as an active dream.

Smaller dreams of cleansing and renewal followed the powerful Field of Body Parts dream, in the now-familiar format of groups of smaller dreams following a Wednesday healing dream. The small dreams presented dark clothing made white when it came out of a washing machine and a wall of blackboards turned white when I began to walk along with an eraser. I took the small dreams, which came like clockwork after the larger dream, and worked them into my now-familiar set of exercises. My favorites became the taped meditations I created and the dream prescriptions. I also discovered, with Robert's encouragement, that I enjoyed turning my dreams into free verse. My poems probably weren't profound, but they invited the dreams to speak in a different creative voice, like the doodling of dreams in the margins of otherwise boring meeting notes.

the fourth treatment

THE FLU-LIKE SYMPTOMS disappeared sooner after the third treatment, and I returned to normal more quickly. On Thursday evening, June 21, I prepared for the fourth treatment and began taking the oral drugs. Summer was approaching. All the trees and flowers were blooming; the sun was shining. The original owners of my nineteenth-century Victorian house had been world travelers; one of them had dabbled in horticulture, and a few exotic trees and shrubs remained from their travels, including a yellowwood tree. Every two years, if the weather conditions were right, this tree would produce a show of unparalleled beauty and aroma; this was one of those special years. White lemon-scented blossoms blanketed the entire tree in long white cascades, filling the yard and house with an exquisite aroma and attracting thousands of bees. The air vibrated with the buzz of bees hanging on the thousands of blossoms. People stopped their cars to ask questions about the tree, admiring its incredible beauty and inhaling its intoxicating fragrance. This tree spoke to my spirit, filling my heart and soul with joy and peace.

It was Friday, June 22, and the fourth treatment was over. I rallied better from this one. The premedication side effects were less severe and, for the first time since the chemotherapy treatments began, I felt victorious. I felt somewhere deep inside that I had defeated the cancer — not just for this treatment, not just until the next treatment, but forever. Dr. Jay had originally said that I would know when the cancer had been destroyed. With this treatment, I felt the destruction of the remaining cancer cells. My post-treatment dreams were humorous: several dreams in which I was wearing my wig, and one in which I was working outside in the hot summer sun, wearing the long country-western-style wig that I'd tried on in the wig salon. In one wig dream, I became confused because I was braiding the hair on my wig, but I didn't know if it was wig hair or my own hair. In waking reality I was still bald, but little fuzzy bits of hair were growing back. More startling than my bald head with tiny fuzzy bits — to which I had grown accustomed — was my strange image in the bathroom mirror one morning. I stared for quite some time wondering why my face looked so odd, rather large and more an expanse of white than normal. Then it struck me — I had no eyebrows or eyelashes. I thought, "Well, of course — the chemotherapy doesn't affect just hair on the head." I had also been vaguely aware, without really concentrating on it, that my pubic hair was thinning. I did a quick check — yes, it was gone too. I had been concentrating so much on my head that I had not even noticed the gradual disappearance of other hair until its complete disappearance made such a dramatic difference in the way I looked in the mirror.

Ron stroked my bald head each evening before I went to bed, which gave me a wonderful tingling sensation on my delicate, fragile skin. It was also an important ritual of having someone's hands touch and soothe my afflicted body parts.

During the third and fourth treatment periods, I used and reused my earlier repertoire of significant dreams, sometimes adding drawing or poetry to my repertoire. New small dreams focused on my wig. The healing rituals continued to be important: the ritual of Wednesday pasta, the ritual of Ron stroking my head, the ritual of using music as a major part of my healing.

I still slept fitfully because of the drugs, but I felt better than usual. I read throughout one night, and finally slept through the next night. Dreams continued to focus on my wearing a wig, some of them mirrors of the anxiety and discomfort I often felt around strangers who didn't know why I was wearing a wig or even that I was wearing one. The fake hair was more obvious to me than to others, but I didn't yet have the courage to be seen in public without it. At home, and in the company of friends and neighbors, I removed the wig.

On the evening of Wednesday, June 27, my healing image dream appeared, on schedule:

CASTING OFF THE WHEELCHAIR

I have a wheelchair available to me, but I am not confined to it. The chair is almost like a stage prop — not necessary to the "play," but available if needed. I take the wheelchair to a sandy hill overlooking a beach filled with people. I am with one other person. I push the wheelchair off the edge, and I stand watching it careen down the hill, crashing and disappearing. I walk alone onto the beach and mingle with the crowd, appalled at how sunburned they have allowed themselves to become. I am more appalled at the lifeguard, whose duty I interpret as not only being to keep the people safe from harm in the water but also from sun damage. I follow two small children up the hill. They are badly sunburned and splotchy red, and I am very angry.

I awoke both angry and empowered by this dream. While recording the dream, I noted that I was an active participant in this change-dream. The dream vehicle — the wheelchair — was a vehicle that I rejected. I chose not to use a vehicle that could be driven or pushed by someone else. In fact, I sent the wheelchair — a vehicle for the ill or disabled — careening down a hill where it was destroyed. Then, no longer confined to a vehicle for the disabled, I took on an advocacy role, mingling in the crowd and identifying a problem. My anger was directed at the "lifeguard," who had failed to protect my body and allowed the cancer to occur. After that, the lifeguard had continued to do nothing to stop the downhill progress of the disease. The cancer had occurred within a normal, healthy body whose natural defenses had turned against it and behaved like an enemy. The sun, usually identified as a natural life-giving element, had become an enemy — against which the assigned guardian had not offered the needed protection.

Smaller companion dreams followed the lead of this new parent dream. My subsequent dreams focused on themes of rebuilding according to a set of plans or influencing other people to build according to my set of plans. The theme seemed to be that "every action has a reaction." Whatever I did influenced the actions of others within the dream, creating cause-and-effect relationships. I drew blueprints for others to follow or created recipes, which an army of cooks would follow in large restaurant kitchens. Perhaps this mirrored the reactivation of my immune system, which had to relearn how to heal properly and copy healthy cells, not damaged cells — how to create rather than destroy. My favorite among this set of dreams was one in which I lived in a suburban subdivision of identical houses (an interesting mirror of cell structure):

I stand at the end of a driveway that looks like everyone else's, but then I use a set of blueprints to begin reconstructing my house and rebuilding a stone wall at the end of my driveway. Others who live on this road, curious, come out of their houses and begin to peer over my shoulder, looking at my blueprint. They like my design and begin redesigning their own driveway gates using my set of specifications.

In these dreams of rebuilding, I was fully involved in the process that began with the big dreams of the Lost Wax Process and the Field of Body Parts and culminated in the dreams of rebuilding cellular structure in a healthy pattern. I only had two remaining chemotherapy treatments. Rebuilding was moving forward.

The summer was also moving forward, and I was invited to a neighborhood Fourth of July picnic for an evening's respite. I was glad to go, but I sat a bit uncomfortably. The humid heat further distressed my swollen arm and hand, magnifying the normal side effects caused by the drugs. I was resting the swollen arm on the edge of the picnic table and listened as a neighbor related the story of a friend who had just died from cancer. I'm sure she did not realize the effect of her story on me at that moment. In hearing about the person's death, I slipped briefly into feeling sorry for myself. I stared at the swollen arm and felt the heavy emotions of the realization that the lymphedema was not going to go away. It was a life problem that I was dealing with poorly. I could no longer wear my wedding ring, and some of my favorite clothes with long sleeves no longer fit properly or, in some cases, did not fit at all. The lymphedema could be managed, controlled somewhat, but would be there the rest of my life as a personal reminder of my illness unless a miracle treatment surfaced. There could be a miracle; I would hold that belief as a possibility. I went home for a few hours, sat alone until I pulled myself out of the funk created by my reverie on my arm, and then returned to the party.

My neighbor's house sat on the top of a ridge just above the main hamlet. The evening progressed into a more refreshing night, and a gentle breeze on the hillside where we sat was accompanied by thousands of fireflies. The children gathered around the adults, piling into available laps, and we all watched as the men lit fireworks: Roman candles, wheels and spirals, all spinning, bursting, and fizzing into the air — a spectacular private show. Two of the children had crowded into my lap, singing softly, talking low to one another, and gasping at each new burst of fireworks. I looked around at my friends huddled in blankets across the hillside. Everything was working toward healing.

Roller-Coaster Days

*T*he last message in the dream of exterminating the bats was that after the room — my body — was clear, I curled up peacefully on the bed and went to sleep. What a simple and beautiful image! How difficult it was to achieve in physical reality. Some days I felt well and at peace with the progress of my healing. Other days I felt drained of emotion. Then on other days — the most dangerous days to give energy to — I felt depressed, alone, and sometimes even frightened of a future I could not physically see or hold.

a reverie on the realness of dreaming

LATE AT NIGHT I found solitude in reading. Sitting on the sofa in the soft light of evening reading other people's words brought home to me the importance of my dream journey, an adventure in healing unlike anything I'd ever imagined. On those evenings of wellness and peace, dreams conveyed a language of healing that became precious and beautiful in the discovery of how perfectly the sleep dream and the waking body could work together side by side. I read late into the night when I could not sleep and discovered remarkable journeys into dreaming in novels, biographies, and poetry. I was learning the language of my own dreams, and I was learning to communicate and translate my night dreams into my waking life.

In *Wind, Sand, and Stars,* I found Antoine de Saint-Exupéry's expression of dreaming particularly relevant to the power I felt in my own dreaming. His main character, an airline pilot, has crash-landed in the arid wasteland of the Sahara, lost in the middle of a great desert because of a collision. There, in dreams that fill his soul and body, he discovers a reality greater than the Sahara. He gives himself over to its magic. In the aloneness of being stranded between sand and stars he takes a mind voyage into his childhood memory of a house which manifests itself in a universe of dreams. There he discovers that the reality of his dreaming is more intense, more personal, and more real — a source that touches the eternal language of soul — than the waking reality of the vast desert and endless starry sky. He finds solace in his dreaming that sustains him until his physical rescue is accomplished.

In this reverie I ventured — in my own dreaming, in shared dreams with others, and in my evening readings — that my dreams, too, brought me to an intense and personal reality that sometimes superseded and always accompanied the reality of my waking life. My dreams were more than mental pictures of a house or car or body parts in a field. When I walked into the "dream study" to discuss Calderón's dream with Robert, I was there in the study. How else would I have remembered from reading the play in college that there was a passage relevant to what I was experiencing now, over twenty years later? When an angel made the waters rush at the Pool of Bethesda, I was there and could have walked healed from that pool if I could have trusted the reality of being there within the dream in the same way Saint-Exupéry's character trusted the reality of his dream house. When I pulled a drowning boy from the shallow water, I recognized him over thirty years later. How could I have dreamed this person when I was nine years old if dreams did not hold some reality far beyond my ability to grasp and — even more telling — how could I have come to meet him thirty years later and both of us recognize the story of my dream being the story of his waking reality at the same time of my dream? Healing within a dream is magic, because it is born in a space lacking the boundaries of physical reality. In that space miracles and magic are normal; the magic can be transferred to waking reality and to the physical body.

In the dark moments — which butted powerfully against the light — I forgot the magic for a time. I wanted to understand how, as a person with breast cancer who was undergoing a treatment regimen that was common to thousands of women, I was still an individual with an individual reaction to my illness, to my pain. I felt in dark moments that I was the only one with the pain, but I knew that I was one among thousands who were — even at that moment — experiencing the same pain, the same illness. Even worse, at unguarded moments I sometimes felt so isolated in my vision of illness that I shut out those who I felt could not possibly understand my pain. I even felt a little superior to them because I had emotions, a pain, and an illness that they had not yet experienced and would never experience in the same way I experienced it. But I could not remain a stranger with a vision of illness, cut off from the world. One person with a vision of illness — the wounded healer, the magic in the dream — had the unique ability to enlighten the world with one individual piece of the puzzle, particular enough to that person to make a difference for someone else who experiences the same illness in the same way. I could offer my individual knowledge of my pain, my illness, and I could be part of someone else's healing if I offered access to my piece of the puzzle, to my dreams.

small glimpses of wellness

DURING THE LAST MONTHS of that long summer, all of my dreams were of final, active healing, some as simple as my hair growing back. These small dreams came in the night as multiple dreams, piling one on top of the other. It was impossible to determine if one might be more important than another. They all bore messages, and the messages were that I was healing — slowly in spirit, somewhat faster in body. In the physical healing, I continued to suffer radical mood swings. But through them all, my dreams presented positive images and predicted a more hopeful outcome than I allowed in waking. They foretold a time when I would feel healed and whole again. In fact, they went beyond the feeling of wellness to a time when I would use my own experience to help other people work with their own cancer. Frequently, the person I assisted in a dream would be a child, and the help I gave focused on problems with chemotherapy or emotional reactions to hair loss and feeling abnormal.

Years later, I recalled one of those dreams when I was training to be a "Make-A-Wish" volunteer, a dream bringer for children with life-threatening illnesses. In the dream:

I am standing behind a young male child who lives in a trailer park. His mom and family are nearby. He is depressed not so much by the illness but by the physical manifestation of the treatment: his bald head. I tell him about my own chemotherapy treatments and my own bald head. I pull my long hair forward for him to touch so that he can realize that his hair will grow back. Thrilled to hear that I suffered the same physical loss of hair and had recovered, he smiles and puts on a hat.

Other dreams presented glimpses of my friends and family offering me help and encouragement. Many of them were simple dreams of various people in my kitchen preparing food for me or assisting me with food preparation, always a theme of nourishment and nurturing in my dreams. Sometimes I dreamed that I was working in a kitchen: a small precognitive view of service to others as well. A neighbor of mine also had a dream in which I took on this role of service: she saw me lying in a circle of mutual friends, but they were sitting and I was wrapped in a cocoon. I suddenly threw off the wrappings and danced into the center of the group, telling stories and sharing wonderful adventures of life and dreams.

the fifth treatment

I HAD TWO TREATMENTS LEFT. July 13 was the scheduled date for my fifth treatment. I asked Dr. Jay if I could move the treatment one week later. He checked my charted progress and determined that moving the treatment would not harm the treatment schedule. I had been invited to speak at a history conference that weekend and wanted, if possible, to have more clarity than I would have at the beginning of a new treatment. The conference focused on a different theme each year, this year's, coincidentally, being medicine and healing. I pulled together research files I had put together on eighteenth-century medicine in the Johnson household and presented my subject to an audience of medical doctors, psychiatrists, and psychologists. During breaks, when presenters became acquainted with the audience, I sat in on conversations that led to discussions of alternative methods of healing in the twentieth century. This presented an opportunity to talk about dreams and healing. I found that the physicians attending the conference were open to the possibility of dreams as a source for diagnosis and for healing imagery. I was pleasantly surprised and pleased at their acceptance of the idea of dream healing. The conference also provided a chance to feel like I was back into a comfortable routine in my life — history conferences and historical research.

I returned home from the conference, buoyed by the positive response to my presentation and excited about the prospect of nearing the end of the chemotherapy. Over the next few weeks, I met several men and women who spoke of their own highs and lows, particularly near the end of their cancer treatments, but theirs were born from suddenly losing the security of the cancer-fighting drugs. I felt anticipation and joy as I neared the conclusion of the treatment drugs; my roller-coaster ups and downs came from another source: the still-tenacious Dance Hall dream, telling me that my life would end within the year.

creating my own dream

THE FIFTH TREATMENT presented the usual litany of side effects — familiar to me now as uniquely mine — but they continued for much longer. The days seemed endless, passing at a snail's pace. As Wednesday approached, I looked forward to my usual post-drug "change" dream; it always forecasted my healing for the treatment period to follow. This Wednesday dream focused on my growing personal empowerment:

CREATING MY OWN DRUM

I am a student, studying in an atrium-like classroom, reading philosophy. The teacher is explaining something that I'm having trouble grasping. I leave the room and go outside where large skins have been stretched on the ground for drying. I clean them and fashion them into a small drum and a large drum. I join a friend and hold up the drums. The drums begin to "drum." It is unclear who is drumming; the real drummer seems to be invisible, a spirit. I reenter the classroom, but now it is filled with people. The teacher announces that I have completed my studies. He tells me to look inside the book. I back up several steps and look into a book that is now open in my hands. I understand that all my lessons have been recorded in this book and that I must choose the ones that apply to my life at that time. I am quite excited. I begin to rapidly circle selected portions of the book that I recognize as choices I have already made, and I place other circles around choices still ahead of me.

I felt buoyed by this dream. Although an invisible hand was drumming for me, I had made the drums and I had control over my choices in my life. My choices were protected by divine guidance from the invisible drummer, but control was still in my hands. I had already made choices that I recognized, good or bad, and I circled them as already accomplished, then moved on to the next choices. There were multiple options. The simple message of this dream was positive: My course of study was complete; I had other choices ahead of me.

In another dream at that time:

I crawl through an undersized door into a future where my body is functioning normally again. When I stand up and turn back toward the door, the door is gone; I did not have to return to the state I was in, the abnormal state of illness and discomfort.

Previous doors in my Dance Hall dreams had led to death and represented going to the "other side." This door presented a positive future. Around that time, I also had dreams of the end of the chemotherapy treatments, and several dreams in which I faced a magic mirror and saw an image of myself with hair.

In waking reality my hair was returning; a light fringe of soft baby-like hair covered my previously bald head. I never wore my wig at home, and I sometimes went to work without it. One of my staff members loved the way I looked with no hair. I thought she was simply being supportive until she cut her own hair so close to her scalp that she had little more than I did; she still wears her hair in that fashion. I wasn't sure what I thought about the way I looked with so little hair, and I often reviewed my face in the bedroom mirror. I didn't care for my plump, round face with just scarves or hats; I thought I looked frumpy and somewhat ridiculous wearing just a hat with no wig. Time had begun to reduce the number of places where I felt I needed the wig, but I always wore it when I ventured out into malls, work meetings, or any place where there were larger numbers of people. As soon as the soft frizz of hair appeared, however, I began to leave the wig at home more often, where it sat on the white rabbit on the bedroom dresser.

the sixth and final treatment

THREE WEEKS PASSED, and it was time to take the Prednisone and the Compazine suppositories in preparation for my last chemotherapy treatment. Dr. Jay was out of town, and another doctor was scheduled to administer my final tests. He walked in for the pretreatment consultation, flipped through my treatment notes and charts, and looked up with a curious expression on his face. He was reading through the list of drugs and the level of chemotherapy treatments I had received. He noted with some humor my incredible ability to ingest large doses of poison and look as though I had eaten a normal meal. The entire set of treatments had been at maximum level; my body's tolerance for them was apparently phenomenal. For the last time, I walked to my seat with a view toward the woods. Usually the hour passed quickly, but today it seemed endless. I watched the drugs drip through the tubes, mentally ticking off their names in my head. Then the last drop of the last drug disappeared into my veins. It was over; the end was anticlimactic.

the treatments are over; why aren't you springing to life?

I RETURNED HOME, and the week progressed in the usual fashion. The side effects were a little more severe, probably lingering a little longer because of the immense buildup of toxins in my body. The fuzz-like growth of hair on my head became thicker, and I looked at it frequently in the mirror, talking to it, encouraging it to grow like a gardener talking to young plants. I was pleased to see eyebrows and eyelashes — and pubic hair — growing back. It was all returning.

I still followed Ron to the church in the evenings and stretched my body full-length on the aisle floor below the organ box, feeling the resonance of the music moving under and through my body, feeling the music fill my body with sound and beautiful, unearthly tones that vibrated through every organ, every bone, every nerve. I would doze for a few moments, allowing the sounds to relax my muscles, to push away the tension and anxiety, to bring healing to my body, and to wash away the effects of the long months of drugs. Although the cancer was gone and my body was returning to health, the return was slow. The build-up of aggressive poisons in my body left me more sluggish and foggy after the last two treatments. Unlike the first four treatments, the drugs seemed to linger, leaving me with the feeling that I was walking in a kind of physical aura.

After the final treatment, my dreams reflected my desire to have a normal day with normal feelings. In some of the dreams I was swimming. In one dream I waded in a grotto, simply listening to people who were walking, sitting, and standing near the grotto, all of the people in the dream having normal conversations about their ordinary daily lives; I felt comfortable in this dream. Several weeks after my last treatment, I dreamed that I walked into the consultation room and saw Dr. Jay reading my dream journal. He expressed some surprise at my having recorded feelings of anxiety, and he told me in a very professional, matter-of-fact tone that I was fine and quite well now and that I had no need to worry. These dreams should have been all I needed for assurance.

unresolved dream of death: the dance hall

I HAD COMPLETELY TRUSTED the early dreams that diagnosed my illness, yet now I searched for a dream that could take me beyond those dreams of healing and wellness. My body was mending well; my mind was not. I had dreamed my death in my forty-third year, and no other dream had convinced me that I had eradicated the message of the Dance Hall dream.

During the next seven months, I found myself on a mental roller coaster. Each day began with feelings of fear and anxiety, sometimes mild, sometimes so intense that I had difficulty breathing. I experienced complete joy at my physical healing, then plunged into the darkest of depressions. Just when I thought I'd conquered depression, a word or thought or action would trigger the depression and fear again. There were seven months left in the year designated in the Dance Hall dream as my year of death, and I had a contract to fulfill — a contract that I must, in some way, renegotiate. I struggled with the belief that my life could not be over. There had to be another option than death. There had to be a reason why I discovered the cancer. There had to be a reason why my body had healed. There had to be a reason why I was still alive.

My dreams had provided a warning of the breast cancer. They had followed me through surgery; they had presented me with pictures for visualization and assistance through the chemotherapy treatments; then they had shown my body healed and given me a picture of myself helping others. But my dreams still had one more scene to play out; I was still living under my original contract. There was something of destiny in the Dance Hall dream that still swept over me in unguarded moments and made me feel that I had one more dream to dream. I began to search for and ask for that dream. With all that had happened — with a healthy body as a result — I still needed to get beyond the Dance Hall. No dream had truly ended that hallway dance. I had to have a dream that, once and for all, closed the door and extended my life.

ANGELS

*T*homas Wolfe in *Look Homeward, Angel* speaks of stone angels
being touched by miracle and bringing magic to the world.
What southern child does not have Wolfe's angels engraved in
her memory? That child knows that angels, whether carved in stone or
in air, exist in the living, breathing shadows of her soul and body, exist in
her nights and in her days, and exist in her dreams. I know that there is
only a fine line between my days and my nights, the realities of each
crossing and recrossing until the lines are blurred and the realities are
meshed into a continuous stream of thought and action. Carved angels,
angels in the air, the penumbra, the shadow of a soul.

But my fear held me in the talons of a dream I could not shake. I
wanted to see angels and hear the voice of my spirit. I doubted my
healing if I could not see some presence or hear some voice. I had experienced spirit and healing in my dreams, but I seemed unable to pull
them forward into my day. I had felt the presence of magic and the
workings of an invisible force many times in my life, but I wanted something bigger than all of that — something so big that all my fear would
dissipate, something so big that the dancers in the hall of the dead
would fade and the messenger of death would find another soul to claim.

I looked for angels — big, glowing angels with outspread feathered
wings. I wanted the largeness and realness of the angels of Thomas

Wolfe, the angels of mythology, Rilke's angels of joy and terror. Wolfe's larger-than-life stone angels found themselves locked out of his life, confined to pace a monotonous circle on an old southern porch. Like his dark angels bound to an endless cumbersome path, I wanted to be invited to find peace within.

In Africa I had walked in a funeral procession, feeling the vibration of the shaman's pounding staff as it beat back the spirits of the dead and their souls to their appointed place, as it beat a protective shield around the living, as the pounding rhythms beat into being the heartbeat of the ancient leopard and brought our steps, one at a time, to the edge of the forest. At the edge of that forest in a small, walled cemetery loomed a giant hovering angel carved by some colonial English hand, an angel of towering proportions. Its wings soared above the scrub brush, above our heads and hearts, beating against the intense blue African sky, transmuting the native beating of the staff into my white southern soul. This angel had seemed so far away from home, I had felt so far away from home, yet I had felt so close under its sheltering wings. Where were these angels? Angels had come to me before when I needed them. I might never have seen them as towering figures with wings, but I felt them in the soft magic of dreaming and coincidence.

angels in my life

AN OLD WOMAN in Arkansas — who greeted me each evening on my walk home from work — predicted the birth of my child months before I was pregnant. I was asked to come inside her house one day and accept some roses she had chosen for me, and I entered through an amazing doorway carved with enormous Wolfe-like angels whose wings touched above my head. Throughout her house smaller carvings of angels sat on tables, hung on the walls, and seemed to be in evidence everywhere I looked. She said I would have a boy child. When my son was born I only questioned why, with so many angels sheltering her house and guiding her life, I had not believed her prediction when it was first given.

When my son was a baby, my car careened off the road along with several other cars, all of us stuck in a blinding snowstorm. I was only half an hour from my destination, but my baby would need a warmer, safer place within a short time, and the prospect was bleak. The sliding cars all sat criss-crossed and sideways on a steep hill surrounded by rolling hills and long fields. Houses were miles away. There was a soft tap on my window and I rolled the glass down. Smiling through the window was a young man with red hair and a red beard. "Follow me," he said. I never questioned why or how. I started the car and followed his car as he led me through the maze of other cars, up the hill and then, remarkably, across a small flat field and back again to the road. The weather changed dramatically as I made my way through the next few small villages. Ten miles farther on, I saw the same young man helping another motorist out of a ditch along the side of the road. I continued on for some miles before it occurred to me that, under normal conditions, I could have never navigated through those cars, could never have crossed into that small field with ordinary snow tires in an ordinary car, could not possibly have seen this young man yet again ahead of me on another road. I could never have reached my destination without divine intervention on some level.

Years later, when my son was a young man experiencing difficulty with school and experimenting with dead-end jobs, I asked what he wanted to do and how he wanted to get out of his rut. We talked about the army and other military service options, but they didn't appeal to him. We talked about a friend in the merchant marine, and that interested him. I looked into it and discovered that the merchant marine didn't even exist as an agency as it once had. Evan sighed with disappointment. I sat at my desk feeling disappointed in my search and sad for my son. At that moment the telephone rang. A brisk voice announced an officer's rank in the Air National Guard and apologized for not returning my phone call sooner; he had been away for a few days serving as a pallbearer for Nixon's funeral. I was startled and told him that I hadn't called him. He said that he had my name and phone number on his desk, so we both went through the scenarios of my phone calls over the previous few days, none of which would have placed me in contact with this man. Then he said, "So tell me your story." I told him about Evan, his history of learning problems, and his search for a way out of his present situation. "I have two sons," the officer said, "one is a lawyer with a fancy degree; the other spells his name backward and loves the Coast Guard." After he hung up, I looked at Evan for a moment. "Coast Guard?" I asked. His eyes lit up. He geared into a level of motivation the likes of which I hadn't seen in years. The gentleman on the phone left no name or telephone number, only a rank. But he changed my son's life. Why did he have my name? Was he an angel for me and my son?

Three months later, Evan had his high school diploma and was packing his bags for Coast Guard boot camp. Just before he left, he told me that he'd had a recurring dream in which there was a long brick building with no doors and no windows; recently the dream had changed, and the building now had windows and two doors, one leading to the ocean and one to the land. Three months later, I was watching Evan on television in the uniform of the Coast Guard Honor Guard. To this day, Evan tells me that he loves every moment of working with the Coast Guard. I believe in angels.

My mother called me when I was wrestling with my need for angels and a conclusion to the Dance Hall dream. She spoke of my father's death, which had left her more lonely and depressed than I'd realized. My father had been the other major person in her life and I, her only child, lived thousands of miles away. I'd been too caught up in my own problems to think about anyone else's. My mother told me that she had been crying every day. My father had begun to appear in her dreams, demanding, gently at first and then more insistently, that she pull herself together and get on with her life. She couldn't do so, and he had ceased to appear in her dreams. "Then one day," she said, "I was standing in the kitchen and began sobbing again. I looked up and you were walking toward me as though you were right there in the room with me. There was light everywhere. In front of you was an angel with enormous wings, but I could see through the angel and still see you; I could see both of you at the same time. The angel wrapped its huge wings around me, and you told me you had brought me your angel to comfort me — that I must stop crying and move ahead with my life." She had stopped crying at that point; the fear and pain left and she slumped into a chair, wondering what had just happened to her and knowing that she could never tell anyone but me this story because people would think she was crazy.

As she told me the story I felt sad, wondering why I couldn't see my angel as clearly as she had. I envied her the visual experience, the assurance beyond herself that she would be able to go forward with her life without fear. I needed that kind of visual assurance to know that I could be well and continue to live. I wanted to see my angel; the confidence of sight would give me confidence in my life.

Then a neighbor called me. Her husband had died in a terrible accident years before. She told me that, early that morning, her child ran downstairs and tugged excitedly at her dress, almost shouting:

"Mom, Mom, you never told me that the people we love come back in our dreams and give us messages. Are they angels now?"

"Yes," she had answered.

Throughout my healing, I had received guidance: dreams of my departed grandmother, dreams of sacred healing pools and safe passages, the dream of my father pushing me away from a place of death (Easter Island), and the message in Africa that I needed for my diagnosis. I had angels all around me, and I wasn't listening. I found it even harder to understand my own role in helping my mother find release through her enviable vision of me with an angel like the enormous stone angels hovering in the African forest.

a conference in Montreal

IT WAS A MONTH beyond my last chemotherapy treatment. Our New York summer felt much like a southern summer, the hot oppressive days moving slowly, blending into humid nights, providing a surreal backdrop for dreams that offered me images of healing and rebirth, slowly chipping away at the anxiety I felt each morning upon awakening.

My dreams focused on my depression, offering me help and guidance in dismantling the paralyzing fear I had constructed. I awoke early one summer morning trembling from a brief dream, not unlike earlier dreams in my chemotherapy treatments of being assisted in my passage or journey by an invisible presence. This one addressed my fear:

I cross a body of water on a high narrow plank, a place of particular terror for me because I am afraid of heights. In my attempt to cross, I begin to slip and my fear is almost insurmountable. I move back and find myself needing to make a decision; I need to cross. I need to move forward, not backward. Then two invisible presences move to either side of me and place rails beside the plank, increasing the width of the passage. My fear subsides, and I cross with no difficulty, other people close beside me.

These spiritual guides prepared a path that would allow me to move forward. But I still wanted to feel the bigness of them.

Around this time, close friends and even family — Ron and Robert — who knew me best were becoming annoyed with me; they expected me to appreciate my survival and to function as I had before. The chemotherapy had ended a month before, and I was expected to show gratitude and joy about my survival. I wanted to feel happy, but I could not, nor could I explain the depression to myself or anyone else. I couldn't find its source. I tried conventional meditation and imagery exercises, but the depression and anxiety were always there, waiting like a shadow for the moment the morning light woke me from sleep.

Ron and I attended an architectural history conference in Montreal, hoping the change of scenery would lessen my depression, but the feelings of aloneness seemed to deepen. The September air in Canada was already brisk. I walked the old city of Montreal and tried to enjoy it, but I was haunted by a vague sense of discontent and worthlessness. I walked with Ron, slightly behind him as he photographed old buildings. The chemical withdrawal from my last chemotherapy treatment flooded through my body at unexpected moments, mingling with my depression. I felt increasingly foggy and disoriented, and I began to hallucinate, seeing an even older city. Women, old and young, emerged from doorways; I saw them as they looked a hundred years before, scenes from their lives passing through my mind. I had walked into a dream. Wandering the streets in a daydream of past conversations, I reviewed the preceding year of my life, reliving specific events and conversations, seeing vignettes of my life everywhere I walked, as though an invisible hand were winding a movie reel. The important and the unimportant blurred together, sentences of spent conversations rippling across time, past scenes brought forward to the present showing me how a word or a thought could change my future and my individual time and space.

I couldn't tell anyone what I was feeling. In restaurants, in shops, on crowded streets my body flushed hot in the cold air, the feelings of misery and discontentment welling up inside me and exploding into tears. My behavior was erratic. Instead of being an enjoyable, relaxing period after the chemotherapy, the Montreal trip was a miserable excursion of foggy memory, sunlight too intense for my eyes, and meetings from which I left early because nervous, vibrating energy would not allow me to be still. This had to be some kind of dramatic letdown period after the ingestion of so much poison, now trying to find its way out of my system. When I told another chemotherapy patient my experience she laughed and called it "chemo brain" — a disorienting feeling of not really being part of the world, which builds as the chemotherapy progresses. She told me that, after chemotherapy, she would think she was talking in complete sentences, only to discover that she'd left out most of the words. She told me it would probably take as long to move completely beyond those feelings as it had taken to undergo chemotherapy — not an encouraging timetable.

Back at home I moved like a robot, responding to the demands of days with no names, forcing myself to laugh and respond to the people around me. My self-demands for normalcy prevented my telling Ron how I was feeling. I wanted so much to return instantly to good health that I refused to acknowledge to anyone the devastation of the leftover chemical fog of the now-ended treatments. Night dreams reflected my days, presenting me with a blurred potpourri of images and emotions, colors, shapes, and scenes of endless choices. One dream showed me scenes from my southern childhood that held special memories, including a chinaberry tree growing and thriving from seeds sown in a desolate environment of sand and dust; when it was watered and fed, the nourishment allowed it to take root and grow. The dreams piled on top of each other, night after night, like an overdose of answers that I could barely sort through by day. They repeated a past theme of safe and unsafe venues, and there was always someone providing a safe and pleasant choice for me. In one dream, I drove my own car down a one-way street to a large chain-link fence that surrounded what I thought would be my access to the larger cityscape. Just as I became discouraged, the gates opened and there were roads everywhere, all leading to the city I sought. Most of the dreams were remnants of memories, little more than shapes and colors when I awoke, but together they felt like a grab bag of pleasant surprises — if I could just pull myself together long enough to reach in and pluck one.

The dreams continued. In one I spoke Spanish, which I don't do in waking life. In the dream I translated Spanish poems into English, including a poem about the sun and the promise of living. In another I played games of chance, tossing tiles back and forth across a board, waiting to see where the next move would lead. In one dream a pyramid of people, who looked like gymnasts, confronted me, one of them holding two signboards, the word "anxiety" on one, "depression" on the other. The one holding the signboards crowned the pyramid. Other gymnasts came and crowded under the bottom row, raising the entire pyramid and pushing "anxiety" and "depression" farther and farther away until they finally disappeared into the sky. I honored the dream with physical exercise, inspired by the image of the gymnasts pushing the signboards of anxiety and depression into the air. The answers seemed so easy in the dreams: just push the anxiety and depression away and they will be gone; exercise in the gym and all will be well. My mind sought angels, and there were none.

visions of my future: the spirited forest

I TOOK THE MESSAGE about the gym into my waking reality. I joined a fitness center and dealt with the internal tension through physical training. As I moved the weights up and down in my hands, as I crunched stomach muscles, I listened to the instructor calling the proper moves and proper breathing — a concentrated process of inhaling and exhaling. The accumulated dreams of a year flooded my thoughts, and I used them with each movement of my body, taking all the dark and desolate pictures and exhaling them with all the strength I could muster. Then I would inhale the images of growth, renewal, and healing into my body. The physical exercise became a healing exercise, another way to actively honor my dreams and physically integrate the dream imagery. I felt that I was breathing life back into my tortured mind and body.

After undertaking this exercise program, I had a dream that explored integration:

THE BALLET

I am working in two places: a long narrow room containing a double row of school desks separated by an aisle, and a furniture factory filled with heavy machinery and heavy carpentry tools. Each place represents a different kind of labor: mental and physical. I leave the classroom late at night carrying an armload of carefully labeled, beautiful old handmade carpentry tools made of wood and brass, including two planes, a level, and a square.

I enter the factory and leave the tools on a table. I remove two of them for my husband and then I turn, startled to see the tools coming to life and glowing with beautiful colors. The life in them becomes more and more vibrant. The levels and squares become the arms and legs of people who begin to dance, performing an extraordinary ballet in the air accompanied by bell sounds and music that seems to emanate from the air. I watch, startled, and move quietly beneath the dancers into a back room where a man is holding a small child in his arms so that he will not get his feet dusty in the sawdust. The child wiggles and squirms until he is placed on the floor, where he scuffles happily in the sawdust.

I leave the factory and return to the classroom, where people sleep at night at the desks, renting them as one would an apartment, learning and resting in the same space. I tiptoe around the sleeping people, gathering more of my things from the classroom to take into the factory where all of the items have gathered. All the knowledge and tools from my dream classroom become part of a living dance, merging and integrating, the mental and physical, each bringing "tools" to the other, each a vital part of the other, each dependent upon the other.

I awoke ecstatic from this beautiful dream of mental and physical integration. The whole system was working in perfect coordination. Everything was alive and in complete harmony, and I awoke feeling joy rather than fear. All the tools available to me were there in the shop. In the classroom, students remained throughout the night and continued to learn in the night — the time when they dreamed. They found solutions to their problems in their dreams, like a modern-day temple of Aesclepius. In the original Hippocratic oath, doctors swore by gods of healing, including the god Aesclepius. In ancient Greece, dreams and visions were the most common method of inquiry into the cause and cure of disease. In the temple of Aesclepius, diagnosis of illness and healing took place in the state of consciousness just prior to sleep, when images come forth like frames of thought projected on a movie screen. This dream was a confirmation that the answers to all my problems could be found in my dreaming.

I still struggled with the problem of how to bring dreams forward into the day to work with my anxiety, how to honor them and make them so much a part of my day that I could eliminate my fear. For reasons unknown to me it was easier for me to work with dreams for my physical healing than for my emotional healing.

a menu from the spirited forest

SOME OF MY DREAMS were light, ordinary dreams that dealt with the day's events, conversations, and small problems. As I began to think more about my daily responsibilities and the need to take care of those around me and pay more attention to their problems and their joy, a dream came in the night that reflected those neglected needs of others:

THE SPIRITED FOREST

A partner and I are hired to work in a restaurant, but something has to be ordered for us before we begin. We look at the restaurant — "The Spirited Forest" — and must decide whether to proceed or to wait. I decide that we will proceed; the place needs help. The cook is a large, happy man with no dishwasher. The dishes have piled up, beginning with just a few, but now numbering 119, piled precariously. Leftover spaghetti clogs the disposal unit, and the cook begins raging. However, the place is not hopeless. It is popular, on a busy corner, quite appealing, located in the old nineteenth-century section of the city. Robert joins me, interested in the area as an investment but bored with the two women showing him and his wife around. As Robert checks on exotic stones strung in a necklace at a street vendor's booth, I move toward my husband. Ron is at the end of the street playing Chopin at a piano set up on an improvised platform. The area is cordoned off from the street traffic to form a stage, and shoppers are listening to him play. He is dressed in a tux for the performance.

I move on toward some undeveloped land, joined by Robert. We cross fields, travel up a small embankment, and move through a fringe of wandering homeless people who follow us along the way, begging. One of the men snatches at my coat and I walk faster, a little alarmed. We come into an open field, and Robert begins to unveil his plans for our development — something that includes me. People begin to fill the area. The plans, on the surface, seem to be physical — real estate or investment plans — but a book idea begins to materialize, peopled in the air and played out on a blank field of dreams.

Meanwhile, to take care of the homeless people, Robert asks a woman to bring in a portable soup kitchen to feed the people. I assist with the feeding and send money back with the woman to supply coffee and other drinks. The people are happy, flocking around the warmth of the soup-kitchen stove, digesting all that we are giving them. I feel a special joy in taking care of other people.

This dream brought me a fully stocked kitchen of motifs connected with food and nourishment. The restaurant kitchen represented my personal environment or, more precisely, my spiritual environment. This kitchen explored problems: food-processing machines were not working and cleansing machines, such as the dishwasher, were also not working. However, the restaurant had a hopeful name — "The Spirited Forest" — and the cook was happy in spite of the problems. Ultimately, I found satisfaction in helping others find nourishment, thereby giving myself joy and fulfillment. The real nourishment in the dream came from activities outside, not inside the restaurant.

There were messages for Robert in this dream, possibly foreshadowing some of his own writing on dreams and dreaming (the "field" of dreams) and interesting associations for both of us with writing and investing. In the dream, we both explored undeveloped territory and avenues for healing and nourishment. Ron discovered fulfillment in playing music for others and even had his own performance stage. In waking reality, his music had power in my healing; this dream expressed the value of music in healing for other people. In the dream Ron was playing Chopin, which he often played late at night in waking reality. The music would travel from the parlor, where the piano was located in our house, up through the air vents into the bedroom where I breathed the music into my soul for comfort. As I drifted off to sleep, the music would blend into the opening of my early evening dreams, becoming part of the magical cocktail for healing and renewal.

The portable soup kitchen in the dream foreshadowed my involvement with others who were going through their own battles with breast cancer, possibly introducing them to dreaming as an alternative means of feeding the soul. There was a message about the inner joy and peace that comes in taking care of the needs of others. As part of honoring the dreams of my healing and recovery, I made a pact to help other people who were going through their own cancer battles. I felt I had discovered a gift in my dreaming and wanted to make other men and women aware that their own dreaming could provide them assistance in their healing journeys. Within a year after having this dream, I had volunteered with several outreach groups and a partnering organization that placed me in direct contact with other men and women who needed to talk to someone who had experienced cancer in her own life.

There was also a warning in the dream — the man snatching at my coat — to protect myself and keep my involvement under control so that I could maintain my own good health and energy. This dream brought together messages of nourishment, of needing and finding assistance, and eventually of opening myself to the needs of others as well as meeting my own needs.

blocked paths

I HAD ANOTHER DREAM only days after the dream of the Spirited Forest that was similar in language to the dreams in which spiritual guides widened my traveling path:

I am walking through construction debris and equipment, all of which is blocking the roadway to a bridge that is undergoing repair. The bridge has a curb on the right and a sidewalk on the left. I place one foot on the curb and realize immediately that it is unsafe and leads nowhere. I walk to the sidewalk on the opposite side and look down and across the bridge. Nothing is in my way; the path is clear.

Dreams with similar — in fact almost identical — themes came night after night. In looking back, I think the dreams held the theme until I finally "got it" in waking reality. The dream of the blocked roadway was one of the theme dreams that came night after night, dream after dream both during the chemotherapy treatments and in the months afterward: roads, safe and unsafe; ladders with broken rungs and solid rungs; countless dreams of choosing a safe, sure path that would lead to my goal. The choice was always mine to make in these dreams, but there was always a safe choice and an unsafe one. In some of the dreams, I not only had the ability to make the correct choice (and the correct choice was always obvious; who would step on a ladder with broken rungs?) but I was frequently given the opportunity to go back and try the other choice or path if the first one didn't work. I was puzzled about what these safe and unsafe choices represented.

Among these dreams was a turbulent, troubling dream that reminded me that I had not yet found the answer I sought for the complete waking fulfillment of body and soul:

CONFRONTING MYSELF

I find myself in a restaurant, holding a bowl of food. Startled by a woman, I drop the bowl and run from the building into the streets, where I begin the relentless pursuit of the woman. I cannot let her get away. She moves in the dark behind houses, through gardens, around buildings. But just as she thinks she is free, I am there. The pursuit ends at a white clapboard house with a long porch. Confused at my own behavior, I look at her and realize, startled, that she is me. We are each vying for control, but we are separate. I walk into the house, look into a mirror, and see a small, unwelcome child attached to my back. I shake myself violently and trick the child into climbing down onto the dresser, where I destroy it. I beg for help, and the child disappears. At first I do not know where the other "me" is and I am afraid. Then I realize that the other "me" helped get rid of the unwelcome child; we are there together.

I awoke frightened and troubled. The restaurant and food in this dream provided no nourishment; I dropped the bowl of food, startled by another part of myself I was unable to integrate. However, when I saw the "unwelcome child" in the mirror, I shifted into a more positive mode and began to violently shake the child off me, eventually using trickery to manipulate the child into a position where I could finally destroy it. I had asked for help in shedding a dangerous and unwelcome attachment: fear, anxiety, and the inability to bring my life together after my physical healing. The help I sought was within me all the time, and I was able to recognize that I had successfully integrated my divided selves in the destruction of the dangerous, self-defeating attachment.

removing the wig

MY BODY slowly began to return to normal and my hair began to grow — not just soft fuzz, but real hair. I felt and looked more normal, which enabled me to look more closely at my anxiety and the rather warped view I held of my future. I was comfortable enough with my physical appearance to remove the wig, but the fall air was cold, an encouragement to continue to wear the wig as a hat to cover my unprotected head.

Thinking about the wig as a hat rather than as a chemo-head covering inspired a new night-dream theme. I had dozens of dreams in which I asserted a style all my own. In the dreams I staunchly defended my new style, refusing to return to a former manner of dress or self-presentation just to please the crowd. In one of these dreams, I stood before a large easel in a painting class, painting my picture in a style unlike any used by the other students. I refused to conform to the dictated painting style.

In another dream, more directly related to my hair, I walked through the same dream sequence again and again, much like scenes from the movie *Groundhog Day*. I strolled down a model's runway, each time sporting a new hairstyle, all of them different lengths and different colors. In the same dream, I tried on many scarves and hats from designer shops, the shopkeepers stood in a reception line "oohing" and "aahing" over my dashing new hat, scarf, or hairstyle.

I told Robert about these dreams and, to honor the dream theme, he took me shopping for a hat. It turned into a fun adventure of trying on hats, posing in front of shop mirrors, and finally selecting a hat that took the place of the wig.

October: national breast cancer month

IT WAS OCTOBER, a month designated a national focus month for breast cancer. The media was saturated with information on the disease; every magazine and newspaper contained articles announcing breakthroughs: gene therapy, new drugs, new treatments, new discussions of causes and cures. News and magazine stories focused on women's demands for more research money and better treatments; they demanded to be taken seriously; they demanded a cure for this terrifying disease. Publicity focused on diet and fat grams and their association with both the cause and the cure. Magazines, TV programs, and news articles forced the public to digest information on breast cancer. Some of the information cheered me; some depressed me. Had I used the wrong treatment or had my child been born too late — should I have breast-fed him in a decade that discouraged breast-feeding? Probably, but it was a bit late now.

Everyone, including me, looked for answers outside themselves about why there was so much breast cancer.

Questions raised by the news media influenced my dreaming as well as my waking. I dreamed of missing links in communication. I began searching for missing objects: In one dream, I searched for a missing stone in a field of diamonds but never found it; in another I combed through clutter and debris in a space that only moments before had been clean, uncluttered, and sparse.

In one dream in this series, I lived in a slum apartment, carrying things up and down stairs, all of them crooked, painted black, and strewn with debris. Among the debris was a telephone with the receiver off the hook; no one could reach me. The debris trailed along the stairs to a clean, sparsely furnished, "put-together" apartment. In another dream, still dealing with the theme of my inability to communicate or be reached, I attempted to find a place to pray with a priest. But a noisy, disruptive family interrupted my conversation with the priest, preventing me from hearing his response. In waking reality, I read and listened to conflicting news reports, but the information was worse than debris; it was contradictory and confusing.

October ended and November began and pressed on. Early one morning, I sat up in bed terrified; I had dreamed, or perhaps just thought (I couldn't really recall a dream) that I had only six more years to live. I was appalled at my inability to integrate my new healthy body with what should have been a healthy spirit. Something was still wrong. I was exhausted from the battle with myself, and I carried both the exhaustion and the battle into my dreams. In dreams, I fought with strangers and with friends; I destroyed the wig over and over, sometimes throwing it away, sometimes burning it, sometimes throwing it at other people.

A year had passed since I first told a doctor that something was wrong with my breast. I was cured of the illness. My body had responded splendidly, and, except for the lymphedema sleeve I would always wear, I looked fairly normal. One day I stood quietly in front of the mirror — the same mirror that had shared a year of changes in my body — and looked hard at myself and at the wig that I now rarely wore — for whom? Not for me, not really. I only wore it for the few people who might still be uncomfortable with that soft new growth of hair that named my illness and announced to them that I was different but not so different; tomorrow or the next day or the next year they might be facing the same disease. One in eight; a scary percentage! I looked at the stuffed white rabbit sitting on my dresser and placed the wig back on his head. Then, a few days later, I removed the wig from the rabbit's head, placed it in its original box, and pushed it back into the corner of the largest, deepest drawer in the dresser; I didn't take it out again. I longed for the day when I could do the same with the dream of my death — the Dance Hall dream. My demon was a dream that foretold my death in my forty-third year. I had worked to change the outcome of the dream, but I had no confirmation that I had changed anything.

On December 7, three months before my birthday, people from the Dance Hall dream appeared again, but the dream had begun to change:

I'M STILL SITTING WITH THE DEAD

I am standing in front of the dresser mirror, but it is a dresser from my childhood. Straightening the shoulders of a new silk dress, I look at my image: my hair is shoulder-length, and my face is somewhat changed. I appear to be my current age. Sitting on the bed are childhood friends, still children and giggling like we did as children and telling me how to arrange the dress. I walk out of the house and enter the side door of another building. I am walking rapidly because I am late. I walk up the stairs with an older man and woman, who assure me that I am on time. The building is my childhood church, but the sanctuary is on the second floor. I walk down the aisle and choose a pew crowded with stacks of hymnals. On the pew sit two girls I knew as a child. I sit down in a space cleared for me, and I look around at the congregation. Friends from college and high school sit around me, waving and nodding to me, but they are still teenagers. The hymnals disappear from the pews.

I look toward the choir loft. The minister announces that the choir will be composed of all the young men who went to war. The young men march down the left aisle, some in military garb and some in white suits with red flowers on their lapels. Martha, a childhood friend who is sitting on a side aisle, taps one young man on the shoulder to tell him to straighten his lapel. He turns back, and I realize that these are the young men from high school and college who died in Vietnam. Some of the people around me died earlier; they are the people from my Dance Hall dreams.

ANGELS

The young men walk to the choir loft and turn toward the congregation, each one softly shrouded in a foggy white light. One by one, they vanish. But this time I do not move. I sit in the pew watching them as they vanish, but I do not disappear.

I am forty-three years old in this dream. I have hair, and I am alive. I do not waltz out of a door into death, and I do not disappear when the young men fade away. I am alive at the end of this dream. Wasn't this the dream I had been waiting for — the dream that changed the ending of the Dance Hall dream? Forty-three years old and alive; the dream that ends my fear. But it is not. There is no mending, nothing that prevents my waking with a jolt and a terrible dread that ties my stomach in knots and closes my throat, leaving my breath short and painful. Hours pass before I can throw off the fear, the gut-wrenching anxiety. Although I am alive in the dream, I'm still participating in a dream among the dead; something is still wrong. Even my family has no idea of the depth of anxiety the remains of an unfinished dream has left in my life. I carefully disguise my days and hide my fear in work and home activity.

My birthday is just months away.

Renegotiating My Life Contract

*I*t is December. A year had gone by, a year since dreams of warning led me to doctors for confirmation and surgery. I scheduled follow-up exams, beginning with a mammogram and a gynecological exam. Uneasy, I sifted through dreams and memories of the past year, including my travels to Asantemanso, the village where no one died, and Esumeja, where my father visited me in an intense dream demanding that I seek help.

A wealth of powerful and empowering dreams had come to my aid in this year and in the two years before. Those dreams stood as companions through diagnosis, through surgery, and through difficult medical treatments and brought me safely, with the guidance of unseen powers, over bridges and across barriers of enormous magnitude. I had come a long way in my healing, but I was still haunted by a single dream that followed me even when my body looked healthy — even when my dreams, which I trusted, told me I was healed.

Perhaps I was completely healed when I took Robert's hand and entered the Healing Pool after the angel stirred the waters; perhaps I was healed when I felt intuitively that the chemotherapy had destroyed all the stray cancer cells. Perhaps that intuition heralded a defining moment when, as Dr. Jay had predicted, I could stand back and say: "I had cancer; now I am healed." But my mind wouldn't rest. It traveled again and again to the dream of death. All those healing dreams and the healing medicine, aided by dreams of energy and life, had not diminished the power of that dream. I was nearing the end of the year of my foretold death. What did I fear — that on the morning of my birthday I would be seized by some giant hand from that dance hall and pulled through the door at the end of the hallway? Perhaps. I needed one more dream. It had to be a dream of such power that it could dislodge forever the hold of the Dance Hall dream. I asked again and again, night after night, for that dream.

the Ghana

IN RESPONSE TO MY PLEA, I received a dream that brought me back to Africa where, in a sense, my healing journey began:

I receive a gift from Africa. I open a large box addressed to me and find inside a large glass jar containing water and a small animal labeled as a "ghana." It is a little animal, but I cannot determine exactly what it might be. I turn the jar around in my hand, trying to see the small creature. As I lift the jar, water pours from several holes in the jar. I try at first to stop the flow of water, then realize that the water must flow out. When I realize this, the water is joined in its flow by strings of jewels and bright metallic geometric shapes strung on chains. Colors sparkle and move in the light. Now I have a clear view of the animal with the curious name. It is small and quite beautiful, with multicolored skin and a dragon-like tail, much like a small harmless lizard that crawled in the West African sand. The vulnerable animal has been protected by a coiled blue snake that leaves once the jar is in my hands. I look up the name of the animal in the dictionary and discover that it has integrated two distinct features in one body; it can live both on the land and in the water. When threatened, it has learned to shield itself with a hard-shelled skin, which is its primary protection.

I felt good about this dream. It was not the dream I sought, but it sought me that evening. The name of the dream animal was also the name of the country in West Africa where I had journeyed shortly before my surgery. I felt a power and a mystery flowing to me from Africa through the dream, and I had vivid memories of my encounters with seers and sacred drummers and the formidable Queen Mother of the Asante people. I also saw the Ghana dream as a mirror for myself and what I was becoming. It coaxed me to release "bottled-up" emotions and move beyond the mental boxes I had constructed for myself. It showed me myself as a vulnerable yet beautiful and exotic creature, protected by a force I didn't fully understand before its release, with the ability to adapt to different environments and muster its own defenses. One of those mental boxes included the Dance Hall dream. One possible message of this dream was that I needed to break out and discover my own defenses. Before I could arm myself, I still needed assistance with breaking the box that held the Dance Hall dream.

the cold room

THE NEED to put on the dream-ghana's body armor became even clearer when, in mid- December, I went in for my first annual medical checkup since my initial diagnosis of breast cancer. The mammogram and other follow-up exams showed no problems. The gynecological exam showed irritation in my uterus and cervix, a result of the harsh chemotherapy, but I was otherwise normal. I felt positive and hopeful; some of my pent-up pre-exam tension eased with the good news.

One week later, I walked into my house after a pleasant day at work and punched the answering machine button. A caller was just recording a message. I picked up the telephone and a curt lab technician coldly announced that I had an abnormal Pap test; she had no information about the degree of abnormality. She then told me that the first appointment available for retesting would be in January. I was devastated. The fear, almost terror, returned in an instant; I could not go through this again. I was numb with fear. I hung up and made some phone calls. I cancelled meetings scheduled for the next day and called the doctor's office again, angrily telling them they must see me earlier, that I could not wait until January. The physician's assistant, using her most professional tone, told me the cells did not "look right," that they should have repaired themselves from the chemotherapy by now, and that my doctor could not see me again before January. I paused, took a deep breath, and tensely told her that I had often driven forty-five minutes to the doctor's office, sat for two hours, and been asked to give up my appointment for someone else's emergency. I had always agreed because I recognized the importance of someone else's fears and needs. This, I told her, was an emergency for me and I expected her to find someone on that appointment list who could do for me what I had done for others for years. She was silent for a few moments, then asked if I could be there within an hour.

The test — a colposcopy — was far from pleasant. A searing mustard-colored cream was placed inside my uterus and cold tools were used to scrape away samples for a biopsy. Staring at the ceiling, I scanned my inner archive of dreams and memories, reaching for something that would help me endure the painful exam. There were hundreds of small holes in the ceiling tiles, small doorways to another dimension. I connected dots, created imaginary landscapes, drew blueprints for houses, painted animals — anything that could place me just outside the experience so that I could relax and endure the pain and discomfort. Afterward, I dressed and went to my car. There was no encouragement from anyone in the office — just brochures and pamphlets on uterine, cervical, and ovarian cancer, all of them coldly breaking the cancers into stages of development.

I sat in the same car I had sat in a year before, in the same parking lot, grasping the same steering wheel, fearing that the same process was beginning again. This time I did not scream. I sat still and closed my eyes, reaching somewhere deep within myself, as deep as the very dreams that brought me life, far beneath the fear and anxiety, and I asked myself to name what I saw. I pulled forward a mental image of my body and placed it on view; I asked myself again what I saw. I must, like the ghana in the dream, use my own resources to find the answers. I visualized my body spinning. I could see both sides, inside and outside, and I asked myself one more time what I saw. I saw nothing wrong; I saw a healthy body. Could I trust a simple image brought forward by my mind by asking a simple question? I could trust a dream, therefore I could trust an image brought to me by my mind's eye.

I went home to await the test results. Although I saw nothing alarming in the scanned image of my body, I could barely eat or sleep. I was exhausted by thoughts of having to possibly go through more testing and exhausted by thoughts of having to wait for the outcome of the colposcopy. And I was exhausted by my obsession with the Dance Hall dream. I begged again for a dream — not just a dream about the test, but a dream that would carry me beyond the dream of my death. Instead, my dream that night told me that my ordeal was not over. Shortly after the dream, I woke in a cold sweat. This dream was not the dream I sought for confirmation of life. This was a terrifying dream that confirmed that my death was at hand:

MY TIME IS UP

I look at the date. It is December 29, and I am still forty-three years old. I am thinking about my life, its value, its length. I seem to be talking about all of this with someone who is very important and who has considerable authority. I try to see this person, but I cannot. The person is telling me that it is time to leave; I have used up my allotted time. I have fulfilled my contract, and it is time to leave. I look everywhere; this person is a messenger for someone else. There is someone more important who has more information for me.

I awoke gasping for breath. The dream experience was entirely real, and I was frantic. I needed to change the ending of this dream and I did not know how. I was not ready to leave, but there was such authority in this person's presence that I knew there was no other acceptable response within this dream. I tried to go back into the dream and change it. This person was a messenger, and somehow I had to go beyond the messenger to that someone else who was out of sight and out of reach and who carried more authority than the messenger. I sat in fear and questioned how to deal with the emotions generated by this dream. Could I do it? Could I change a life contract that I had made at some time, perhaps before my birth? I had just been told by a dream messenger that I'd reached the conclusion of an agreement I'd made before my physical life began. I had to find the authority beyond the messenger. But how?

I shared this terrifying dream with Robert. I also told him about the colposcopy and my new wait for test results. He'd had to cancel a business trip to the Bahamas. He asked if I would like to take his ticket and his place at the hotel in the Bahamas and sort out some of the negative stuff in my life. I told Ron I thought perhaps I would take Robert's offer and go spend a reflective weekend in the sun, alone and in a bright space where I could sort through dance halls, messengers of expired contracts, and the dilemma of new medical tests. After some fancy talking at the airport, Robert accomplished the impossible; he convinced the airline manager to find a way to allow me to use Robert's unused ticket. I left on this short, unexpected trip to the Bahamas, not knowing the test results, shadowed by the terrifying realization that I might not have the choice of life.

The sun, the beach, and the strong young strangers playing in the sand and water should have lifted my spirits, but they simply became blurred, jumbled images to me. I found myself entering their space, intrigued by their momentarily carefree lives. Watching them playing out a few moments of their lives within my view, I had the sense of millions of people like me across the earth, all clamoring for answers to each of their particular problems, all seeking their place and purpose, all seeking a response from the same higher authority. How important was I among all these people — important enough to go beyond the messenger? I walked back and forth between the beach and my room several times during the day, attempting to reach the doctor's office to ask about the results from my tests.

I enjoyed the time alone to think and communicate with myself, but I discovered that communication with the people who were supposed to give me my test results was impossible. The doctor had just left; the doctor was with a patient; there was no answer; the office was closed for the day. I left phone numbers and messages, ate dinner, left more messages, and paced the exotic lobby, unimpressed by tanned bodies and beautiful clothing. I talked to Ron, and he also had been trying between meetings and job hours to locate someone with my test results, but ran into the same dilemma.

The moon shown full that night in the branches of the palm trees outside my window. The ocean glittered and danced with silver streaks of moonbeams and stars. I felt so far away from people who cared about me; I felt an immense sadness that no tropical breeze could lift, and I felt small, so small against the backdrop of palms and moonlight and ocean. Perhaps this trip alone to a beautiful place to work out dreams and test results was not such a good idea.

Three days later, the taxi to the airport jauntily bounced past expensive vacation homes juxtaposed against tents for the homeless erected in palm groves. The radio endlessly named attendees at christenings, weddings, wakes, and weekend funerals, punctuated by intervals of thirties blues and Sunday gospel. The world marched on in spite of me: life and death, paying no heed to one small person returning home.

Home was unusually stifling. Communication with my doctors was impossible; every imaginable barrier seemed to come into play. Ron even stopped by the doctor's secondary office, where he was told that he would find my gynecologist, only to discover that she had left on an emergency.

Finally, after almost nonstop phone calls, I reached my gynecologist's colleague, who told me that she had the test results but couldn't interpret them for me since I wasn't her patient. It was the proverbial straw that broke the camel's back; I exploded in anger. I shouted at her, relating in quick, angry sentences the days of missed telephone calls, the anxious days and nights of missing the exact moment when I would have had the opportunity to speak with my doctor. I told her that I had just come out of an entire year of chemotherapy only to find myself faced with the possibility of another kind of cancer. I stopped talking. I was exhausted and could think of nothing else to say. There was a moment of silence. The doctor on the telephone looked quickly through my folder and responded in a soft, quiet voice: "You are fine. Are you listening? You are fine. You must do some follow-up tests for us so that we can monitor you, but you are fine. There are no cancer cells. Are you listening? Please tell me that you are listening to me. I had no idea what you were going through. I am so sorry. There are no cancer cells." I thanked her. I relaxed. There were no cancer cells, but what else was going on? Was my life over anyway? The dream of a contract that was "up," the higher authority. Could I reach that authority? Could I talk to God and make God hear me? I was so exhausted.

My dream that night mirrored my insane plunge into a desperate search for the authority beyond the messenger:

I dream that I am running from danger. After hiding for days with friends and a large wolfhound, the dog and I find the path out: a narrow footpath through an alley that will lead us out of the city and into the open countryside, where I can escape the danger.

A narrow footpath — a narrow chance for safety, but who or what would lead me there? I stumbled through the days, unable to shake myself free of the dream that told me my time was up or the belief that my contract was ending. I tried desperately to revisit the dream, to talk to the messenger, but I could not bring back the dream.

The winter moved on, but I hardly noticed. Each night I asked for my dream guides to take me beyond the messenger, to allow me to view my contract, to permit me to discover the key that would turn a year of positive healing dreams into a future, to allow me to back away from the door at the end of the dance hall. Instead, I dreamed many dreams about the peopling of places familiar to me. I dreamed one dream in February about the village where I lived and of all of its inhabitants, each of them performing their ordinary daily activities, myself included. Then a second dream drifted in like an overlay, softly creating an alternative reality in which the same people lived in different houses, in different economic situations, performing the same daily activities but in a slightly different environment because of different choices they had made somewhere, some time in their lives. In this overlay I, too, was different. I was less caring and less generous, and I liked myself less.

I awoke from this dream realizing that I had chosen well so far; my life choices were good ones. However, I had regrets. I wanted more: more choices, more chances to enjoy my family and friends, more opportunities to make a difference in other people's lives. Could I change the contract by changing my direction, by creating new paths and opportunities? Or had I already changed the contract? Was that less caring person the person who could not go beyond the messenger? Was the dream of my contract expiring about her or about me? What did a year of sacred healing dreams have to do with this contract? They had to be gifts from the authority who was now teasing me in such a terrifying way. Were my guides and angels so fickle that they would take away all the gifts in a single challenging dream about my life contract that was linked, in my mind, to the Dance Hall dream?

January and February kept me in the teasing and unnerving suspense of asking for a dream not yet received. I moved through work and at home as though I were indeed walking down a Dance Hall waiting for an answer about the wooden door at the end.

March 9 arrived. I was born at midnight on March 10, and I would end my contract the next day unless I could change it. I was alive, not feeling that I was living on borrowed time, and yet the "contract" dream continued to haunt me day and night. In its simplicity and vividness, it became a constant part of my life, reminding me daily that I had an important unresolved issue that I must confront before I could feel that I'd come through this illness well, whole, and mentally and physically intact.

I carried the dream of the contract with me all day. Whether or not I had exaggerated the importance of this dream, it seemed to hold the key to the resolution of the Dance Hall dreams. I fell asleep that night, thinking about the messenger and the higher authority, asking one more time for permission to go beyond the messenger, asking one more time whether I had already reached the end of my life.

signing my new sacred contract

IT WAS EARLY MORNING when the dream I'd been waiting for occurred. I had asked for this dream, but I never expected a dream of such power, such terror, and such overwhelming support for my life.

I was asleep and then, in what seemed like only moments — the same kind of warp-speed passing of time I experienced in my surgery — I came awake, sitting up in my bed sobbing, not understanding where I was or what had just happened. I could not separate the waking from the sleeping, the sleeping from the dreaming. Ron asked over and over what I had dreamed. I desperately tried to hold every detail, tried to fully grasp the most incredible experience of my life, not even sure if what I had experienced was supposed to be fully remembered. The dream seemed to be dissolving, details vanishing in my desperate attempt to retain it all. The dream was overwhelming, empowering — the beginning of my life, not the end. I picked up my paper and pencil, but my hands were shaking so badly that I couldn't write or think. Ron sat silent, waiting for me to capture whatever I needed to capture from the night. I was awed; I had gone somewhere in my waking and dreaming where I had never gone before, somewhere I would never have believed possible. I had reached beyond the messenger and encountered a presence so terrifying in its beauty, power, and light that I was sure I was not supposed to remember all of the experience, but I remembered enough of the power and magic to know that I had another chance at life:

WINNING A LIFE EXTENSION

I am moving up a mountain more rapidly than I have ever moved in a dream. I seem to be borne by some invisible hand, and at the top of the mountain I am at the feet of a powerful being. I cannot even look at this being. There is light — incredible light, the likes of which I could not even have begun to imagine. I try to look. Is this my angel? It must be. I cannot see a face or even a body. There seems to simply be light — immense, indefinable light. But I am aware that this is more than light, that it is Presence. I then realize that I am pleading, begging for my life at the feet of this Presence. I argue, weep, beg, and lie sobbing and ter-rified at its feet, but I am never so frightened that I back away. I have gone somewhere in my mind beyond the fear. I have finally gone beyond the messenger, and I must make this Presence understand.

The Presence moves slightly, and when it moves it moves in waves of energy and light. It almost has a form, but not a form I can name — not a form like any I could ever imagine. Thought seems to transfer across the waves of energy, but I never hear a voice. This Presence seems to transfer emotion without speaking. Sometimes it is solemn as it listens to me; sometimes it is bemused at my frail attempts to explain why I need to remain on earth. I speak more and more rapidly, and the Presence seems to become more and more bemused by my frailty.

I acknowledge that I had agreed, before arriving on earth, to leave when I was forty-three. This Presence holds a contract in front of me — a contract with a signature that I identify as mine. I am pleading again. I am bargaining, telling this Presence that I had not wanted to come here, to this earth, but that now I have a family and friends I love and I want more time with them. I argue with the Presence that it must already real-ize this, since it has allowed me to make this contract and allowed me the warning dreams about my illness. If this entity had granted me the warn-ings, then it must intend to grant me life. Time elapses — time that seems both an eternity and only seconds. A new contract is presented with a new date — a date I can't recall when I awaken, but it is far into the future — a date I can have no argument with.

I collapse at the feet of the Presence, and I feel myself coming awake.

I needed to be alone with my dream, and Ron understood that. I went downstairs. I sat alone downstairs in the parlor for hours, holding pencil and paper, sometimes trembling and sobbing, sometimes shivering with either cold or confirmation of this enormous dream. Ron quietly joined me after awhile and sat quietly in a chair nearby, understanding that I needed to sit separately for some reason. This was not a dream in the way our society understands the word "dream." This was unlike any experience in my life. I had been awake and asleep at the same time; I had entered another reality. The renegotiation of my contract had been real; I had moved beyond the messenger to a supreme spiritual authority who had allowed me to add another lifetime to my life. This new contract would carry a different kind of responsibility: the responsibility of understanding why I was here. Perhaps I was waiting for a dream to remember why I was here — not that I was healed of a disease but why I was here on this earth in the first place.

The need to accept the responsibility of why I was here was not stated in words in the dream; it was implied in the granting of a new contract. I knew without hearing it said that when I accepted my new contract, I also accepted my new life with new purpose and new responsibility to the world; whether the world be my hamlet or the larger world community of men and women, I could give something back in return for being on the earth a while longer.

The fear and the tension were completely gone; they disappeared with the renewal of my contract. This was the dream that not only went beyond the messenger with the original contract, but finally and completely dissolved the hold of the Dance Hall dreams. I was convinced that I would never again experience fear in quite the same way. Spiritual and physical integration was completed in that dream; the diverging paths had come together, and the door at the end of the dance hall was closed. I was alive because I dreamed. I had renegotiated my life contract in a dream with a Presence — a spiritual being as terrible and wonderful as any angel imagined in a southern child's dreams, a towering Presence that left me whole in the shadow of its wings.

I took a few days to digest this dream and then I shared it more fully with Ron. We talked about it for a long time, both of us aware of its enormous import in my life. Then Evan and I discussed his own dreams for his life, not yet in a form tangible enough for him to recognize. One morning I traveled to Robert's house, about an hour away, made myself comfortable on the floor, and retold my dream. We discussed where I was in my life contract and began unraveling what that contract might hold for me. Robert was just beginning to write about techniques he used in working with dreams, and he was experimenting with presenting workshops on dreams. He had just held his first workshops and had invited me to speak to people about my experience with dreams and healing. In this way I had already begun to find my voice in working and sharing with Robert. I was finding my voice in other ways as well. I was volunteering for fund-raising walks with the American Cancer Society, speaking to other people facing cancer that I met almost everywhere I went, plus, as a natural part of living in a very small hamlet, talking to people in the hamlet's old-fashioned general store — where everyone gathered at some point on a weekend — about dreaming.

Robert reminded me that our first experience of working together with dreams came when he was researching Iroquois material in the colonial documents. Some of those associations had been with a mountain. We attended workshops in Iroquois stories and dreaming led by a Mohawk, Tom Porter, at Mount Lebanon, the old Shaker community, turned Sufi retreat, mentioned earlier. My new dream of renewing my contract had led me once again to the top of a mountain. Important assignments have been given throughout history on the tops of mountains. Moses himself brought commandments for living back down a mountain after an extraordinary experience of his own. Mystics, philosophers, ancient gods: an endless host of good company found answers and their place in history as a result of life-changing experiences on tops of mountains, some sought for, some received unbidden. I felt intensely in the entire experience of being before the Presence that I had been given an assignment on my mountain, not to be healed — that had already happened — but to speak, to live, to give back all that I had been given.

"What kind of dreams do you dream?" my grandmother had asked. Now I could answer, "I dream my life."

Part 3

BRINGING DREAMS HOME

SHE WHO DREAMS

J no longer ask myself why I needed so badly to have one more dream for my life. I needed that dream to remind me that, although I was doing nice things for myself, my family, and my community, I could go farther. I had entered life with a purpose and a responsibility. In renegotiating my life contract on the mountain I needed to give voice to my dreams, and move into a larger role of bringing my own lessons forward into my family's lives, my friends' lives, my community, and beyond to a larger community. And it was no coincidence that Robert's dreams had led him to the Mohawk Valley to research a historic figure whose house I managed — where I finally met Robert, the drowning boy of my childhood dream.

As I focused more intently on my life's purpose, I spent some time reflecting on the early days of my friendship with Robert, and on why those first few weeks of getting acquainted were so powerful.

Perhaps our lives had come together for an even greater shared purpose: to continue the exploration of dreaming and to teach and guide others to deepen their relationship with their dreams. We had no idea at that time that I would face the challenge of illness and the renewal of a contract to remind me of my soul's purpose — or that Robert, using his dreaming experience and research, would develop original techniques for guiding others to see the world community as a dreaming society.

As we shared dreams, and as I slowly shared my fears of illness with Robert, he encouraged me to focus on my soul's purpose on earth. Just days before I left for West Africa, he wrote a quotation — which he shared with me — from Plotinus in the margin of his journal: The soul has the power to conform to her character the destiny allotted to her. This was a theme that came home to both of us in my healing dreams and in Robert's support of my healing. Robert was part of my dreaming destiny. I believe that his role in my illness was to constantly remind me of my life's purpose, which, in my opinion, was to remind people of the limitless resources for spiritual and physical healing within the dreamspace, while learning about his own life's purpose as well, and to teach me how to find my voice within my dreams.

As that role became increasingly clear, Robert searched back in his dream journals and shared another quotation he found in the margin: The shaman is, above all, a sick man who has been cured. This was a definition of the wounded healer by Mircea Eliade — a foreshadowing that would resonate for both of us as dreams revealed themselves along my healing journey.

moving ahead to honor a contract

I WAS NOW REQUIRED to honor the terms under which my life was extended. I needed to move beyond my reticence and take an active role in the lives of other people — to share my story and, with it, the gifts of dream healing. To my surprise and delight I found that, as I did this, I became what Robert calls a "dreambringer" — a person who can bring dreams to people who desperately need them for their own life journeys.

Robert's workshops were expanding from the first few experimental evenings at a local arts organization. At Robert's invitation, I accompanied him to some of the dream workshops he was teaching, where I told the story of how my dreams had healed me and transformed my life. I experienced the joy of people discovering healing paths and direct lines to the sacred through their own dreams. As Robert experimented with new techniques in his own work, we continued a long tradition of dream-sharing.

I continued to develop confidence and experience in working with my own dreams and in helping people work with theirs. My staff began to share their dreams and we would work with them using Robert's technique of asking questions of the dream. Confidence gave me the voice I needed to go beyond recording dreams in a journal and sharing them with old friends to encouraging new friends — and often complete strangers — to share their dreams with me. I put together a small workshop of my own which was held in the store space of a New Age book and gift shop. It filled quickly; people were anxious to hear about healing in dreams and anxious to share their own stories. I quickly learned that one of the greatest gifts we can bring to others is to open a safe space where they can share their dreams and become open to the guidance and healing of dreams.

inviting a group into my dream of a sacred contract

TWO OF MY DREAMS have been particularly useful as sacred spaces for community dreaming: my dream of the Healing Pool at Bethesda and the powerful dream of renewing my sacred contract. These dreams speak to people who need to find healing in their life, whether their challenge is illness, emotional pain, or a need for life guidance in renewing their own sacred contract.

In a particularly moving workshop, Robert invited people to share in a weekend entitled "Dancing with the Bear: Recovering the Arts of Dream Healing." Over twenty people participated in journeys of shared dreaming for transferring energy, recovering soul, and healing mind and body.

Robert prepared a center space with a cloth, candles, and a few objects that had personal and group dreaming significance. Others placed objects that were meaningful to them and their dreaming in this center space. Berries were placed on the cloth for the bear. After everyone was seated in a circle, Robert announced that he would drum for a few moments so that everyone could reflect on their need for the weekend and possibly recall a healing dream that spoke to them.

Robert uses a round frame drum in his workshops and maintains a steady monotonous rhythmic beat, like the steady beat of a heart, frequently used in shamanic journeying. The opening drumming is softer, lighter, and less lengthy than drumming for working with a dream. After the drumming, we stood in a circle and performed an opening ritual that invoked the spirits of dreaming and life and closed the gates of the circle to those who wished to do harm. A song solidified the words of power and brought in the energy of the bear:

> *Don't cry, little one.*
> *Don't cry, little one.*
> *The bear is coming to dance for you.*
> *The bear is coming to dance for you.*

The day progressed with dream sharing and working in small groups with specific dreams. Then Robert asked people if they would like to go into a group dream, to reenter a dream of healing and power where they would journey to a sacred place and renew their soul's contract.

Robert set out some guidelines for the journey: I would relate my dream; the dream travelers could then ask questions to clarify anything they felt would help them on their own journey; they would then get comfortable and reenter my dreamspace, with my permission, and seek their own answers or find a dreamspace familiar and specific to themselves.

I shared my dream of meeting the awesome Presence of Light who allowed me to renew my contract and my soul's purpose. Robert reminded the dreamers that they were not interpreting my dream. They were exploring the dream as though it were their own. In this way they could feel the full impact of my dream as their own journey, at the same time seeing new scenes that might or might not resonate with me as additional information I neglected to see in my dream.

After the participants asked questions and got comfortable for their journey, Robert asked me if the group had permission to reenter my dream. I said "Yes," and he responded with, "Let's go on a journey." He drummed. The rhythmic beating of the drum carried people back into the words of my dream and on beyond until it became their dream and a place where they could seek their own answers for their own healing.

When Robert beat a recall on the drum — a series of short beats — everyone gradually returned to the room. They sat up and wrote notes in their journals, then Robert asked if anyone would like to talk about their journey.

Several people volunteered to share their experiences. Some had met departed relatives who had messages for them. Some recalled and revisited places from history or from their own past. Some brought back general messages of healing and peace. Some brought back information about their own healing or for a family member or friend. One young woman, currently going through chemotherapy for a particularly stubborn kind of cancer, visited her own guardian and received a radiant message of hope and healing.

Robert asked the dream travelers to find ways to honor their dreams of renewing their sacred contracts. The woman who visited her guardian wrote a poem about the visit, which she said she would keep near her bedside. Some drew pictures; others said they would bring their dreams of healing to friends or family for whom they had journeyed. Some would seek representations of animals they saw on their journey. All found the most sacred way for themselves to use, honor, and respect their journey into my dream of renewing a sacred contract.

bringing dream gifts to others

As ROBERT's DREAM workshops expanded and more and more seasoned dream travelers emerged, Robert felt the need for a central space where these "frequent flyers" could come together several times a year and explore dreams. The place that presented itself through dreams and synchronicity was a beautiful turn-of-the-century lodge in the Adirondacks, on Gore Mountain. There are no televisions, radios, and only one telephone. The lodge sits on a garnet mountain overlooking Thirteenth Lake over a vast expanse of evergreens, the perfect space to move inside dreams without interruption. Twice a year Robert hosts a weekend, by invitation, for these experienced dream explorers. They now come there from around the world to gather and explore both personal and community dreams. Robert often asks me to share a dream for group travel, like the Healing Pool dream or the dream of my sacred contract. On one of these weekends, I shared a complicated but magnificent dream with Robert just days before leaving for Gore Mountain. During the workshop, Robert asked me to share the dream for a group dream journey.

RESTORATION THROUGH THE CELL

THE DREAM — Restoration through the Cell — was a complicated but very graphic dream, powerful and empowering. I captured a "motto" from the dream just as I awoke: "The power of intention can be defined in some cases as moving the signature of the cell to wholeness." The dream concerned the ability of cells to change, restore, and become whole. The dream action shifted between two venues — a modern city and a city of the past — with a bridge as access between the two. The city of the past was crumbling and deteriorating, but it seemed to improve each time I visited it in the dream. I crossed and recrossed the bridge many times; each time I crossed, the buildings in the old city took on more character and definition, like a painting coming to life. There was an unknown person in the dream monitoring part of the rebuilding. There were many elements in the dream: coins or large, ornate door keys brought from the "past" side across the bridge to the "future," cubes depicting scenes from the past, and a scene indicating that the cubes could be manipulated by the keys, much like a computer. There was a telepathic element to the manipulation and a hint that one must be careful in the manipulation so that something bad wouldn't be created. I was sitting in the future (the new city) and creating renewal in the past (the old city). The cubes were not creating permanent constructions or models; they could be changed endlessly, creating change in the environments they represented. The changes translated across time and space, moving effortlessly back and forth, responding to intention.

This dream seemed to have import for a world community and for world thought, as well as for a personal journey. We journeyed together with this dream, and the dreamers shared their experiences with it, some of them almost as complicated as the original dream.

One dreamer went to what she described as "the heart" of the house — a kitchen area — and explored the work within the nucleus of the building, or nucleus of the cell. She received pages of structural detail, which she recorded: "Each detail affects the whole. The construction or marriage, strong or weak or anything in between, affects the whole." Another dreamer found her message in the removal of debris for the restoration of the cell city and wrote a message for her life: "The old junk I am storing in my body needs to be cleaned out — some of it examined, and some of it flushed away." Others found meaning in returning to the "blueprint of their soul" and in personal healing.

One person's journey with my dream touched my heart. When she visited the old city, she was reminded in her journey that she had an "old" problem to deal with in order to make her own "new" city: she had been told that she needed surgery for an ovarian cyst. She resented having to take time away from her family for surgery. She took my dream home with her, and dreamed her own night dream of the restoration of the cells in her body. In that dream she went inside her body to her ovary and, using energy that shone light like a flashlight, pierced and shriveled the cyst. She later told me that she awoke the next morning feeling great relief, knowing that something had changed. She made an appointment with her doctor; he examined her and, much to his surprise, decided that surgery was not necessary.

This woman had found a connection between my dream and her healing capabilities. She had not shared her dream with her doctor but told me that, since meeting other people who shared dreams, she now understood that healing in a dream was not far-fetched. Her final comment touched me even more deeply: "Thank you for so much more than this dream; you have the ability to bring healing to the world with your dreams and experience."

As I came to see how powerful my dreams could be for other people, I began to offer more of my dreams as journeys for others. I was always surprised and delighted with the healing opportunities for others within my dreams. Particular favorites were the Field of Body Parts, the Healing Pool of Bethesda, and the small dreams in which an invisible guardian placed planks across unsafe places to give me safe passage. The Ballet dream, in which tools came alive and my body spun around in the air for viewing, became a wonderful dream for exploring body scanning. Reentry into my dreams made them personal to the dreamers, who came away from them with visualizations of healing for themselves. The Healing Pool of Bethesda often morphed into streams, rivers, lakes, ponds, or pools from people's personal experience; dreamers rediscovered places that were special to them at various times in their lives, or they found mystical pools in their dream imagination. The energy in a big dream can bring many people to healing and understanding for themselves and their communities. The ability to share a healing dream of our own with others — and even to take them inside the dream for energy and guidance — is a gift of the dream and the dream bringer.

Bringing Dreams
to the Community

*B*ACK IN MY OWN COMMUNITY, people knew my story of healing and dreams. My neighbors had followed my story from the moment they cleaned my house upon my return from the hospital just after my surgery. I had told a few dreams as the months went by, and then they began to bring me their own dreams. Some were of contracts spent and lives ready to close. Some were poignant; some reminded me that not all contracts were renegotiated.

An elderly woman in my hamlet was dying. She was one hundred years old. Her family and friends gathered around in her home where she lay in bed drifting in and out of sleep. She had wonderful gifts of caring and love, which she had shared abundantly during her life. Never confined to wheelchairs or disabled in any way other than the slowness of aging, she had baked cookies and taken meals to those less able than herself until just weeks before she died. She also demanded the same level of service from others. She would call me and tell me that she needed two dozen cookies and where I should take them. I would bake those cookies, and I didn't even bake cookies for my own family. One day she opened her eyes briefly and pulled her daughter's face down close to her own. She was beaming:

"I'm going home."

Her daughter thought that perhaps her mom's mind was drifting. "You are home; you are in your own house," her daughter replied.

"No," her mother said gently, "my contract is up; I'm going home. It's beautiful. I've seen it."

re-burning the ashes

ON ANOTHER OCCASION an elderly man who worked at odd jobs in my neighborhood stopped to talk to me. He had lived a hard life, both in his childhood home in Ireland and later in this country. A year or so earlier, he had told me a story about growing up in Ireland in such poverty that his family stayed warm in winter by collecting the fireplace ashes thrown away by others and burning them again in their little stove. On this visit, he told me he'd had a dream showing that he had "dark stuff inside." "I'm going to die," he said. "I won't be able to re-burn the ashes much longer. I saw that in the dream." I felt incredible sadness. He died a few weeks later. His contract had been a tough one; ending it brought him peace.

The personal stories blossomed. Everywhere I went, people wanted to tell me their dreams or wanted me to share my favorite dreams with them. Dreaming after my illness became a navigational guidance system that was always true. Many people shared dreams about illness — dreams that I knew could be turned into dreams of healing. I began to talk with people about changing the outcome of their dreams.

finding my own voice

WHEN ROBERT'S BOOK *Conscious Dreaming* first appeared in bookstores, a few local reporters noticed my story in his chapter on healing dreams and requested interviews with me. I had participated for the past five years in Robert's workshops, telling my story as a part of his healing dream workshops; but my story was still confined to Robert's workshops, to people who shared their dreams with me in my workplace and hamlet, and sometimes in conversations where discussions of dreams arose as part of the evening. It was not until the publication of my story in Robert's first book on dreaming that I began to find my public voice.

Furthermore several reporters shyly confided their own dreams, intrigued by the idea that dreams can bring healing. Interviews were often interrupted by personal confidences that typically began, "I don't usually remember my dreams, but there was one dream..." A male reporter, eager to share a dream but nervous of being tagged as less than hardboiled, walked me a hundred yards from other people to whisper his story.

Seeing my name associated with dreaming in print gave me the courage to approach organizations that took a traditional approach to breast cancer. I began to volunteer. First I spoke to a gathering of the local branch of the American Cancer Society. My story made some of the people fidget with their dinners; people in professional health organizations sometimes scoff when prodded to look for healing in visions and dreams. However, someone found my story interesting; a few days later, I received a phone call asking if I would help with the annual Relay for Life, an American Cancer Society overnight event designed to celebrate survivorship and raise money for research and programs. During the event, teams of people gather at schools, fairgrounds, or parks and take turns walking or running laps. Each team tries to keep at least one team member on the track at all times. The event represents the hope that those lost to cancer will never be forgotten, that those who face cancer will be supported, and that one day, cancer will be eliminated.

The next year I was given another opportunity to find my public voice when Relay for Life representatives asked me to speak at their event as a survivor. On the opening day, I spoke to hundreds of cancer survivors and their families about courage and hope, and particularly about dreams. I related three of the dreams that were central to my own survival. I told them about how I had come home from the doctor's office, frightened and angry, and dreamed of draining a breast-shaped cone — a dream that had given me both an image I could use in self-healing and an exact picture of the location and nature of my disease. I told them about how, when my body was filled with poison during chemotherapy and I was close to despair, I drew courage and hope from the dream in which I walked through a field of body parts and reconstructed my body from the pieces I harvested. Then I shared the biggest of all my big dreams: the dream in which I was brought into the intimate presence of my death, and was finally allowed to renegotiate my life contract.

The applause that day brought me to tears. The applause was for my victory and, more importantly, for the victory of a larger community of men and women who were using all the resources available to them for survival. When I joined the other cancer survivors for the first lap around the track — known appropriately as the "Survivor's Lap" — dozens of men and women pressed close to tell me their own stories of survival, and many of them shared dreams.

A tall, thin elderly woman introduced me to her husband, who walked alongside her on the Survivor's Lap. She told me that she was a survivor because her husband had encouraged her to pay attention to a dream that pinpointed the location of her tumor. In an experience eerily similar to my own, a doctor had told her that she had nothing to worry about — that her concern over a small lump was needless and that she should go home and "watch it" for a year. Her dream told her otherwise, but she almost ignored the dream because a doctor had told her to ignore her fears, to ignore her intuition, to ignore her dream. However, she had told her husband her dream, and he made the appointments with not one but two other doctors. One of those doctors performed a biopsy and found the tumor that had been diagnosed in her dream. That doctor told her that "watching it" for a year would have been a deadly mistake.

While attending planning meetings for Relay for Life, I became involved with a dietary study sponsored by the medical profession in which groups of people followed various low-fat diets to determine the relationship between fat and cancer recurrence. My role was to visit the study participants and encourage them to continue with their prescribed diet. I met several women who were having more difficulty dealing with the side effects of cancer than dealing with their participation in the dietary study. They were relieved that I was a survivor, and they asked me to tell my story of survival. When I told them my story, they shared their dreams. And when they shared their dreams, they discovered a crucial ingredient in their own healing.

A woman I'll call Ruth was in a severe state of depression, suffering from lymphedema and other side effects. She had been told that the swelling would disappear after chemotherapy with the help of diuretics. Instead, the swelling became worse. She shared several dreams that had given her clear and correct information on how to control lymphedema.

In one dream, she was lying on a long table and someone was pushing and kneading fluid through her arm. I recognized a form of lymphatic massage that I had experienced at a clinic in New York City. Years after the end of my chemotherapy, my oncologist directed me to a wonderful facility in New York City; he had seen a television interview with its founder, Dr. Lerner. The facility was treating lymphedema using European methods that were new in this country at that time, though they're common now. Patients with lymphedema in their legs who arrived in wheelchairs were leaving Dr. Lerner's facility walking unaided. People with severe lymphedema in their arms who arrived wearing huge sweatshirts left wearing clothing with normal-sized sleeves. Dr. Lerner was offering miracles to many and hope to even more; lymphedema, untreated, could become dangerous and even deadly.

I spent three weeks at Dr. Lerner's facility working with therapists who used foam padding and lymphedema massage techniques to manage and control the affected limb. At the end of the three weeks, Ron was taught how to perform the special massage techniques on my arm at home.

While I was at Dr. Lerner's facility, a breakthrough in my lymphedema treatment appeared in a shared dream between myself, my doctor, and my therapist in which each of us envisioned a solution to the edema in my fingers. The dream came after a long day of failed attempts to reduce the swelling in my hand so that I could wear a small glove, called a gauntlet, to control the swelling during the day. They had tried all their usual treatments. The next morning, the three of us excitedly reported our dreams, all presenting an identical treatment method: a different way of cutting the foam base used under the bandages. The foam "hand" dreamed by all of us involved cutting the foam separately for each finger and covering the top of each finger with it — an exact duplication of the top of my hand. We tried it, and it began to work immediately. I was fitted with my new glove and arm sleeve. The day I left the city, Dr. Lerner came out of his office and asked me to come with him into the waiting room. There he told all the new patients the story of the dream solution to my stubborn hand.

I gave Ruth the name of the clinic, which at that time was the closest location for effective treatment of lymphedema. The woman was excited that she had dreamed of a technique — previously unknown to her — that was available in ordinary reality. She immediately made arrangements to attend the clinic. Three months later, Ruth's lymphedema was manageable and she was relaxed about participating in the diet study.

the *Dream hot line*

Between 1996 and 2000 I was a telephone hot line volunteer for an organization that put survivors in touch with people newly diagnosed with cancer. As a volunteer, I provided the newly diagnosed patient with medical information about the physical properties of their disease, but more importantly I talked with them about what they were feeling and answered their questions. I never met any of the people who called, and I only had one conversation with each of them, but I hoped they carried away more than a resource list of medical options. Many of them moved easily from talking about emotions to talking about their dreams. The sharing of dreams on the cancer hot line became a wonderful healing exercise for the new patients, and it helped me grow in my own ability to work with my dreams and theirs. Often we talked about dreams that conveyed messages that demanded a response. The callers' responses were as varied as the people themselves. Later in their treatment, some of them gave me permission to tell others their dreams. Here they are.

My Grandma Refused to Give Up

A young woman named Helen had been diagnosed with breast cancer and was undergoing chemotherapy. She had very small breasts, which had previously been "enhanced" with surgical implants. After having problems with the implants, she requested their removal and was left with scar tissue, which was not perfectly smooth. She felt a lump in the scar tissue for several months, but she ignored it, believing that it was part of the scar tissue. She also began to have "peculiar" dreams that she didn't understand, but later believed to have been about the cancer growing in her body. She ignored those, too. The summer months brought Helen to her annual vacation spot in Florida, where she began dreaming of her dead grandmother. She ignored those dreams because they made as little sense to her as her other "peculiar" dreams. The dreams were insistent — some of them frightening — but Helen could not, or would not, understand them. In the midst of her usually enjoyable vacation, Helen contracted a serious case of cellulitis with severe itching and redness on her face — a case that would have sent an ordinary person to the doctor. Not

Helen; she returned home and insisted on being her own doctor, her face slowly recovering from the uncomfortable rash.

A few days later, Helen was walking down the stairs in her home, and — just for a second, just out of the corner of her eye — was absolutely certain she saw her dead grandmother on the stairs. As Helen's eyes widened in the shock of recognition, her grandmother stuck her leg out straight across Helen's path, tripping her and causing her to fall down the stairs. This time Helen was forced to go to the doctor; her face was bruised and swollen, and she feared that her nose had been broken in the fall. There was one thing she could not tell the nurse when asked what had happened: her beloved dead granny had purposely tripped her and caused her to fall down the stairs! The doctor walked in, looked slightly puzzled and asked, "Have you had a mammogram recently?" Stunned by the question, Helen demanded to know why he would ask such a thing when she had come to him for something quite different. "Because," he replied, "an old woman, I believe somehow associated with you, showed up in my dream last night and said you needed a mammogram."

Now Helen got the message of the dreams she had been shutting out. She told me that she believed her grandmother had passed on a health warning to the doctor — who fortunately paid attention — because Helen had ignored the messages in her own dreams. Her granny may even have tried to send her to a doctor with the unrelated problem of the cellulitis rash, but that hadn't worked. Maybe granny had actually been instrumental in the fall that brought Helen to a doctor who remembered his dreams. Helen agreed to the mammogram, which revealed that she was in an advanced stage of breast cancer. Subsequent surgery revealed that six lymph nodes were involved. Helen chose to participate in a clinical trial, for which her dreams — now no longer rejected — had also prepared her. The clinical trial would investigate new healing technologies involving the use of stem cell therapy. Helen's prognosis was hopeful; her subsequent dreams, which she recorded faithfully and worked with daily, predicted full recovery and a cure.

Recognizing the Intruder

Ellen, a woman in her late thirties, dreamed that a threatening intruder walked into her house and pointed a gun at her breast. She was sensitive to dream imagery and knew intuitively that the dream was warning her that she might have developed breast cancer. She immediately sought medical help. Ellen's cancer was discovered in its earliest stages, thanks to the fact that she remembered her dream and acted on its warning. Her problem was solved with a simple lumpectomy.

LEAVING VIRGINIA

SOMETIMES A DREAM is so powerful that the dreamer holds the memory of its details for years until waking events catch up with it and reveal its meaning. Lorraine lived in Virginia and was married with grown children. One night, she woke up in the middle of the night frightened, with the details of a terrifying night dream clearly in her mind:

LOSING BOTH MY BREASTS

I am standing naked in front of the mirror, and both of my breasts have been removed — both painfully, but the pain is different for the removal of each. One seems to be a physical pain — the left breast. The other seems to be a mental pain, intense anguish — the right one. I have just moved to upstate New York in the dream. I am no longer living in my home in Virginia. I am alone, so very alone.

Lorraine was frightened by this dream but didn't understand it. When she woke up, her first thought was that nothing could ever cause her to leave Virginia. One year later, she was diagnosed with breast cancer and her left breast was removed. Several months later, her husband left her, unable to come to terms with a wife without a breast who had changing needs and newly discovered strengths. The pain in her right breast was the emotional pain of her husband leaving. Lorraine had no skills and no money, so she turned to her sister, who lived in upstate New York. She pursued a college degree in New York, completed the cancer therapy, bought a small house, and found a satisfying job. On a cold winter night, she opened a novel she had been reading in Virginia and found the scribbled notes she had written the night she awoke from her dream. Every element of the dream had been fulfilled.

Bringing Dreams to the Community

Hippo and Elephant at the Door

BARBARA HAD RECORDED her dreams for many years and had, like many of us, failed to recognize the initial dreams that warned of her impending illness. Her big dream — the one that got her attention — was very direct. In the dream, a friend telephoned her and told her that she would die if she didn't have her breast removed. Barbara acted on her dream immediately and was undergoing chemotherapy when she first met her healing guides — two animals — in a dream. Animal helpers and guides take many forms, but Barbara's helpers seemed particularly interesting; they had a directness and humor that reflected itself in Barbara's attitude toward her recovery. The helpers — an elephant and a hippopotamus — introduced themselves by knocking on Barbara's door and inviting themselves in. She was concerned because the animals were large and her door was of a normal size. The hippo made it through with only slight difficulty, but the elephant struggled and got stuck, and Barbara was obliged to shove him the rest of the way through. In very deep voices, the animals argued with each another, intelligently laying out Barbara's options and presenting their differing points of view to assist in making decisions. Barbara suggested that future meetings take place in an environment more natural to them so that she wouldn't have to be concerned about their comfort. They agreed, and they continued to meet her throughout the period of her chemotherapy, offering her options for each new phase of her recovery. The animals disappeared when Barbara no longer needed them.

Bears in Red Collars

DOROTHY LIVED in rural Virginia. She did not recall any of her dreams before her illness, but during her recovery she experienced hundreds of dreams about two little bears with matching red collars. They brought her healing through simple play and childish joy. They danced for her, played with her, cleaned her house, and took care of her daily chores. They prepared her meals morning, noon, and night, dancing and play-ing all the while. She felt no fear when she fell asleep, because she knew her little bears would be waiting for her. She woke each morning filled with joy and hope because she had spent another night with her little bears. "I know," she said, "they will be gone when I am completely well, but they will come back if I need them and they will only be a thought away; I will recognize them by their joy and their little red collars." Dorothy survived breast cancer because two little bears took the daily stress from her life and brought her healing through their joy.

A WARNING THAT COULD NOT BE BRUSHED OFF

MANY CANCER PATIENTS with whom I talked told me that they never dreamed. They meant, of course, that they had never developed a habit of dream recall. What I found interesting with most of those women was that, although they didn't remember their dreams, something in their subconscious still kicked them awake and made them aware of their health problem. I was convinced that such intuitions often flowed from denied or unremembered dreams. One such example occurred in 1999 in a workshop I was attending on historic paints held in North Carolina. Somehow the luncheon conversation there turned to dreaming. Several of the restoration specialists were discussing work-related dreams, and then the dream discussion turned to healing dreams. A woman named Gloria overheard me talking to someone else about dreams. She hesitantly approached me when no one else was around and told me that she admired my ability to discuss illness and dreams with strangers. She wanted to tell me a story, but she said it wasn't about dreams; it was about her illness. She had worked all morning to summon the courage to tell me her story, and she decided that since I had the courage to talk about my dreams, she could muster the courage to talk about her story of discovery.

Gloria had studied art in school, but had put her talent aside to raise a family and provide for several children in the absence of a husband. A second marriage also ended in divorce and, in the difficult period afterward, Gloria decided to take an art class to reclaim some of her talent. She placed her pad in front of her on the first night of the class and, barely hearing the assignment, began to draw ovals with a dot in each. She drew them over and over, the dot always in the same place inside the oval. She went home and pulled out canvas and paints and began painting larger ovals, now looking more like breasts, with the same dot in the same place. She seemed to have little control over the repetitive geometric patterns. She got the message and made an appointment with her doctor.

Gloria completed radiation and chemotherapy; a canvas of ovals and dots had saved her life. She insisted that dreaming had nothing to do with her discovery of her illness, yet she recalled, just barely, a dream involving an art classroom. She had brushed off the message of her dreams, but it returned through her artist's brush. As Robert says, dreams and intuition come from the same source.

Barnacles on the Whale

Not all dreams lead to physical survival; some lead to spiritual healing before physical death takes place. A young woman who worked with me developed an aggressive lymphatic cancer that invaded her organs. Her upbeat personality and her supportive dreams carried her almost a decade beyond the time when she was expected to die. She had attended the workshop I gave in the New Age bookstore. She said very little in the workshop, but she went home and began to work with the techniques I taught. When we talked about healing dreams only a year before her death, she shared a short dream that she used in her healing meditations. In the dream, she saw herself scrubbing barnacles off the body of a whale. That was the entire dream but, upon awakening, the dream felt wonderful and cleansing. She decided to tape-record the dream to play back when she drove in her car. She attributed the constant repetition of this small dream to the extension of her life far beyond its predicted end.

A Coat of Mirrors

In Make-A-Wish, a volunteer organization that brings physical reality dreams to children, I met a woman whose child suffered from an aggressive cancer that required several surgeries and multiple levels of in-hospital chemotherapy treatments. She was desperate to find any solace for her child and talked to me about sleep dreams. She could recall no dreams of her own that related to her son's condition, nor was she accustomed to sharing dreams with her child. On the night before her child's next round of aggressive chemotherapy, I went to sleep with the intent of a dream for her child's health. I saw her child in the bed receiving the chemotherapy and, in the dream, I gave her mother a beautiful, heavy, red robe with thousands of tiny geometric mirrors sewn into it. I was told that the coat of mirrors would protect her child through chemotherapy and help her avoid at least some of the surgery. I immediately called the mother after I woke up and shared the dream. She took the dream to her child in the hospital and told her the dream as a story. Her child cherished the dream story and took it into her own mind as though she had dreamed it herself. By focusing her own intention on my dream for her she endured the chemotherapy with fewer side effects. Then the child's mother received the best news of all: further surgery would be unnecessary. Was this the result of a gift of a dream? I don't know, but I believe that by focusing all of her attention on a beautiful story aided in her healing. The daytime imagination is as powerful as a sleep dream.

village of Dreams

SOME OF MY MOST MOVING experiences of dream-sharing and dream-bringing were played out with my neighbors in Glen. I live next door to the general store, in one of two houses originally owned by the founder of the hamlet. Food and gossip have been served around the potbellied stove in that store since the town was a bustling commercial center in the days of dirt roads, gaslights, horses, and wagons. In those days, a local study club was formed, like hundreds of others in outlying farm communities. In the early twentieth century, farm women felt isolated and sought ways to come together. Men had agricultural meetings, which provided social life for them; women wanted something of their own, so across America, study clubs began to form. The women read books and reported back at regularly scheduled meetings. Sometimes they painted or sewed. The meetings became opportunities to share, learn from each other, and find companionship. Some of these clubs continued even though their original purpose — to escape the loneliness of being miles away from each other on a farm — no longer applied. They still read books, did book reports, sewed, and painted; but now they sometimes invited speakers to talk to them about topics of interest.

After the publication in 1996 and 1997 of Robert's books on dreams, the remaining members of the local study club invited me to read chapters from his books at one of their meetings. I read my own story from *Conscious Dreaming* as told by Robert, and rapidly became known as "the woman who dreams." Many Saturday afternoons, when I walked across my lawn to the store and sat down with sandwich and soup, someone would approach and share the long table. After a few comments about deer and hay and the weather, the question often came:

"Aren't you the person who dreams? Can I tell you my dream?"

"We all dream," I would say, and then I would listen.

By the end of the dream-telling, the store staff would join the conversation to play "if it were my dream" or to tell a dream of their own that seemed related. I have listened now to hundreds of dreams, wonderful dreams: visits by dead relatives come to accompany someone to their next home; warning or advice; solutions to health problems; or just solutions to daily problems at work or at home. Precognitive dreams abounded. One man's dream predicted a heart attack, and a second dream gave him instructions for preventing a second, fatal heart attack. The second dream even named the amount of insurance his wife and young child would receive if he didn't lose weight. He changed his diet and began to ride a bicycle, both activities that were suggested in the second dream.

When neighbors can't find me in the store, they telephone and ask, "Do you have time for a dream?" I always have time for a dream. In a hamlet as small as mine, we all dream for each other; the caller could be dreaming my life, too, so I need to have time for their dream. I've discovered that we are beginning to dream like native populations who lived close to the land and close to one another. We dream daily events: a storm gathering over the horizon, a problem being discovered by a neighbor and not yet shared, the haunting remnants of lives from houses long destroyed or abandoned, and even the activities of wildlife and animals in the area. I have a neighbor who sits on a special boulder where h   e had a visionary experience as a child; there he brings his problems or, during hunting season, daydreams the locations of animals. He is a caring hunter who hunts for meat and blesses the animals he kills.

My husband Ron still plays the organ in the hamlet church. It has become a special instrument for community dreaming, beyond my experience of lying on the floor and allowing the resonating music to flow through my body during chemotherapy. An elderly woman waited for Ron after church one Sunday. She had been wrestling with the meaning of a dream in which she was instructed by her dead mother to contact a sister she had not spoken to in decades. She tried to ignore the dream, but she continued to dream it night after night. She would have continued to ignore it if Ron hadn't changed his prelude (which was listed in the program) at the last moment and played a somewhat unfamiliar hymn —

which, as it turns out, had been the elderly woman's mother's favorite hymn. When Ron began to play the hymn, chills ran down the woman's spine and she knew it was a sign that she needed to honor the dream.

My favorite community dream was also shared in the church. Another elderly woman approached me before the Sunday service and asked, "Aren't you the woman who dreams?" Her story was a marvelous tale of a dream she titled "Mr. Death." She had been sleeping next to her husband several evenings before and saw a dream vision of a tall, dashing gentleman. He came into her bedroom wearing a beautiful pinstriped waistcoat and an elegant tuxedo with tails. He walked over toward her, and she joyously said, "I know you; you are Mr. Death." He was somewhat surprised at her recognition. She asked if he had come for her, and he told her that it wasn't quite time for her to go, but that he would accompany her when she was ready. He simply wanted her to recognize him when he returned so that she wouldn't be frightened. She assured him that she would not be frightened and asked if he would like to talk to her husband. He declined. When she shared her dream with her husband and children, they were appalled. The children were frightened, and her husband was angry that she had sent "Mr. Death" to his side of the bed. I was delighted with the dream, and she was delighted to find someone who was as thrilled with the dream as she had been.

I love this question my neighbors ask of me: "Are you the one who dreams?" I presented a dream earlier of my hamlet as an overlay of two separate communities. Both were my hamlet, but I had lived in the hamlet and shared my life with its residents in only one of the overlays. In the second overlay I was not part of the life of the hamlet, and there were changes in both people and places that I didn't like to see. This dream was like the movie *It's a Wonderful Life* — a review of life without me. Fortunately, my presence seemed to have made a positive difference. I was even a little embarrassed by the presumption in the dream that I was so important to my community, but I also realized because of that dream how important each of us is in the lives we touch. We have the opportunity to choose how we touch those lives and what kind of imprint we leave behind.

I met Robert when I needed to find my dreaming partner. I have a family that shares their dreams every day. Dreaming shared dreams and learning to share dreams brought me through illness to healing and finally to the renewal of my sacred contract. In that renewal, I made a life promise in the new contract and then began taking my dreams to a larger community. These experiences with the men, women, and children I met within the larger community — in workshops, in planning meetings, on hot lines, and in my workplace — gave me a voice and gave me the experience I needed to speak with people about their dreams, to bring dreams to them when needed, and to help them open the door to exploring and working with their own dreams. Some of these dreams could easily be called miracles, but they are miracles that are available to us all. I am alive because I dream. More important, my dreaming has led me to a life of sharing and exploring every day the dreams that call all of us, every night, to remember our soul's purpose and to walk with greater courage and passion on this good earth.

HEALING WITH
DREAM IMAGERY

*M*Y OWN EXPERIENCES with dreaming led me to study more about dreaming in the ancient world, when people routinely sought healing guidance from dreams and from the divine power that showed itself in dreams.

In the original Hippocratic oath, doctors swore by gods of healing, including the god Aesclepius.

In ancient Greece, dreams and visions were the most common method of inquiry into the cause and cure of disease. In the temple of Aesclepius, diagnosis of illness and healing took place during that state of consciousness just prior to sleep, when images come forth like frames of thought projected on a movie screen.

Galen documented and recorded a description of the effect of images and the imagination on health. He believed that one could study the records of a patient's imagery and dream content to glean important diagnostic information. Such inputs would help doctors help teach their patients to learn how to heal themselves, and help patients bring their bodies and minds back into balance.[4]

The Renaissance physician Paracelsus credited his own understanding of the laws and practices of health to his conversations with women

---

[4] John Coxe, M.D., ed., *The Writings of Hippocrates and Galen* (Philadelphia: Lindsay and Blakiston, 1846), pp. 215–16, 620–21.

healers. He wrote a book entitled *Diseases of Women,* in which he noted man to be his own doctor. We can find the physician within ourselves and all things for healing within our own nature. He believed, correctly, that the imagination, the power of the mind, could both create illness and cure illness working singly or together with medical remedies and the spirit within.

the body believes in pictures

THROUGH MY WORK with dreams, I've developed a number of exercises that can help you access the power of your own dreaming. Two most powerful methods I've used are what I call "Intent" and "Prescription and Medicine." *Intent* is your personal statement of either your desire for a dream or a statement of what you wish to receive from a dream. You might wish to have a healing dream or wish to state a more specific need. You can write it down and place it under your pillow before going to bed. This keeps it in your memory: "I want a dream of healing." "I want to be free from fear." "I want a dream on what to do about my upcoming surgery." The intent can be anything you need. You can use the same statements when meditating for a dream or meditating for a particular need. You state what you wish to know.

I used the words *Prescription* and *Medicine* often in the previous chapters. When I think of a prescription, it is the piece of paper the doctor gives which defines the kind of medicine and the dosage. In dreaming, the prescription is the dream itself and it can be transferred upon waking to one or two sentences of description (i.e., *I walked through a field of body parts; harvested them; washed them in hyssop; and reconstructed a new body*). When those dream sentences are then used as a message, whether it be a taped message, a drawing, a poem, or something else that works best, they become a medicine based on the original prescription, and must be used like a prescribed medicine as long as needed until the next dream of healing presents itself or until you feel that you have moved beyond the need for that particular dream. The prescription is the brief synopsis of the dream. Its use for active healing is the medicine working in the body. Waking or sleeping, imagery — mind mental pictures — is the way we send messages to our body. The pictures we send can be used to harm or to heal. When they are used consciously for healing, we release the most creative and powerful potential of our subconscious mind. When healing pictures come in a dream, they are gifts. Mind mental pictures, whether from our waking reality or from a sleep dream, provide an intention for healing that empowers the imagination to transport healing messages to the body. These messages become an active prescription for healing.

It is important to realize that healing is not always the lengthening of life. Sometimes healing is the final balancing of life. Healing is as important in the preparation for death as is the healing of the body to continue in active life. We need to learn how to use healing imagery for both a return to active life and for preparing the mind and body to enter a new passage. I hope the following exercises help you in your quest for healing.

EXERCISE 1:
GOING INTO A WAKING DREAM

EVEN IF YOU HAVE DIFFICULTY remembering night dreams, you can ask for a waking image for healing. Try the following exercise:

1. **Find a quiet place** and get into a relaxed position. If you prefer meditative music, candles, or special objects as a background, select your music and prepare your space in a way that feels best for you. Have a pad and pencil nearby, perhaps a bandanna or scarf to cover your eyes, and anything else that makes you comfortable.

2. **Close your eyes** and breathe deeply several times.

3. **Choose something to work with.** Let's use *anxiety* as an example.

4. **Think about the word** *anxiety.* Translate the word *anxiety* into a picture that best describes the way you feel when you are anxious. For example, you might see a rope tied in knots or a person wringing their hands. You might visualize an entire situation that makes you anxious. Whatever you see is the image that will work best for you.

5. **Now claim your image;** it is your personal gift. It might be so unusual that it doesn't fit what you would think of as a normal image for anxiety, but it will provide its own magic if you work with it in healing.

6. **Open your eyes** for a moment and think about your image. If it is a positive image that makes you feel free of anxiety, you will be able to use it as a mental picture of yourself without anxiety — for example, you as a child running free across the grass. I sometimes use the dream image I mentioned earlier in which I saw myself sitting on a hillside holding a group of balloons. I had written the words *fear* and *anxiety* on the balloons. Then I released them one at a time into the universe.

   If your image is one that defines your anxiety, like that of the knotted rope or the filled balloon, think now about what would make that image the opposite of what you see: Untie the knot; untwist the rope; burst the balloon or release it.

7. **Close your eyes again.** Take three deep breaths and release them slowly. Spend several minutes with your positive image (the child running across the grass, untying the knot, untwisting the rope, or whatever works for you). Allow your mind to work freely with your image until you feel a sense of release.

8. **Open your eyes** and record your experience with your image. Write it down, draw it, tape-record it, or find some other method that will allow you to come back and use it again.

9. **You now have a healing prescription.** When you begin to use it, it becomes active healing medicine. You can use it as a meditation when you feel you need it, or you can use it throughout your day. You do not have to close your eyes to use it. Think about it while at work or at home. Use it while you are driving the car or sitting in a bus, subway, or train. Use it while you are washing dishes or in a quieter special place at home. Just let it drift into your thoughts for a moment, and you will find it as effective as sitting quietly with it for longer periods of time. Use it until the intention, the thought, the image becomes active within you.

This exercise can be used with any dream or image from the waking imagination. For me, simple dreams worked best because they were easy to turn into a mental image and easy to turn into a few sentences for a taped message. Dreams such as the Field of Body Parts, the series of dreams of safe and unsafe passages, ladders without and then with rungs, all lent themselves to becoming healing exercises. The colleague who dreamed of scrubbing the barnacles off the whale successfully used her small dream as a taped message and as a simple meditation for healing.

Exercise 2:
Turning Dream Prescriptions into Medicine

As I described earlier, the day I was diagnosed with breast cancer I came home and walked into my house alone, angry, afraid, and confused. I lay down on the sofa and desperately tried to think of what to do first. I closed my eyes, drifted into sleep, and had a dream in which I held a cone-shaped sponge over a pan of water, turning it over, identifying the exact location of the cancer, and squeezing the cone object like a sponge into the water, dark fluid flowing into the bowl. That dream located the source of my cancer and provided the mental picture of squeezing the cone until the poisonous liquid flowed into the bowl. When my surgeon told me to go home and do something to begin my healing, I took that dream picture of the cone and consciously used the image of squeezing the dark liquid into the bowl as an element of my healing process. I used it every day and every evening until the day of my biopsy. I treated my dream as a prescription and turned it into medicine for healing.

With a few variations, you can follow the same process for developing a dream prescription as you did to find a waking image in Exercise 1. It is important to trust in your ability to heal. When you work with an image, either from your waking reality or from a sleep dream, you are actively speaking to your immune system. You are giving your brain messages that can be translated into healing in your body.

Always keep a pad of paper and a pencil handy near the place where you dream; that will make it easy to collect your images while they are fresh. Here's how to gather a dream prescription (the dream message itself) and turn it into *medicine* (using it for active healing):

1. **Before going to sleep,** ask for a dream of guidance. State your intention for the evening (i.e., "I want to be healed," or

something specific, like, "I want to know what to do about my aching knee"). A dream question can incubate during the night and produce answers in dream imagery.

2. **Once you have your dream,** reenter it to get specific information. In a general healing dream, you might want to know more about a place or a guardian you see. An animal or a special plant might appear. For example, I asked for a dream to help heal my lymphedema, and my grandmother appeared showing me a plant that grew near a limestone wall. I relaxed, went back into the dreamscape, and asked questions. I had recorded the dream when I awoke but looked again at the dream, closed my eyes, and began to revisit the dream, scene by scene, until I had all the information I needed. I opened my eyes and wrote down each scene in the dream that answered the questions I asked:

> ❧ *What kind of flower does this plant have? My grandmother had shown me the leaves: wide and flat, with a forked end and furry underside. There was no flower.*

> ❧ *Where does this plant grow? My grandmother had shown me more details of a limestone wall against the side of a mountain.*

> ❧ *In what season will I find this plant? I followed my grandmother over wet snow with small flowers and green grass showing beneath, as in early spring.*

I opened my eyes from my second visit with this dream and was able to find the plant: the hart's tongue fern. I have a number of herbals and books on plants that have drawings and photographs. The visual image of the plant was so vivid I was able to locate the plant rapidly. A brief history of the plant noted that it had no flower, grew along the base of limestone walls in moist areas, and was called the hart's tongue fern because the forked end of the leaf looked like a hart's (deer's) tongue. When I went on a search for the plant I discovered it grew well in Tennessee, where I was born, but also in western New York. It was also rare, so I had to actually buy a plant from a nursery on my next visit to Tennessee. I had one set of herbal volumes from the early twentieth century that included recipes for tea from the hart's tongue fern leaves. I dried the leaves and turned them into tea — it tasted a bit like chamomile. The tea is said to aid in vascular health in the body.

Turn your prescription dream into medicine. With my dream of the cone-shaped breast, I took the dream — the prescription — and turned it into medicine by writing a few sentences and taping them to the dashboard of my car to remind me to use the dream. Repeating these sentences became so much a part of my day that I replayed them over and over in my mind as a simple intention until they became a positive healing image. I used them until I felt that I could move on to a new image that offered the next step in my healing.

Dream prescriptions can be honored and turned into medicine in many ways: meditation, writing poems, physical activity while thinking about the message in the dream, and personal or group reentry into the dream for continued healing or further messages of healing.

the pool of bethesda

If a dream in *She Who Dreams* speaks to you, use it as your own healing dream; change it as you see fit to make it work as your own healing prescription. Let's take as an example one of the more powerful dreams in my healing repertoire of dreams. You can use it as a starting point for healing, and change it to fit your special needs as you explore your own images of a healing pool. I will recount a portion of the dream again, omitting names of people so that you can insert names of your own:

I walk with a guide to the healing pool at Bethesda. There is a long row of steps with a columned arcade above, and I meet an angel who says its name is Eliseus. I ask the angel for help, but no one seems to come. I hold my guide's hand as a child would, and I move cautiously into the edge of the pool. Another angel moves forward, perhaps the same one, and stands beside me. This angel tells me that I will find healing in the "rushes" or "rushing." I walk with my guide into the cleansing water of the pool, and I feel that I am healed.

$\mathcal{E}$XERCISE 3:
MAKING ONE OF MY DREAMS YOUR OWN

1. **Look at this healing-pool dream.** Think of a special place — a river, a swimming hole, a place by the ocean — any place that will work as your own healing pool. Follow the steps in Exercise 1 to work with your own healing-pool dream; you can explore it alone or you may ask friends to explore it with you.

2. **Relax with music,** candles, whatever feels most comfortable for you. Have your pad of paper and pencil nearby.

3. **In your mind, travel to your healing pool.**

4. **Look for a guide** — animal or human — who will go with you into the healing pool. Travel to my healing pool and wait for the rushing of the water with your guide or travel to a place special to you. Remember everything you see, and bring back your own personal set of healing images that you can claim as your own healing-pool meditation.

5. **Write your meditation.**

6. **Revisit your healing pool** whenever you feel the need. Use your healing pool as a prescription or as a special location for future exploration.

$\mathcal{E}$XERCISE 4:
USING YOUR HEALING IMAGE
AS A LONGER MEDITATION

YOU NOW HAVE HEALING IMAGES from both waking and sleeping dreams that you can use to speak to your body in a number of ways. You have used these pictures with *intention*. If you wish, you can now choose your favorite dream or healing image and incorporate it into a longer meditation. In a recent dream, I saw myself walking through the woods to a meadow where I came upon a small person who held a key and a box. The dream was quite long and lent itself to a longer meditation that I could use in a quiet space. You can use any dream, but let's use the woods as an easy meditation. If you don't feel you can hold a longer dream in your mind as you sit in your quiet space with your favorite music, you might wish to tape the dream against a background of your favorite music and play it. Have your pad and pencil nearby.

1. **Go to a space** where you know that you can have undisturbed quiet and that the telephones are turned off.

2. **Find a comfortable position,** either sitting or lying down.

3. **Play your favorite music** for meditation.

4. **State your healing intention** and close your eyes.

5. **Visualize a favorite place** — in this meditation, a forest — and embark on your journey:

    Walk slowly and quietly through the forest, looking at everything. Remember the kinds of trees you see, the kinds of plants, and any special flowers; they might hold healing messages for you. If a flower seems to speak to you, pick the flower and carry it with you. Walk until you come to the end of the path.

    You see a meadow before you. Enter the meadow and look around. Look for a person or an animal; approach that being and state your healing intention. Spend the next few moments exploring your environment with the person or animal. Remember everything given to you, everything said to you, and all the places you visit.

    After you have explored your landscape for a few moments, return the way you came: across the meadow, through the woods, and back to your entrance to the woods. Bring favorite things back with you from your journey.

6. **Comfortably return** to the waking reality of your meditation space.

7. **Write down the details** of your journey, and separately write down the healing images you were given: the special flower or tree you saw in the woods, a special place you saw in the meadow with your guide, a gift from your guide, or perhaps a song — anything that is given to you.

8. **To honor your meditation,** use the song or gift in ways that feel most appropriate to your healing. If you have been given a special flower or tree, look up its healing properties and discover ways to honor its gift. Plant the flower or tree. Buy a bouquet or find an essence that will make you feel comfortable or contribute

to your healing. A fragrant essence is usually available in oils or potpourri. An actual flower essence has no scent but might be given to you in your meditation as a healing option. If so, you might wish to explore popular books or websites on the properties of flower essences. Be creative. Draw your journey or write a poem.

9. **If you liked the meditation,** use it again or expand it into a different one using your new gifts.

10. **If you enjoy using meditation in a quiet space,** experiment with your dreams and change your taped messages frequently, using the gift of your own dreams as the journey for your meditation. You will be surprised at how much more effective a meditation becomes when it is your own dream in your own voice.

EXERCISE 5:
VISUALIZING YOUR BODY (BODY SCANNING)

IN THE MIDST OF MY HEALING, I had a wonderful dream (described in Chapter 12) in which I was in an enormous room filled with tools. The tools took on a life of their own, and in the end of the dream I joined them in a magnificent ballet of active healing. The ballet was performed in the air, and the entire dream was so permeated with magic and healing that I felt that there was no barrier between my mind and my body. I felt the two could work in a magical harmony to effect the healing and balance of both.

When I awoke from this dream, I was more aware than ever of my ability to look at my body from many angles, both inside and out. In periods of healing, we often become anxious and frightened about how we are doing. Learning to scan our body to check on whether small aches and pains or feelings of anxiety have any basis can help us separate fears from useful messages from our body. Based on my dream, I developed a simple exercise in which I made my body spin and dance in my mind's eye, as in the ballet in the air so that I could scan it inside and out:

1. **Relax in your special place.**

2. **Create a mental picture** of your body.

3. **Pull this picture** of your body up into the air — a small version of yourself.

4. **Move your visualization** of your body in a slow, spinning motion so that you can see it from every direction.

5. **Look at it** from every angle as it turns.

6. **Now go inside** this image of your body. Turn it around and around. Check everything inside, from its toes to its head, and feel what you are seeing.

7. **If you see any area** that is dark or discolored or that doesn't look right, you can work toward healing that part of your body. Consult a doctor if necessary, and begin to work with anything of concern from your scan using your dreams and images and the other exercises in this chapter.

forming a circle of dream helpers

FORMING A CIRCLE of dreamers offers many benefits. Sharing dreams in a group and reentering dreams for further exploration within the comfort and safety of a dream family magnifies the experience and the energy of the dream. A circle of dreamers can support healing and bring information back to the dreamer that the dreamer may have overlooked. The emotional support of a dreaming family often brings spontaneous emotional and physical healing.

Some circles simply share dreams or put together a few simple rituals: singing an opening song or creating an altar with candles and personal objects — perhaps those that represent a special dream. Some circles use taped meditation music, and some prefer the shamanic style of rhythmic drumming using a round frame-style drum and a single monotonous beat to bring energy to the dreams. Do whatever works best for your group to provide a place for sharing and bringing the energy of your dreams together for yourself and for others.

more tools for self-healing

PHYSICAL EXERCISE

IF YOU GO TO A GYM or do physical exercise as any part of your routine, make it part of your healing ritual. Working out in a gym is an excellent place to practice active meditation. You are already working with your body; all you need to do is to add your favorite simple meditation for expelling what you do not want inside your body and inhaling healing and light. Any exercise instructor will tell you to breathe in during the relaxed part of your exercise movement and breathe out for the strenuous part. You can use that breathing process to incorporate your healing images. Let's use sit-ups as a simple example:

1. **Lie on your back** on the floor, knees slightly bent, hands behind your head.
2. **Lift your head** straight up toward the ceiling using your stomach muscles.
3. **As you lift,** breathe out; as you go back to the floor, breathe in.
4. **Now make this a healing exercise.** As you lift, expel all the darkness from your body in your expelling breath. As you lower yourself to the floor, breathe in light and healing.
5. **Repeat this process** with every exercise you perform.

Prepared Recordings

I purchased a tape of ocean sounds. Then I placed a small tape recorder near my pillow and listened to the tape each night before I went to sleep. I also developed a simple mental exercise using the ocean sounds on the tape; it relaxed my body and mind and allowed me to sleep after some of my more anxious days. Here is the exercise:

1. **Imagine** that you are lying on a beach.
2. **Allow the ocean waves** to move up over your body and back down again.
3. **With each movement** of the waves away from your body, see tension and darkness leaving your body.
4. **With each movement** of the waves over your body, see healing, light, and release moving into your body.

Making a Tape from Your Own Waking Image or Sleep Dream

After several months of using a recording prepared by others, I decided that the best way to talk to my body's immune system was to use the words given to me in my own waking and sleeping dreams. I chose a favorite dream and rewrote it until it sounded like a meditation. I borrowed a second tape recorder and played the ocean tape on one recorder as a background while I read the dream onto a new tape. My dream then became a meditation read against the backdrop of the ocean sounds. Then I played my own dream using my own voice as a night meditation for healing. I felt that my body would respond well to hearing its own voice reciting a healing message given back to it from its own waking and sleeping images. I changed the tape as my dreams changed and as my healing progressed.

Go Fly a Kite

SHORTLY AFTER MY CHEMOTHERAPY was completed, I was visiting a neighbor on a windy spring day. He put together a kite, and we walked to the top of a nearby hill to fly it. After a few moments, he had the kite so high it was almost out of sight. He then asked me to hold the large plastic spool of string. He had brought along pieces of paper. He cut one piece into a geometric shape, then cut a simple line into its center and made a small hole at the center. He asked me what I wanted to release, and I said "anxiety." He wrote the word "anxiety" on the piece of paper, then told me to imagine that the piece of paper held all my anxiety. He slid the paper onto the kite string, making sure the string was inside the small hole. Then he let go. The string was fully released. The paper immediately began whirling and twirling straight up the kite string and disappeared out of sight, sent to the top of the string near the kite by the wind. I felt such childish joy as I watched the simple magic of the piece of paper whirling into space that I asked him to do more. We used all the pieces of paper and watched them carry all of our negative feelings and statements of intention into the universe one by one.

Turning Dreams into Poems or Prose

IF YOU ENJOY WRITING, turning a dream into a poem or story is easy and fun. You simply take your favorite dream and rewrite it either as rhymed or free verse, or write it into a longer story. As you write and explore, you will discover more nuances in the dream.

One of my favorite experiences with using this technique involved a wonderful dream that was part of a series of fantasy dreams that I titled *The Sisters.* I chose one of the dreams from that series to turn into a poem. Here it is as a dream:

THE BATTLE OF THE KINGS: THE DREAM

The scene is a dense, dark forest. The tree trunks are enormous, and there is a musty smell to the earth that recalls a time many centuries ago. In the forest, two young kings are searching for each other. Both were once leaders of legions, but now they are in a battle that has become personal and singular. They represent distinct forces of good and evil but, like those qualities, they appear to be shadows. Clothing and features are difficult to distinguish.

They come upon each other and fight with intensity, using weapons that seem to be drawn from the earth and sky itself: thunderbolt-shaped wooden branches and lances that look more like tree limbs than shaped tools of battle. One king is wounded — the one that represents good — but the other presents him with gifts: seven black sheep and seven black horses.

The wounded king takes his gifts and backs away, leading the animals into the depths of the forest. His wounds are mortal, but as he is dying one of the black sheep approaches him. It seems to gag slightly, opens its mouth, and places on the ground a brilliant blue stone. The dying king places his hand over the stone and wraps his fingers tightly around it. He arises in a blaze of white light. The animals seem to vanish, but the blue stone remains near the base of a young tree.

You don't need to be a great poet or even a good poet to realize that turning your dream into a poem gives it new meaning and new life. The creative process of poetry allows you to explore your dream and go deeper into it.

THE BATTLE OF THE KINGS: THE POEM

The young kings, shadows of good and evil,

split from one,

battle with tree and thunderbolt for the life of the universe.

Gods and magicians, unseen powers,

choreograph a battle no one dares to win.

Or lose.

Thunder rumbles through the ancient forest,

dark with virgin oak, pine, and ash.

Berries of life and death, beauty and horror,

trembling on the magic Rowan

as the winds herald

the clash of gods in the shadows of the man-creation.

Valiant men whose legions

await the triumph of one, shadowed in silhouette against the other,

mirror good and evil, twin spirits, one within the other.

Lightning and shadows form the path,

as currents of energy surge across the sky.

Tree lance and thunderbolt of magician's wood

bring the earth and sky

to bear the burden of a universe at war.

Stars fall, casting their precious treasures to earth

to be born in magic

as hero of light tumbles to the ground near death.

But victory for one cannot be, else death will come to all.

The dark side sends forth a gift:

seven black sheep

seven black horses

Bearers of gifts of life to a universe that must not die.

Magicians tremble in the near-disaster of their own making,

and a single sheep,

gasping near the felled man/god,

coughs into his dying hand the blue Roc of life and healing.

This dream could also be turned into a longer adventure story, with all kinds of possibilities for episodes between warring brothers who represent the light and dark sides.

the wounded healer

I HAVE TOLD THE STORY (in Chapter 10) of the spontaneous initiation of a Samoyed shaman. The man was described as stricken with chicken pox. He remained unconscious for three days. Nearly lifeless, he had visions of going down to hell where he was carried to an island upon which stood the Tree of the Creator of the Earth. The Creator gave him a branch of the tree with which to make a drum. Moving on, he came to a mountain. Entering a cave, he saw a naked man who chased him, caught him, and cut off his head. The naked man chopped up the shaman's body and boiled the bits in a kettle for three years. Then the shaman reassembled his body and covered it with flesh.

When the man awoke from his unconscious state, he discovered that he had the ability to heal others. This is not an experience reserved for distant cultures. The "wounded healer" is often found within ourselves. As I mentioned earlier, when I was working with my own dreams through the long months of chemotherapy, I was given a special dream in which I went through a plowed field strewn with body parts, tissue, ligaments, bones, organs, and flesh. I gathered all the necessary parts together, washed them individually in a bucket of water and hyssop, then reassembled them into my own healed body. This dream provided powerful images for me during this period of my healing.

People in what we describe as "primitive" cultures universally believe that those who survive an illness can then walk among the ill and treat them without fear. A brush with death from which a person emerges with knowledge of the encounter marks the person as one with a calling for healing others.

While engaged in a healing process, many people have some kind of dream or experience in which they find themselves dying and then reassembling. My dream of reassembling became one of my most important dream prescriptions. You may use my dream in your healing process, or you may use your own dream of dismembering and re-membering. Often a dream such as this is the final step in your healing and the first step in working with others for their healing. The wounded healer is the most important kind of healer; he or she brings experience and knowledge to healing.

I am alive because I dream. My maternal grandmother returned when needed in dreams — after she passed — to give advice on the nature of the soul's journey. My dreams gave me specific warning of my disease a year before its diagnosis. My dreams introduced me to deep sources of wisdom and energy, pulled me out of the trough of despair and finally allowed me — in the most literal sense — to renegotiate my life contract and become a dreambringer for others.

Now, if I were to make a bumper sticker from my dream experience, I would choose this one from an old dream journal:

"I'm not only alive because I dream, but I am the dream I choose."

Sources and Resources

workshops with Wanda Burch

Arts in Healing Weekend with Wanda Burch (dreambringer), Hannah Cole (yoga instructor), Peggy Lynn (Adirondack songwriter/musician), and Fran Yardley (storyteller)

An annual fall weekend retreat designed to give women with cancer or chronic disease an opportunity to meet other women with common experiences. In a rustic wilderness setting, the participants are offered workshops in storytelling, songwriting, dream work, and gentle yoga. Shared meals, music, firelight, and guided meditation help create strong bonds between participants. Some scholarships available.

Location: Sagamore Institute
PO Box 40; Raquette Lake, NY 13436; (315) 354-5311
www.sagamore.org
sagamore@telenet.net

Dreaming Well: Using Healing Imagery from Dreams

A one-day workshop of personal dream exploration into how we can use our dreams for self-diagnosis and self-healing. Through dreaming we can grow more creative relations with our physicians as well as our families, draw on energy and guidance from deeper sources than the everyday mind, and connect with the deeper story of our lives. When we share and use the images given to us in dreams, we find that we open ourselves to new possibilities of healing.

Location: Great Hollow Wilderness School, on nearly nine hundred acres of beautiful nature preserve.

Registration: Please contact Irene D'Alessio (203) 264-0319, e-mail: umadurga@earthlink.net.

Queries about additional workshops, presentations, or general information may be directed to e-mail address: ronwan@capital.net

materials by Robert Moss

BOOKS AND TAPES

Conscious Dreaming: A Spiritual Path for Everyday Life
(New York: Three Rivers Press, 1996)
    A unique nine-step approach to understanding dreams, using contemporary dreamwork techniques developed from shamanic cultures around the world.

Dreaming True: How to Dream Your Future and Change Your Life for the Better (New York: Pocket Books, 2000)
    Explores how we can "dream with the body" in order to stay well. Simple and practical techniques for working with a dream journal to catch — and act on — messages about the distant future and tap into our creative source. How to dream toward a better job, a better relationship, and creative fulfillment.

Dreamgates: An Explorer's Guide to the Worlds of Soul, Imagination, and Life Beyond Death (New York: Three Rivers Press, 1998)
    Exciting new techniques that can launch you into other worlds and the farthest reaches of your imagination. A complete training course for opening the dreamgates and embarking on the most rewarding of all forms of travel.

Dream Gates: A Journey into Active Dreaming (audio)
(Boulder, Colo.: Sounds True, 1997)

A complete training course for the inner adventurer. You will learn, through guided dream instructions and exercises, how to traverse the uncharted expanses of dream reality.

Way of the Dreamer (video series, with Wanda Easter Burch)
(Milford, Conn.: Psyche Productions, 2003)

An inspiring and beautifully produced eight-part video documentary series on Active Dreaming that includes Robert's account of his personal dream odyssey and the "Secret history of dreaming" across the ages, as well as instructional tapes on dream sharing, dream reentry and tracking, working with precognitive and early warning dreams, dream encounters with the departed and spirit guides, and healing through dreams.

Classes and Workshops

Robert Moss also offers workshops and, for the serious dreamer, advanced programs. Information on all of these programs is available on his website: www.mossdreams.com.

The Robert Moss School of Active Dreaming

The Dream School is dedicated to the rebirth of a dreaming society, in which dreams are shared and celebrated and used as sources of healing, guidance, and creativity everywhere, every day.

Depth Workshops: Robert leads weekend and longer workshops at Basic, Intermediate, and Advanced Levels.

Dream Teacher Training: Robert leads five-day intensive trainings for dream teachers.

cancer support

The American Cancer Society is a voluntary health organization dedicated to eradicating cancer as a major health problem. It provides research, education, advocacy, and service. For more information, call the toll-free hot line at (800) ACS-2345 or visit www.cancer.org.

BREAST CANCER SUPPORT

Breast Cancer Action carries the voices of people affected by breast cancer to inspire and compel the changes necessary to end the breast cancer epidemic. For more information, call (877) 278-6722 or visit www.bcaction.org.

MAMM magazine is the nation's only consumer publication for women living with breast and reproductive cancers and their families and health-care providers. For more information, write to MAMM at 54 West 22nd Street, 4th Floor, New York, NY 10010; call (646) 365-1350 or visit www.mamm.com.

National Alliance for Breast Cancer Organizations® (**NABCO®**) is the leading nonprofit information and education resource on breast cancer in the United States. NABCO provides information to medical professionals and organizations, patients and their families, and the media. For more information, write to NABCO at 9 East 37th Street, 10th Floor, New York, NY 10016; call (888) 80-NABCO; or send an e-mail to nabcoinfo@aol.com.

National Breast Cancer Awareness Month (NBCAM)
For the past sixteen years, the National Breast Cancer Awareness Month campaign has been dedicated to increasing public knowledge about the importance of early detection of breast cancer. Today, NBCAM continues to work to increase the number of women who are receiving mammography screening and learning good breast health practices. To find out more, go to www.nbcam.org or contact Susan Nathanson, national coordinator, at (312) 596-3557.

The National Breast Cancer Coalition (NBCC) includes more than 450 member organizations and 58,000 individual members. It is dedicated to research, access and influence, and other issues related to breast cancer. For more information, write to NBCC at 1707 L Street NW, Suite 1060, Washington, DC 20036; call (202) 296-7477 or visit www.natlbcc.org.

SHARE provides free support services for anyone affected by breast or ovarian cancer and promotes public awareness and early detection of both diseases. Services include information hot lines in English at (212)

382-2111 for breast cancer and (212) 719-1204 for ovarian cancer and in Spanish at (212) 719-4454, survivor-led support groups, public education, advocacy, and wellness programs. For more information, call (212) 719-0364 or visit www.sharecancersupport.org.

The Susan G. Komen Breast Cancer Foundation is dedicated to eliminating breast cancer as a life-threatening disease by advancing research, education, screening, and treatment. For more information, write to The Susan G. Komen Breast Cancer Foundation at 5005 LBJ Freeway, Suite 370, Dallas, TX 75244; call (800) 462-9273 or visit www.breastcancerinfo.com.

Y-ME National Breast Cancer Organization provides breast cancer information, support, and referrals through its national 24-hour toll-free hot lines in English at (800) 221-2141 and Spanish at (800) 986-9505. The hot lines are staffed by trained peer counselors who are all breast cancer survivors. For more information, write to Y-ME at 212 West Van Buren, 5th Floor, Chicago, IL 60607; or visit www.y-me.org.

Young Survival Coalition is a volunteer network of survivors and supporters whose goal is to increase awareness of the issues surrounding breast cancer in women age forty and under. YSC focuses its support on increasing breast cancer research, technology, education, and outreach for young women. To learn more, call (212) 577-6259 or visit www.youngsurvival.org.

Lymphedema Support

Lerner Lymphedema Services

Dr. Robert Lerner is the pioneer in lymphedema treatment in the United States. Throughout his career as a surgeon, he has been intent upon finding a solution to the under-served and often ignored lymphedema problem. Over some forty years, he has been treating and studying the condition known as lymphedema and started the first lymphedema treatment facility in the United States in 1972. During this time, he has tried pneumatic pumps, has developed and used various microsurgical procedures and finally, in 1989, discovered the effectiveness of a simple treatment known as Complete Decongestive Therapy (CDT) and Manual Lymph Drainage (MLD). He founded the Lerner Lymphedema

Services organization in 1989 where he has successfully spearheaded the use of Complete Decongestive Therapy and Manual Lymph Drainage.

As of January of 2000, Lerner Lymphedema Services has treated over six thousand patients with this procedure. For over a decade through his school, the Lerner Lymphedema Services Academy, Dr. Lerner also has been training therapists in the CDT/MLD technique from all over the U.S. Students have included the entire staff of the Mayo Clinic and many other prestigious health care institutions. He teaches a two-week certification course for therapists, nurses, physicians, and other health care professionals in locations throughout the country that has been featured in the 1998 American Cancer Society Lymphedema Workshop.

Dr. Lerner is also on the board of the Lymphedema Association of North America (LANA), which is seeking to establish teaching standards for CDT/MLD in the U.S. and Canada to ensure the quality of all training programs. He continues to lecture widely, publish studies, treat those suffering from lymphedema, and train others in the technique that has brought so much success toward helping those with this condition.

Lerner Lymphedema Services, specializing in state-of-the-art care for lymphedema patients, certification training for CDT/MLD for therapists, and bandages for use in the treatment of lymphedema, can be reached at (800) 232-5542 or you can visit their website at http://64.26.53.29/faculty.htm.

National Lymphedema Network
Latham Square, 1611 Telegraph Avenue, Suite 1111
Oakland, CA 94612-2138
Hotline: 1-800-541-3259 or 510-208-3200
Fax: 510-208-3110

appendix:

DREAMING OUR WAY
TO THE HEART OF THE WORLD
BY ROBERT MOSS

*I*f we could fold time, travel forward a century or two, and then look backward, I believe we would find abundant confirmation that the rise of the dreamwork movement is one of the most important developments of the modern era.

In my brighter vision of what is to come, our society will be guided by dream helpers who are dreaming with and for the Earth itself. Their constant work is to help those around them to use dreams for guidance and healing, as a direct line to the God/Goddess we can talk to. Dream helpers play a central role in healthcare; now it is recognized that dreams diagnose problems before they manifest and that dream imagery and conscious interactive dreaming offer vital tools for healing. Dreamworkers help the dying to prepare for the afterlife journey by following the path of the soul in dreams, and in this way they learn to go through the swing-door of death with confidence and grace. In the workplace, the day begins with dream leaders helping colleagues to share their dreams and to grow community visions. In our schools, our children become storytellers, communicators, and creators by sharing and giving creative expression to dreams — and get credits for doing this.

SHE WHO *Dreams*

In this happy future, dream guides are valued because they midwife creativity and healing, but above all because it is understood that they help us to connect with soul, and that this is vital to our survival as an evolving species in balance with our environment. Dream travelers are respected because it is now common knowledge that they have direct access to the flux of consciousness that particle physicists found to lie at the heart of matter — more specifically, to the "hidden" six or seven dimensions of the multiverse identified by superstring theory — even before the end of the twentieth century.

In my darker vision of what is to come, I see dream travelers and dreamworkers helping to rebuild our world after a catastrophe. In spontaneous dreams and visions over many years, I have found myself traveling into a possible future in which an order of priestess-scientists are trying to repair the havoc caused by the ignorance and violence of men of power who did not listen to dreams. The dream priestesses of the future have perfected the arts of community dreaming and group dream travel, and have been able to access immense sources of energy and knowledge at the heart of subatomic space. Dreaming, they reach out to educate and inspire those who will help humanity to find its way.

In a recent dream, I found myself voyaging into the world of the Kogi, a dreaming people who live on a sacred mountain in Colombia and succeeded in isolating themselves from the outside world until the 1980s. I made my dream journey to the Kogi at the invitation of a friend who had spent many months with them and had brought me a personal message from one of their shaman-priests. I met a being who showed himself first as a giant bird, then as a man in a conical hat. I saw vivid scenes of his people on the mountain they regard as the heart of the world. Then he opened a vision gate for me, inside the dream. To my surprise, I found myself looking at seemingly ordinary, middle-class Americans going about their daily business. I was catapulted into the mind of one of them — and I was horrified. Here was a decent family man, trying to do his best, in utter ignorance of what was happening to the forests and the seas, of the psychic forces that bred hatred and violence, and of the nature of the soul. In that moment, I understood the immense cost of our Western ignorance, from the point of view of an indigenous dreaming people. And I knew that the return of the dreaming ways is the antidote.

Dreamworkers may follow many different approaches to dreams, but by my observation they agree on the following:

1. Dreams are important!

2. The only "expert" on a dream is the dreamer.

3. Dreams connect us to sources of guidance that are wiser than the everyday mind.

4. Dreamers should help each other, wherever possible, to open a safe and sacred space where dreams can be shared and the dreamer can be offered nonintrusive feedback and guided to take appropriate action to honor the dream.

5. Dreaming is for the community as well as the individual.

We need many more dream helpers from all walks of life, contributing a panoply of rich and varied perspectives, personalities, and life experiences, to bring the gifts of dreaming to people where they live.

The next step, it seems to me, is very simple and hugely important. If we are going to become a dreaming society again, we need ways to make it easy and safe — and fun — to share dreams with other people, anywhere, any time. Our first service to others, as dream helpers, is to confirm and validate other people's dream experiences and to encourage them to claim the full power and energy of their dreams. And we need to be able to do this in the thick of the hurry-sickness and manifold distractions of contemporary life.

lightning dreamwork

OVER MANY YEARS of teaching and practice, I have evolved the simple and powerful method for everyday dream sharing that I call Lightning Dreamwork. Like lightning, it is very fast and it focuses extraordinary energy. In the workshops, we allow just eight minutes for the whole process to be applied to a single dream. This does not mean that we can't spend an hour — or a day — with a dream when we have time and the dream invites that depth of exploration. It does mean that when we use this process we always have time to share our dreams, no matter how busy our lives may be.

The Lightning Dreamwork process makes it possible to share dreams and receive helpful feedback just about anywhere — in the office, in the emergency room, at the family breakfast table, or in the checkout line at the supermarket. The guidelines make it easy to share dreams with complete strangers or with intimate friends and family.

This process incorporates the "if-it-were-my-dream" protocol for commenting on someone else's dream developed by Montague Ullman, which has been a tremendous gift to dreamworkers all over the map.

There are four key steps in the Lightning Dreamwork process. I have written the instructions as if you are working one-on-one with the dream. In a dream circle, one member would play "lead partner" in guiding the process, with the others contributing their suggestions and associations in the "if-it-were-my-dream" phase.

STEP ONE: TELLING THE DREAM AS A STORY WITH A TITLE

THE DREAMER tells the dream as simply and clearly as possible. The dreamer should always be encouraged to leave out his/her autobiography and tell the dream as a story, complete in itself. When we do this, we claim our power as storytellers and communicators. We also avoid the appearance of giving a license to others to probe into our personal lives, which must never be permitted in dream sharing.

The dreamer should be encouraged to give the dream a title. It's amazing how the deeper meaning and shape of dream experiences jump into high relief when we do this.

STEP TWO: THE PARTNER ASKS THE THREE VITAL QUESTIONS

IF THE DREAMER has forgotten to give the dream a title, the partner should ask him/her to make one up. The next step is for the partner to ask three key questions:

1. **How did you feel when you woke up?**

    The dreamer's first emotional reactions to the dream are vital guidance on the basic quality of the dream and its relative urgency.

2. **Reality check**

    The reality-check question is designed to establish whether the dream reflects situations in waking life, including things that might manifest in the future. Dreams often contain advisories about the possible future, and it is important not to miss these messages. By running a reality check, we help to clarify whether a dream is primarily (a) literal, (b) symbolic, or (c) an experience in a separate reality. In practice, the dreamer may need to ask several specific reality-check questions focusing on specific elements in the dream. Here are a couple of broad-brush reality-check questions that can be applied to just about any dream:

- *Do you recognize any of the people or elements in the dream in waking life?*
- *Could any of the events in this dream possibly happen in the future?*

3. **What would you like to know about this dream?**

This simple question to the dreamer provides a clear focus for the next step.

Step Three: Playing the "If It Were My Dream" Game

The partner tells the dreamer, "If it were my dream, I would think about such-and-such." The partner is now free to bring in any associations, feelings, or memories the dream arouses, including dreams of their own that may contain similar themes. Often we understand other people's dreams best when we can relate them to our own dream experiences.

It is very rewarding to receive a totally different perspective on a dream, so sharing in this way with strangers can be amazingly rich — as long as the rules of the game are respected. One of those ironclad rules is that we never presume to tell someone else what a dream means for them; we say only what it would mean for us if it were our dream.

Step Four: Taking Action to Honor the Dream

Finally the partner says to the dreamer, "How are you going to honor this dream?" or "How are you going to act on the guidance of this dream?"

Dreams require action! If we do not do something with our dreams in waking life, we miss out on the magic. Real magic consists of bringing something through from a deeper reality into our physical lives, which is why active dreaming is a way of natural magic — but only if we take the necessary action to bring the magic through. Keeping a dream journal and sharing dreams on a regular basis are important ways of honoring dreams and the powers that speak through dreams. But we need to do more.

- Turn a dream into a bumper sticker. This is always helpful. When we write a personal motto from a dream, we not only distill its teaching; we begin to bring its energy through.

- Create from a dream. Turn the dream into a story or poem. Draw from it, paint from it, turn it into a comic strip.

- Take a physical action to celebrate an element in the dream, such as wearing the color that was featured in the dream, traveling to a place from the dream, making a phone call to an old friend who showed up in the dream.

- Use an object or create a dream talisman to hold the energy of the dream. A stone or crystal may be a good place to hold the energy of a dream and return to it.

- Perform the dream through spontaneous dance or theater.

- Use the dream as a travel advisory. If the dream appears to contain guidance on a future situation, carry it with you as a personal travel advisory.

- Go back into the dream to clarify details, dialogue with a dream character, explore the larger reality — and have marvelous fun! In my workshops, we practice dream reentry with the aid of shamanic drumming — and enter each other's dreamspace (with permission!) as trackers, to support the dreamer's journey and to bring through additional guidance.

- Share the dream with someone who may need the information.

to the place of the heart

SHARING DREAMS in this way opens paths to limitless adventure and healing. Once we have mastered the Lightning Dreamwork process, we can play the role of dream helpers and dream ambassadors (quite literally) on any street corner.

We soon find that dreams bring us, and can bring our communities, back to the place of the heart. When I was teaching in California in October 2002, I found myself in a dream that made this very clear:

MOUNTAIN LION PULLS ME UP TO THE PLACE OF THE HEART

I am climbing a slope that becomes steeper and steeper, carrying quite a lot of stuff. I have to lay down my baggage in order to keep ascending. Now I am carrying just one item, a small white box. The slope becomes a vertical cliff, very difficult to scale. Someone at the top lowers a beaded strap to me. When I grasp it, I am startled to see that the other end is held by a mountain lion. The mountain lion pulls me up, immensely higher than I had expected, until I am on a lofty peak with a commanding view over the coastline and nearby towns and forests. Now the lion directs me to open the box, and I take out a beating red heart. When I place it on a boulder at the summit, the heart beats steadily and powerfully. I know that the heartbeat is reaching people across a great distance. I feel the heartbeat shepherding them toward healing rhythms in their lives, and recalling them to the wisdom of the heart.

I shared this dream with a circle I was leading. We did more than discuss it. We agreed to travel inside it, in a conscious group journey assisted by shamanic drumming. We identified the baggage we needed to put aside in order to make the ascent. We climbed the mountain to receive healing and guidance in the realm of the animal guardians and the place of the heart.

The heart center is where we find courage and reconnect with what truly matters. Our role, as dream helpers, is to encourage each other to go there — and move beyond our conflict and confusion to the heart of the world.

© Robert Moss, 2003

This article was first published in *Dream Network* magazine, vol. 22, no. 1 (2003).

acknowledgments

$\mathcal{I}$ am deeply grateful to Robert Moss, who is truly the brother I never had. Together we have dreamed and together we have learned how to work with our dreams and use them in our lives. Robert first encouraged me to record my dreams and then encouraged me, when home from breast cancer surgery, to begin putting together a chronology of dream diagnoses from my dream journals. It was Robert who first suggested I might have a story to tell that might be helpful to others and Robert who first called my jumble of pages a book. Thirteen years later Robert encouraged me to approach New World Library with my manuscript and helped me put together a proposal, which became *She Who Dreams*. I am blessed to have found a brother whose incomparable friendship has never failed to support my dreams and my life purpose.

Thank you to Marcia Moss for sharing her family, her home, her wonderful meals, and her love for so many years, for challenging all of our dreams with new ways of seeing. I also thank my god-daughter Sophie for the blessing of her birth when comets shot through the sky and for the gift of her music.

I am blessed with a family, which includes Ron, my childhood friend and life partner, who has supported the manifestations of all my dreams, including moving from the South, where both our roots lay, to the Northeast, where we followed separate paths that mirrored similar interests in history, preservation, and early architecture. A strong dreamer himself, Ron listened to my dreams and encouraged me to follow their lead even when they spelled a difficult path through illness and recovery. His special gift of music, which meant so much in my healing, and a magic touch with plants still bring me joy and comfort in my life.

Thank you to my son Evan, who has dreamed with me and for me since he was a child. His own dreams led him to a career he loves and to the woman he married. I am grateful to Evan and Ophie, his wife, for their love and to my beautiful grandchildren, Madison and Joshua, who already shares their dreams in a continuing tradition of dream-telling.

I would like to thank Georgia Hughes of New World Library, who accepted my book and set in motion the process of birthing and refining *She Who Dreams*. I thank my editors Katie Conolly and Carol Venolia, whose queries and re-phrasing have beautifully shaped and structured my book. Many of their queries reminded me how much one assumes from one's own generation that needs to be explained.

Thank you to Patti Prime and Linda Peterson for the unique experience of learning to use my dreams in conjunction with aerobics and weight training. "Closing up Shop" will always have special meaning to me.

Thank you to Byron and Susan. I met both of you on the first day home from my surgery when an incredible full-course meal was delivered elegantly in a large box. From there we have explored all kinds of dreaming, wonderful creative Thanksgivings and dinners on the hill, being a "companion" in food reviews, and in all the adventures of trying to make Glen the hamlet of our dreams.

Thank you Bonnie, Wade, and Lauren for sharing dreams with me and allowing me to share dreams as a daily part of our workspace.

Thanks to all the people of the hamlet of Glen who have participated in dream-telling and a special thank you to Gloria who believed most strongly and consistently that I had a book that would be published.

Thank you, Carol, for evenings of dreams and humor and for asking questions destined to be a book of her own.

Acknowledgments

Thank you, Cara, for sharing adventures in dreaming and adventures in Peru; for encouragement and cat-sitting and sharing knowledge of flower essences and plants.

Thank you to my parents and grandmother for their continued presence in my dreams when I need them.

And thank you to all the dreamers who have supported my dreaming and my book with their love and encouragement.

index

Index

INDEX

b

INDEX

about the author

*W*anda Burch is a thirteen-year survivor of breast cancer. She comes from a long line of strong Irish-American women in the Alabama hills. The first person who encouraged her to dream was her maternal grandmother, a "wise woman" who, after she passed away, returned to Wanda in dreams to show her healing plants and to advise her on the nature of the soul's journey. Wanda's dreams introduced her to deep sources of wisdom and energy, pulled her out of the trough of despair, and finally allowed her — in the most literal sense — to renegotiate her life contract and become a dreambringer for others.

Wanda Burch has worked for many years as the curator of an important historical site in upstate New York, in an area that is rich in the traditions of the Iroquois Indians, with whom she has shared deep experiences of dreaming. She lives with her husband, Ron, in the tiny hamlet of Glen, New York, where neighbors have taken to sharing dreams with her on an everyday basis, weaving a fascinating web of interlocking dreams that guide and energize their lives. Wanda has published articles on colonial medicine and on dream diagnosis and healing. She is an advocate for breast cancer research — chosen to attend the National Breast Cancer Alliance LEAD workshop in the northeastern region in 2000 — and, as a hot-line volunteer, has talked to women about their dreams while sharing stories of her own. Wanda writes from the depths of her personal experience, and, as she says in *She Who Dreams*, she is alive because she dreams.